D0338815

ART CZAR

Also by Alice Goldfarb Marquis

Marcel Duchamp: The Bachelor Stripped Bare

Art Lessons

The Art Biz: The Covert World of Collectors, Dealers,
Auction Houses, Museums, and Critics

Alfred H. Barr, Jr.: Missionary for the Modern

Hopes and Ashes: The Birth of Modern Times, 1929–1939

ART CZAR

The Rise and Fall of Clement Greenberg

a biography by

Alice Goldfarb Marquis

MFA PUBLICATIONS
a division of the Museum of Fine Arts, Boston

MFA PUBLICATIONS
a division of the Museum of Fine Arts, Boston
465 Huntington Avenue
Boston, Massachusetts 02115
www.mfa-publications.org

© 2006 by Alice Goldfarb Marquis

All rights reserved. No part of this book may be reproduced in any form or by any electronic or mechanical means, including information storage and retrieval systems, without written permission from the publisher, except in the case of brief quotations embodied in critical articles and reviews.

The Museum of Fine Arts, Boston, is a nonprofit institution devoted to the promotion and appreciation of the creative arts. The Museum endeavors to respect the copyrights of all authors and creators in a manner consistent with its nonprofit educational mission. If you feel any material has been included in this publication improperly, please contact the Department of Rights and Licensing at 617-267-9300, or by mail at the above address.

For reasons of space, photograph credits appear on page 320.

For a complete listing of MFA Publications, please contact the publisher at the above address, or call 617 369 3438.

ISBN 0-87846-701-7
Library of Congress Control Number: 2005938088

Book design by Mark Polizzotti

Available through D.A.P. / Distributed Art Publishers
155 Sixth Avenue, 2nd floor
New York, New York 10013
Tel.: 212 627 1999 · Fax: 212 627 9484

FIRST EDITION
Printed on acid-free paper
Printed and bound in the United States of America

CONTENTS

v

FOR MY VIRTUAL FAMILY
Charlotte and Martin Stern

Prologue

THE INDISPENSABLE CRITIC

CLEMENT GREENBERG'S LONG LIFE spanned the most eventful years in the history of American art. He was central to the movement of American innovators from the periphery to the hub of the western art world. Greenberg was the key supporter, promoter, and propagandist of the kind of art that capped the development of modernism and perhaps pushed it over the brink into history. His strong support for artists like Jackson Pollock enhanced his reputation for predicting the rise of new artists, bringing them to the attention of art dealers and museums and increasing the market value of their works.

This outspoken critic also played a negative role, in that he deplored much of the next wave of art, a diffuse set of forays, feints, and experiments that mimicked the ways of science even as they mocked it. The new art, collectively called postmodernism, confronted every standard of aesthetic value, criteria that had prevailed for millennia in the Western world. In that scramble of theory, politics, interests, and (let's face it) money, Greenberg played his second important role—as a target for a new, better educated, and more tolerant generation of art historians. They were able to sharpen their skills by denouncing his judgmental rhetoric, his evident elitism, and his strong brief for values.

But despite the sometimes strident catcalls, Greenberg remained indispensable to discussions of American art in the twentieth century. Many first-time readers of Greenberg's writings were struck by his frequent references to the avant-garde, beginning with his first significant article, "Avant-Garde and Kitsch," published in 1939 in a small highbrow periodical. At that time, "avant-garde" was a military term drafted by left-wing radicals into political service. In Britain, a few critics had linked avant-garde to the arts, but Greenberg was the first American not only to use the word repeatedly in his reviews of new art, but also to develop a complex theory of how avant-gardes develop.

Greenberg began writing about contemporary art at a time when only a handful of Americans did so, and when the overwhelming mass of the public was preoccupied with the privations of the Great Depression and the looming European war. Most people had neither the money nor the impulse to become interested in art: weren't Norman Rockwell's folksy tableaux enough, and freely available on the cover of the *Saturday Evening Post*? Those who did have an interest in art tended, like the Museum of Modern Art during its first ten years, to eschew American artists in favor of Europeans like Picasso and Matisse, whose seminal creations were already passing into history. Greenberg's innovation was to devote this kind of attention to contemporary Americans. Many of his early readers were city people, children of Jewish immigrants like himself, who were the first in their families to be interested in art. For this secular congregation, Greenberg became a rabbi, a leader and adviser with a weekly sermon. Along the way, he amassed a valuable art collection and a body of writing that is frequently quoted today.

Starting out as a small voice published in periodicals of marginal circulation for a handful of culture enthusiasts, Greenberg eventually developed into a towering figure whose views influenced artists and their dealers, museums and their public, as well as a growing throng of Americans newly interested in art. Greenberg's timely focus on Jackson Pollock as the central figure among the Abstract Expressionists persuaded many art world insiders to heed his words on the next big thing. Greenberg's rise was built upon his prescient words about the abstract new art of the 1940s and 50s. Likewise, his stubborn grip upon the abstract art of the 1960s and beyond set off a fall from his lofty perch. Greenberg suffered for his inability to adjust his views to contemporary tastes. Nevertheless, younger artists and would-be critics sought him out, basking in his onetime glory and hopefully rereading his statements.

Greenberg continues to be relevant in the world of art because he offers a thoughtful alternative to the ironic, anything-goes sensations purveyed in the current milieu, not only by dealers but also by museums and academics. While championing the new art of his time, he exercised discrimination, following the best of traditional art critics. While the clarity of his writings seems spontaneous, he was an obsessive editor and rewriter, amassing mountains of manuscripts. He was the last of the "amateur" art critics, succeeded by a mass of university-trained art historians flaunting advanced degrees. The paradox was that the amateur boldly— even aggressively—issued his verdicts, while the more educated writers flinched from overt judgments. This contrast exposed Greenberg to some violent attacks, in which he was tarred as a dictator, or worse. Yet, more than a decade after his death in 1994, hardly a week passes without a reference to his writings, a record of influence seldom surpassed.

While his writings are widely available, Greenberg was extremely guarded about a biography. He once upbraided John O'Brian, the editor of his essays, for asking too many questions. Later, he wrote to the same O'Brian, "One's life is supposed to be an open book. I'd prefer to open it myself." Unfortunately, Greenberg died before opening that book, and it fell to others to explore his fascinating life. The present volume is not the first such attempt at exploration, but I believe it is the most complete and fair-minded to date.

The author has many institutions and people to thank for help, guidance, and friendship over the many years this book was gestating. Among the participants, observers, bystanders, coaches, and sympathetic ears were John Blankfort and Nell Parker, Liliane Choney, Joanne and David Cooper, Hilde Cytryn and Enrique Heller, Ann Elwood, Anne Ewing, Joanne Ferraro, Jane Ford, Reva and Gerson Greenburg, Aline Hornaday, Laurence Jarvik, Brian Keliher, Sue and Larry Keller, Luisa and Paul Larson, Jean Mayer, Laurence McGilvery, Kay and Harold Orlans, Goldie Rothenberg, Laurence Suid, Patricia Terry, Bill Thoma, Sue Whitman, and Dennis G. Wills. Caring organizations include the San Diego Academy of Arts and Letters, San Diego Independent Scholars, and the Art and Architecture Area of the American Culture Association. The University of California at San Diego was supportive as always; the Department of History there allows me to be a perennial visiting scholar, while the Geisel Humanities Library satisfies my every scholarly whim. The Special Collections of the Getty Research Center provided me with every possible convenience as I plowed through forty-five boxes of Clement Greenberg Papers. The New York Public Library was my first resort in New York: the reference librarians (in particular David Smith and Stewart Bodner, associate chief librarian of the Center for the Humanities) can access uncanny quantities of data; the art and architecture section seems to have kept clippings about every New York arts person or event; and the Jewish studies section presides over vast stores of publications, some ephemeral, some unique, all quickly available. Other helpful libraries were the Rare Book and Manuscript section of the Butler Library, Columbia University, and the New York Academy of Medicine Library, where Thomas Adrian was a thoughtful resource.

Sarah Greenberg Morse, whom I interviewed several times, was extremely helpful. Others who kindly consented to interviews were Virginia Dorazio, Arthur C. Danto, Stephen Flanagan, Piri Halasz, Glenn Horowitz, Ivan Karp, Rosalind Krauss, Jacquie Littlejohn, Amy Newman, Norman Podhoretz, Irving Sandler, Natalie Greenberg Stern, and Robert Storr.

I owe a special debt to John O'Brian, professor of art history at the University of British Columbia and the editor of four volumes of Greenberg's *Collected Essays and Criticism*. He not only shared the critic's letters, but also let me "debrief" him for two days, while I was a guest at his home in Vancouver. Two other colleagues were eager to help: Helen A. Harrison, director of the Pollock-Krasner House and Study Center, Stony Brook Foundation, and Elaine King, professor of art history at Carnegie-Mellon University, Pittsburgh.

My indispensable guide as a writer and friend is Mark Polizzotti, the master of *le mot juste*, editor and director of publications at the Museum of Fine Art, Boston. Others splendid contributions were made to this book by copy editor Robert Hemenway, proofreader Marlowe Bergendoff, and the resourceful photo researcher Caroline Kraft.

La Jolla, California
October 2005

ART CZAR

Chapter I

WHO AM I?

ONCE THEY WERE HUDDLED MASSES. Now they constitute a visual cliché: faded photos of nameless people trudging out of rusty boats, crowding into the vast echoing halls, then new, of Ellis Island. They parade mutely, some perhaps catching your eye, making you wonder what became of them. Few were aware of what awaited them in the new world, but they marched resolutely forward, convinced that what lay ahead would be better than what they had left behind. Gold in the streets? Maybe not. But a chance for a decent life—and with luck, maybe more? That was worth the arduous journey.

Clement Greenberg's parents were part of that hopeful, energetic mass of Jews from Eastern Europe who poured by the millions into New York City between 1880 and 1915. His mother, Dora Brodwin, arrived with her family in 1899, when she was eleven years old. She was among more than 163,000 arrivals that year from Russia and central Europe. His father, Joseph Greenberg, followed an older brother, Isidore, arriving in New York in 1904, at age twenty. That year's influx topped 322,000. Their son much later described their origins as "a Lithuanian Jewish enclave in northeast Poland," then under control of the Russian tsarist regime. Fleeing religious persecution and a bleak future, they defied even the naysayers they left behind, people who commonly described them, in Yiddish, as *"shnayders, shusters und ferdganovim"* (tailors, shoemakers, and horse thieves).

By the time they met and married in 1907, Dora was nineteen

years old and Joseph, at age twenty-three, already an entrepreneur. He managed what was commonly called a candy store, actually a grab bag of neighborhood needs: newspapers, magazines, cigarettes, fountain drinks, candies, stationery, and toys. When their first son was born in 1909, they moved to Alexander Avenue in the Bronx, a neighborhood rapidly becoming an escape valve from the teeming slums of Manhattan's Lower East Side. Clement Greenberg's first memory, he told an interviewer, was of standing on the candy store's counter and naming comic-strip characters pointed out by his father.

In 1914, the entire Joseph Greenberg family, now including two younger boys, Martin and Sol, moved to Norfolk, Virginia, where Joseph's older brother Isidore was having trouble managing the expansion of his women's wear stores. With the navy base booming as the First World War broke out in Europe, the OK Brothers, as they styled themselves, eventually owned a chain of five stores, the OK Outfitters. Greenberg later minimized that achievement by saying that his father "had a clothing store and then he got another one."

This remark, made in old age, highlights Clement Greenberg's lifelong struggle to come to terms with his parent. Throughout, the son carried on an interior dialogue with his father, wavering between murderous contempt and a touching desire to please. Such a conflicted relationship was by no means exceptional among immigrant Jewish families. Irving Howe, the most acute participant/observer of these families, described the searing confrontation between the American-born sons and their old-country fathers: "Denial and suppression, embarrassment and shame: these words would not be too harsh."

At home both parents spoke Yiddish, and this was Clement's first language as well. They were not observant Jews, but maintained an inbred distance from a non-Jewish world that, for count-

4

less generations, had locked them out of most attractive opportunities—studying at the best universities, jobs at large corporations, and even housing in upscale neighborhoods. But Greenberg's parents also brought with them a powerful element of "Jewish" values: respect for education, strong family ties, a desire to "make it." Much as Clement resisted—even hated—that legacy, he was irrevocably marked by it.

By the time the family returned to New York from Norfolk in 1915, Joseph Greenberg was a substantial businessman, ready to forsake the "rag trade." He turned to more promising enterprises, such as a metal goods factory and lucrative forays into real estate. He was so successful that Greenberg could not remember "there ever having been any worrying about money" or any family member "lacking for anything. Which is not to say we were rich." Nevertheless, his grievances against his parents, especially his father, shaded his later recollections of growing up. Looking back, he saw himself at the age of four or five as "an artistic prodigy" who could "draw photographically," as he told an interviewer in 1987. As late as 1991, at the age of eighty-two, Greenberg was still bitter that his parents had ignored the drawings he produced. They were "barbarians," he fumed, who threw out his "every last scrap of artwork."

The child may have been difficult to raise. When he was five years old, on a family vacation in the Catskills, his cousin Sonja saw him beating a goose to death with a shovel handle. Near the end of his life, Greenberg also recalled the incident but explained it quite differently: he was afraid of the big bird, so he killed it with an axe. A reviewer of the book in which this incident is described seized on it immediately to foretell "the slow escalation in targets, the growing taste for blood, the rise to bigger and uglier assaults, the sordid end. The die is cast; the boy will become an art critic."

Greenberg's explanation of terror at a large bird attacking him fits into emotions felt by others raised in the Jewish immigrant world. Irving Howe, who was Greenberg's near contemporary and who also grew up in the Bronx, noted that such a background "left us with a large weight of fear. Fear had seeped into Jewish bones over the centuries, fear had become the intuitive Jewish response to authority, fear seemed the strongest emotion that the very world itself, earth, sky, and sun, brought out in Jews. To be Jewish meant . . . always to live on the edge of foreseen catastrophe." He cited a Yiddish proverb: "A Jew's joy is not without fright."

Greenberg, like Howe, wrestled all his life with his Jewish heritage. Howe once wrote that "feeling Jewish is something that occurs to people only when they already see some alternatives to being Jewish." At the age of twelve, Greenberg was allowed to take the five-cent subway ride to Manhattan (a privilege that he later characterized as "mistreatment"). He told an interviewer late in life that he yearned to visit the non-Jewish world to arrive at an identity, to "make yourself into yourself." Getting off the subway in Manhattan, he could "see the crowds of gentiles—and it was liberating."

Greenberg was by no means alone in this point of view and the future it might foretell. In 1919, the acidic observer of America's leisure class Thorstein Veblen described from his own experience the exceptional fate of many a Jewish intellectual: forced to abandon his traditional culture, such a person would find his place in the wider culture equally insecure. This propels him to become "a disturber of the intellectual peace, but only at the cost of becoming an intellectual wayfaring man, a wanderer in the intellectual no-man's-land."

Perhaps it was Greenberg's glimpses of that insecure yet dazzling world at the heart of New York that prompted him to rage later at what he insisted were his family's paltry provisions for his care. His parents had never taken him to a doctor, he told an interviewer late in life, until he complained of persistent headaches and was given aspirin. But he also recalled having his buck teeth straightened back in the early 20s, "the dark ages" of orthodontia, and "the results were plausible." Any kind of dentistry was rare then; as late as 1929, the annual per capita outlay in the United States for all dental services was $3.90.

While some relatives hinted that Greenberg's mother favored him over her other children, he himself complained of her ill treatment and neglect—even though she had persuaded his father that the boy had artistic talent and should receive further training. Before he was sixteen, he was attending drawing classes at the Art Students League, taking the subway to its Fifth-seventh Street building in Manhattan two evenings a week, after high school. His teacher, Richard Lahey, told him, as Greenberg quoted almost sixty years later, "Obviously you have talent, but there's more to it than that." Greenberg said his ambition was to paint like Norman Rockwell. His father was shocked that the boy was drawing—even photographing—a live, nude model. "Had I known that," Greenberg recalled his father saying, "I wouldn't have let you go to art school."

In fact, Greenberg attended art school for less than three months. His mother had been ill with a recurring infection diagnosed as "blood poisoning." When she died in 1925, at age thirty-seven, he quit the art lessons. Soon after, his father pulled him out of Erasmus Hall, a public high school in Brooklyn, and sent him to the private Marquand School for Boys, operated by the Young Men's Christian Association in a spacious new high-rise at 55 Hanson Place in downtown Brooklyn.

The school offered a rigorous college-prep curriculum, but also had business-oriented courses—typing, shorthand, office practice, and bookkeeping—for students not bound for college. Its program was "non-sectarian but thoroughly Christian," with daily chapel devotions followed by a sermon from "a prominent man on business or other matters." The goal was to develop the "well-rounded moral, social, physical, and intellectual character" of each student. The typical student's day included six periods of recitation, eighty minutes for physical education, and an hour of supervised study, ending at 5 P.M. The VIth (college prep) Form, which Clement would have attended, included three hours of English, with concentration in written and oral composition, plus typical readings: Edmund Burke's "Speech on Conciliation with America"; George Washington's "Farewell Address"; Daniel Webster's "First Bunker Hill Oration"; essays by Carlyle, Macaulay, and John Milton, Shakespeare's *Macbeth*, and a history of English and American literature. In addition, students took five hours each of math, Latin, French, or German, plus chemistry or physics. With various fees added on, tuition cost almost $200 per year.

Greenberg had little to say about this education, except to complain that his father, ever a shrewd businessman looking for a bargain, expected him to finish his last two years of high school in one: "He was in a hurry to get me out of the house." A less jaundiced interpretation might be that Joseph Greenberg hoped his oldest son would develop a respect for business, and might even join his varied enterprises. He could also have been motivated by a desire to prepare his son for success in the non-Jewish world.

In the fall of 1926, Clement Greenberg left home for Syracuse University, a private institution in upstate New York. Thanks to his year at the Marquand School, he received advanced placement credit for a year of ancient, medieval, and modern history, for biology, and for two years of Latin and three years of French. To have a place to live, he joined a Jewish fraternity, the ETA chapter of Sigma Alpha Mu, but was shy and made few friends. However, one of these friends, Harold Lazarus, would become a confidant and willing foil for Greenberg's intense critical judgments about both literature and art, as well as his emotional agonies. Their relationship was so close that Greenberg would pepper Lazarus with detailed multipage letters when they went home for the holidays. Though they saw each other infrequently after graduation, these letters went on for some fifteen years, chronicling what was certainly the closest friendship of Greenberg's long life. Harold's physical distance may have emboldened Greenberg to unburden himself in page after page of fine Spencerian handwriting, often in pencil and often on cheap paper or hotel stationery. Harold kept all of the letters until the day he died; unfortunately, Greenberg kept none of Harold's.

Reportedly, Greenberg arrived at the Syracuse campus carrying a lacrosse stick, perhaps a souvenir from high school days. He also boasted of being on the university's swim team, when in fact he had simply tried out and never made it. Academically, however, he shone. He took a broad array of humanities courses, starting out as a middling student, with a fair number of C's (a perfectly respectable grade in those pre-inflation days). His major was English, where he took nine courses and garnered mostly A's. But he also impressed his professors in history and, apparently, was so pleased with his performance that he kept some of his papers to the end of his life. One, written in his junior year and called "The Dionysiac Cult in Greece: Athens in Particular," starts with an epigraph in Greek and was carefully revised and neatly written. The spelling and punctuation are flawless, a discipline that would carry over into every word Greenberg ever wrote. The professor left not a single comment or criticism on it, except an elegantly laconic "A."

Clearly, Greenberg was an academic star, but he was also perverse. He spent time drawing figures and also wrote poetry, mostly derivative, traditional, pessimistic, and, reflecting the author's age, sophomoric. In a green spiral-bound notebook, he wrote, polished, and rewrote:

Substance is neither permanent nor sound;
It has melted from your touch and taste; all
Your haste could not save even a small
Dusty from your grand fiction's funeral mound.

Greenberg's letters to Harold during his college years highlight how he had redirected his own discomfort with Judaism against his father and all he represented—which to Greenberg meant Jews who spoke with an old-country accent, moneygrubbers, and crass peddlers of goods. Unspoken but nonetheless present was Clement's belief that his father had betrayed his mother, dead less than two years, by getting remarried to a distant relative, also named Greenberg, and soon having another child, Natalie. And in addition, Clement focused onto his father his own anxieties over what he would do once his brilliant college career ended, when his lack of ambition might find him remaining idle. In the summer of 1929, Greenberg wrote to Lazarus that his father "spends sleepless nights over the fear that I may turn out to be a weakling in life." Lacking religion, "he can only think of the glory and sweet fruition of the strong man who stands on his own two feet and batters the moon with his fists . . . O papa, if you could only read poetry." More than two years later, he was still languid and jobless, agonizing to Harold: "What to do that's right? . . . I lack direction."

Lazarus was the only figure in Greenberg's life who could appreciate his overwhelming affection for literature. Home for the summer after finishing his sophomore year, Greenberg had exulted to his "soul-mate" at having pocketed the train fare by hitching a ride home in a friend's car. He spent some of that $10 on "one of the most obscene and at the same time best-written books I have ever read," Petronius's *Satyricon*, as well as a volume of Sophocles plays, both acquired from "a quaint truck bookstore on Sixth Avenue." At a "quaint French bookstore" on Sixth Avenue, he bought some Molière plays, chatting with the clerk in halting French. He left "feeling very cosmopolitan."

He started out that summer laboring (or pretending to labor) in his father's overheated plating factory. Only a week after starting the job, he complained that "the acids were making my head even balder" and abruptly quit. In the evening, he would join his younger siblings, Sol, sixteen, and Martin, twelve, and their new stepmother, Fan, in apartment 6D at 736 Riverside Drive in Manhattan. While he would have preferred to spend the entire summer in New York reading an assortment of classics, he was shipped off to Camp High Lake in the Pocono Mountains of Pennsylvania as a waterfront counselor. "Ah, woe is me!" he moaned to Harold. "Squalling Jew bastards from the very best homes in Long Island, are my fate for two long months." His daily assignment: "seeing that no children of the circumcised fall into the lake." Enclosed were two sketches featuring himself, one holding an oar and wearing bathing trunks drooping at the crotch, the other visiting a nearby girls' camp decked out in a blazer, knickers, and fancy socks, a pipe in his mouth and a shock of hair on his head. The drawings are amateurish but they represent the artist's wish fulfillment: a full head of hair for a fellow already losing his, and weighty sexual equipment.

By mid-July, Greenberg was trying to goad "refractory bitches into increased activity . . . Some *disgusting* adult perversions would be very refreshing." He was spending his nights "trying to seduce the waitresses . . . and the days thinking about 'how to do it.'" For the boys in his charge, Greenberg had only contempt, calling them "snotty brats with names like Seymour (ugh), Alvin, Stanley, Irving, Sidney, etc. . . . typical of . . . Jews that wear jewelry, golf hose, smoke cigars, play pinochle, spoil their children, and indulge in loud horseplay."

The following summer, Greenberg came home a few days

before postcards arrived with his grades from Syracuse—A's in two English courses and B's in two others. To that, his father remarked: "If only you were sure of $15 a week after you graduate I'd be satisfied." Clement was supposed to find a summer job, but had other plans. After sleeping until noon every day, he tried poetry:

> The sun over the Palisades
> Is like a Florida orange
> But the stink in the subway Is
> Awful
> Besides There are too many Jews
> In N.Y.

He spent the rest of his waking hours smoking and fantasizing on how he would spend the money if he did find a job. Until such a miracle materialized, Greenberg was content to enjoy his stepmother's "clean tablecloths and bacon for breakfast every morning." His father called him "a lazy son of a bitch," but Clement didn't dare to disagree, he told Harold, "because I like him too much." He would have liked to feel "hurt and misunderstood," but could not. "My bed is too soft and clean, my meals agree too well, the shower-baths are too fragrant, everything conspires with lamb chops to make me feel that as long as I've got my hair, life is OK."

His father had other plans for him. By July, in that ominous summer less than three months before the bottom fell out of the stock market, Clement worked as a clerk at Planet and Abrahams, a law firm where his father was a likely client; he was paid $12 per week. "I take orders from a man who never read Shakespeare," he complained to Harold. "I sit around on my can all day long, drawing pictures that shock the office girls." By August, he was disillusioned with a law career. "My heart's just not in anything but enjoying myself," he told Harold, "but I don't want to eat in the Automat for the rest of my life."

Perhaps Greenberg trusted Lazarus with so many confidences because they were both aspiring intellectuals. But there were other reasons as well. Harold was gay, and Greenberg played on what he saw as a contemptible vice; he repeatedly sent Harold letters mocking his own encounters with "queers," "fairies," and the like. On the other hand, Greenberg was mesmerized, perhaps frightened, by the intensity of his own affection for Harold. As school was starting again in the fall of 1929, he confided that he couldn't wait to get back to the campus. "O to be in Syracuse, now that autumn's here!" he exulted, echoing Robert Browning. "Won't it be great, sitting or laying all over a double bed and shooting our heads off, squabbling, agreeing, discussing and disgusting, and you'll be vive and I'll be gauche, vice versa, etc."

The final year of college had confronted Greenberg with choosing a career. But, after graduating in 1930, cum laude and Phi Beta Kappa, he couldn't even find a summer job, and instead thought he might spend the holidays at the beach in Far Rockaway "among the lower middle classes." (With typical contrariness, he allowed his name to be included in the hefty Phi Beta Kappa directory, 1776–1941, but, unlike almost every other living member, omitted his address.) "Everything is a delightful uncertainty," he told Lazarus, except that the book he was reading, Dostoevsky's *Crime and Punishment*, gave him his "first literary thrill . . . in a long time." Later that summer, he had "a mystic revelation . . . my 'true happiness' lies in sitting on my ass and letting life come to me . . . slowly, reasonably . . . ballasted by regret and made beautiful by indecision and German poetry." Like every budding writer, he was trying out the styles of others, this time a Joycean stream of consciousness. Another time, he would reach for T. S. Eliot, a Surrealist takeoff on "The Love Song of J. Alfred Prufrock":

Among adolescent maids who've never prayed
William P. Yerington finds his earthly troubles.
Physio-chemical engineers
Who pressure to vent skeptical sneers . . .

and so on for another thirty-six lines.

In July 1930, diploma in hand, Greenberg applied for a job at IBM as editor of the company's internal weekly newspaper, but he wasn't offered the position. In September, he was fired from "the lousiest job ever conceived by the million commercial demons of America," investigating credit applications. He envied Harold, who was starting on his M.A. in literature at Harvard in the fall. The family moved from the Riverside Drive apartment to a two-family house at 539 Ocean Parkway in Brooklyn. The house was spacious; in it he "had a room of one's own according to the lady essayists"—a reference to Virginia Woolf. Many years later, Greenberg would reminisce about the seasonal changes he experienced there: "Spring and summer would never come to me elsewhere," he wrote to the editor of his writings more than fifty years later, "as they did on Ocean Parkway in Brooklyn when I was in my twenties."

While Harold tackled his studies in Cambridge, Greenberg was bemoaning a job that he'd taken because "I need money badly awful badly." He would do clerical work for a near-blind salesman at a paper and twine company, "amanuensis for a pleasant dodderer." Further, he fantasized about shooting his stepmother while also reading Henry James's *The Europeans* and Isadora Duncan's autobiography. By the end of October, Greenberg had also read Thomas Mann's *The Magic Mountain*. He was again unemployed, hence had time to take in exhibitions at the new Museum of Modern Art. Far from simply acquainting himself with the modest array of art shown there, Greenberg leaped to judgment:

"Gauguin is overrated," he wrote to Harold. "Pascin is French, and Rouault's big canvas in blue, black and glaze is the best picture in the House, with Matisse, Cézanne, and Dufy next in that order. Picasso is simply Decadent!"

This fragment may have been his first stab at reviewing art, written for an audience of one. A few months later, he offered another verdict on a MoMA exhibition. The Daumiers, in a mild and hardly modern show of Daumier and Corot paintings and graphics, gave him "that artistic thrill of plucking every chord." These and other youthful judgments indicate how deeply and how early Greenberg developed intense opinions about good, bad, or execrable art, long before he developed a theory to support them.

Considering that the Depression had thrown more than 30 percent of the work force into unemployment, Greenberg—or, more likely, his father—was lucky to unearth yet another job for Clement in mid-November. He was paid $15 a week by the Home Title Insurance Company, "Brooklyn's Atlas," to dig out "antiquarian facts" about local real estate for the company's advertising. His boss was a Harvard man, magna cum laude, who had "set out to Write" [*sic*] but was now "3/4 barbarian." Greenberg stuck it out until mid-January 1931, when he was fired. His boss made good on a promise to get him a job at the *Brooklyn Eagle*. There he began writing "piece news"; paid by the column-inch of printed matter, he might net $12 a week. But by the end of February he was fired again, supposedly because he misspelled the name of a prominent judge, but actually because he handed in a story written in a style that Harold called "the close harmony of modern poetry." Even worse, he had left the office before the copy editor approved it.

Like many people who first learned to speak another language, Greenberg was a lifelong collector of obscure, sometimes even nonexistent, words in English. Henry Adams, he wrote to Harold, "animadverted" [disapproved] of Harvard." A college acquaintance was "more 'lymphatic' than ever." Current poetry had "nowhere 'vernal' [spring-related] subjects." The nakedness of fan dancer Sally Rand was "too 'lubric' [lubricious] for words." Another son of Jewish immigrants, the literary scholar Morris Dickstein, recalled his own fascination with his second language, "trying to expand my vocabulary through a forced march" as a high school senior, in order to score better on the college board exams. For Greenberg, obscure words were a lifetime fascination and represented more than a scholarly quest: using such baffling verbiage also intimidated the reader.

*   *   *

While the rest of the family vacationed elsewhere, Greenberg stayed home alone that summer of 1931, devouring German fiction, poetry, and philosophy. Years later, he would often cite Kant's *Critique of Judgment* to support his own theories of modernist art. Plowing through German greats and eventually arriving at Goethe's *Faust*, Greenberg liberally levied judgments: "Stefan George . . . greater than anything so far in English . . . Werfel not as good as fifteen poets I can name . . . Hamlet + Stavrogin = Faust." But no amount of German literature could relieve the piercing loneliness of spending a whole summer "in a big empty house" eating meals in restaurants and following "women home from the subway station."

In September 1931, more than a year after acquiring his B.A. from Syracuse, Greenberg wrote that it "begins to bother me that I haven't produced as the World knows it." He worried that someone meeting him for the first time would say, "An interesting prick but I could push right through him with my little finger and meet air on the other side." His father had "the delusion" of worrying about him, which, understandably any father would, as he saw his son sleeping until noon, chain-smoking cigarettes, and reading for most of the day. More than twenty years later, Greenberg wrote that such inactivity may have "looked like idleness," but that in fact he was studying Italian and extending his command of the other two languages he had started to learn in college, French and Latin.

In the fall, Greenberg went south to stay with his aunt Fanny Galin in Portsmouth, Virginia. Less than a month later, he was back in Brooklyn, replete with tales of blacks picking cotton, sailors being tattooed, and observations on classic travel literature. But he had still found no direction or plan.

After a visit from Harold in December, Greenberg appeared to hang dependently on this relationship. Harold had brought along gifts for all the children in the family, and Greenberg reported that even his father "felt that we were all unequal to your presents and to yourself." The visit prompted Greenberg to write two poems, one of which he sent to a barely known publication, *Pagany*, with, he confessed to his friend, "an awful craving" to see his work in print: "I want fame, then I'll have money, then I'll take my father out to a swell dinner and introduce him to swell blondes, then I'll sleep till three o'clock instead of noon, till next January, even."

Meanwhile, he was trying out some art reviews on his tolerant—and only—friend. On a visit to the Brooklyn Museum, he contemplated African sculptures, and touched on a concern with the flatness of paintings that would later reappear in his reviews. All sculpture could be traced back to Africa and the Egyptians, he wrote to Harold. "They never allow themselves to slip into the flat," a quality he later insisted on in paintings. By contrast, sculptors like these Africans were correct in always stressing "the whole three-dimensional thing." He was also enormously impressed with a figure whose penis was so large that "sticking out straight ahead, two lines drawn from the point to the head and toes respectively would make an equilateral triangle."

While still devoting himself to language and literature, Greenberg continued his judgmental strolls around the tiny New York art scene at the beginning of the 1930s. He found the Whitney Museum, then housed in a Greenwich Village town house, "rotten . . . private taste should never make a museum out of itself. And [John] Marin's watercolors would be much better if hung alone; watercolors can't stand each others' company." He also visited the nearby gallery 291, where Marin watercolors were selling for $350 and oils from $35,000 up. He met "an old, doddering white-haired bird who takes care of the place and buys the best pictures for himself." Two weeks later, Greenberg identified "the old fish" as Alfred Stieglitz "the famous photographer. Also husband of Georgia O'Keefe [sic] the hothouse weed. She is lousy, by the way."

The summer of 1932 was nearly identical to the one before it: hanging aimlessly around the house, sleeping late, and reading, and sharing his two-year-old sister's routine of lunch (lamb chop and mashed carrots), nap outside; supper at six, and amusement. Clearly upset about his son's baby-routine, Joseph offered to send Clement to Europe, provided he could support himself there. Even this prospect left Greenberg lukewarm: "The express companies don't want me, neither do the press bureaus." Yet Greenberg was apparently too accustomed to "lamb chops and mashed carrots" to try bumming around Europe.

His patience at an end, Greenberg's father shipped him off that winter to St. Louis, where he was to manage a wholesale neckwear business, one of a chain his father had created. Greenberg complained that he "was just beginning to get going" on his writing: like many an aspiring writer, he had "dozens of things" in his head clamoring to be "written down." On arrival, he seemed to get involved in the business; when he passed a men's haberdashery store, he looked "pertinently" at the ties displayed and arrived at how much they cost. He could tell Harold "about grosses and dozens and turnover and profit; income and net cash off and on the spot." He was living at the Hotel Missouri in a snug room, toilet down the hall, "half of a dive, lousy with whores, actors and traveling salesmen." In the night club on the roof, he heard Sophie Tucker.

Leaving New York seemed to trigger a spate of literary pastiche, a mélange of Joyce, Carl Sandburg, possibly Brecht, all aimed at Harold. "St. Louis, Armpit of the West, city flowering smoke, who sticks her dirty fingers into the craintive [*sic*] sky . . . whores in roadsters, thick as lice; Jews are still called sheenies instead of kikes, and lots of low Jews who eat their own snot . . ."

In May, he was shipped to Cleveland, where another of his father's stores required family attention. Charged with managing the business, Greenberg was sick at the responsibility: "I'm always afraid I've forgotten something," he wrote to Harold. He was living in a $30-a-week room at the Allerton Hotel downtown, registered as Clement Green to elude a neckwear manufacturer with whom his father's store was now competing. Business was bad, he told Harold, people owed him money and he suffered from "concrete loneliness." In mid-July 1933, he was summoned home, probably for a business briefing from his father. He stopped off on the way to see Harold in Syracuse. Later, he described the New York visit as "terrible—I felt and still feel . . . nowhere." But returning to Cleveland was no better. Chronic indigestion prompted him to self-diagnose a "pre-ulcer" condition and put himself on a milk diet. "I don't know what to think of myself," he wrote Harold.

In mid-August, his father picked him up in Cleveland and drove him to Chicago. There, they visited the World's Fair, which Clement viewed with a critical eye. "Spectacular and lousy," he concluded, "looking very, very cheap in the daylight and like a swell soda fountain at night." After two hours at the fair, his father delivered him to the train that would carry him to his next assignment, San Francisco. Another neckwear outlet required Clement's attention. He interrupted the long train ride in Ogden, Utah, a bleak assortment of railroad-related businesses and modest clapboard homes some thirty miles north of Salt Lake City. Forming a judgment after only a few hours in town, he wrote to Harold that the Mormons were as "strange" as the Arabs described by Charles Montagu Doughty in his 1888 book, *Travels in Arabia Deserta*. After twelve hours of contemplating cowboys, girls riding ponies bareback, and the backdrop of craggy mountains, he reboarded a westbound train, and paid an extra $20 for a berth in the tourist sleeping car. "It's intended that I stay in Frisco for three months and then go to Los Angeles for the rest of the year's exile."

In a short story written some time later, Greenberg described his arrival in San Francisco. "It is summer and clad in summer clothes as he stands on the upper foredeck of the ferry crossing the bay, he is suddenly greeted by a cold bitter wind that sets him to shivering in every bone." Like many another traveler from the East, he expected balmy California sunshine and was unaware that San Francisco had the coolest summers in America. Lodged in the Pickwick Hotel in the heart of downtown, he was desolate. "I get drunk every other night," he wrote to Harold. "All of a sudden I see why such a fuss is made over [inebriation]. It's a wonder they don't make more of it, so precious it is." He was sleeping until 9:30 a.m. every day, "so fucking unhappy there's use in nothing else but saying it." The figure in his short story is "walking the streets alone, with a loneliness doubly driven into him by the blank faces he sees on the street." He finds the beach too chilly for swimming and the park shrouded in clammy fog. "Four months pass like this," he writes, "until the misery of loneliness and neglect becomes the only abiding sentiment and mood, staining all things the same color."

That August, he focused desperately on women, while giving Harold some cocky advice: "Look: you meet a woman and take her

out seven or eight times . . . Then you find out a moment when
you're twisted and twined in each other's mind, like winter snakes
. . . trying to realize that you now know every inch of her."
  Such encounters may have inspired more poetry like this:

> In peeping down your open dress
> Oh lady, what reassures I see
> What before was hard to guess
> Now the plainest reality.

> As the pilgrim lifted up
> When at last he sees his rest
> So do I rise up
> Seeing the shade of your breast.

  In November 1933, such fantasies seemed to approach reality.
"I've met a girl with her own roadster and three dogs," he wrote to
Harold. "She has unknown amounts of money, I hear. She even
has shares on the market that go by her father's name. Meanwhile
she likes me and calls me Clement, instead of Clem."

Chapter II

WHAT NEXT?

WHILE HE WAS KISSING HER, she had suddenly cried, Greenberg wrote in a short story he hoped to publish. She was sobbing that one day he would break her heart. He was "shallow," she had said, and he had smirked. So went the fiction. Later, he matter-of-factly described her to Harold: Gentile, twenty-six years old, divorced for three years, and her name was Toady Ewing. Greenberg confessed: "Lord, Harold, I'm lost."

So besotted was he that for the rest of his life, he kept a beginner's poem Toady sent him:

> I washed my face in water
> That'd neither rained nor run
> I dried myself on a towel
> That was neither wove nor spun.
>
> Now tell me true
> How was that done?
> I can't believe it none.
> I washed my face with the morning dew
> And dried it in the sun.

In the fictionalized account of his romance with Toady (renamed "Sarah"), Greenberg wrote that she lived on Russian Hill in San Francisco with her widowed mother and worked for a substantial firm of attorneys. She had "a perfect kind of prettiness," he wrote, "each feature delicate and precise" and a voice that "turned deep through the telephone, which set him madly in love every time he heard it." Her friends were people from Stanford University and included "musicians and artists and landscape gardeners and reporters." Sarah and her mother drove Greenberg down the Pacific coast past fog-shrouded Half Moon Bay to the beach at Santa Cruz. He was living "from weekend to weekend." Soon, they were parked at Land's End in her mother's Ford, getting drunk and lingering until early morning in fervent embrace.

In the story, which Greenberg also kept with his papers until the end of his life, Sarah possessed a "sexual sureness" that the unnamed hero attributed to her having been married before; it "allowed her to do things that would have shocked him in a virgin. Her curiosity and her pure objective joy in physical sensations was like a man's." She soon told him that the previous year she had been secretly engaged to a young law student at the University of California at Berkeley; the engagement ended when a doctor told the young man that marriage might aggravate his "touch of TB." She told him of other disappointing liaisons, to which he responded by "feeling bad that there were so many before me." "What did you want me to do?" she asked. "Go into a nunnery?"

He "became sensitive in matters of fornication. When he saw a movie in which a man forgave a woman her transgressions, he would get hot with rage. When he read about such things . . . he would pencil his curses on the margin." When she was boldly sexual, he imagined her previous "trail of concupiscence, a well-stocked rich, sinful career . . . mysterious, undivinable that he would go mad trying to penetrate." When she fell into baby talk after their first kiss, he found it "queer and exciting."

A month after they first met, they drove south on a serpentine, often fog-shrouded road high above the ocean, past small settlements left over from the Prohibition-era booze trade. At a deserted beach they parked and, "hidden from the sight of the world, they lay in each others' arms." They drove back to San Francisco, reciting poetry to each other. But Greenberg (assuming it was indeed he, rather than his fictional stand-in) was troubled by her lack of shame, remorse, or modesty. She now struck him as "too old a hand at these pleasures," even though her behavior filled him with "a queer pleasurable excitement."

Then Toady's mother went out of town, leaving them alone in the apartment for two days. In the story, it is at this point that Sarah tells the narrator about her prior marital infidelities and says, "I'm going to marry you." Laughing, he replies, "I haven't any money. I haven't enough money to marry." But she is adamant. "Down from the elevations of his drunkenness . . . he forgave her," Greenberg wrote. "He was looking forward too much to the night in bed to worry about his prayers and his psalters and the autobiography of his passion." But after leaving the next morning, he agonizes over her defects and his lack of funds, realizing that "if he didn't marry her he would have to go away still loving her and to leave her to someone else's arms and that would equal the agony of realizing her past."

To Harold, Greenberg wrote that he couldn't help but "sound inordinately smug" after spending the night with Toady, "going home at 7:30 in the gray cowpiss California morning—all passion spent and reeling with bliss." But he discouraged any contact between Toady and Harold because "that sort of thing would tangle my heels when I make my eventual escape—shame on me for that . . . Please, you don't know how in this case I hate myself."

The letters to Harold now were devoid of literary or artistic allusions, but focused entirely on Greenberg's romance. One from March 1934 was filled obsessively with details about Toady, her auburn hair, "mottled" blue eyes, five-foot-two height, "short upgoing nose," faint eyebrows, and "small always red mouth . . . good legs . . . a couple of moles on her forehead." She read slowly and talked "in a monologue, so that I can listen whenever I want to," implying that he frequently tuned her out. A grandfather had been a judge and the ex-husband "was a tall, handsome shit." Toady had graduated from Stanford, where she was "one of those snappy, high-toned Kappa Alpha Theta girls." By the time the letter reached Harold, Greenberg wrote, he and Toady would be married: "I couldn't help myself."

After a two-day honeymoon in Yosemite, Greenberg moved into Toady's apartment at 1644 Taylor Street; her mother had recently moved to a cottage in Carmel, a charming seaside town about one hundred miles south of San Francisco. In the newly-weds' honor, the son of the president of the Southern Pacific Railroad threw a cocktail party, at which, Greenberg reported, he met "some few choice shitheels and many pricks . . . some of the best people." Four days later, he was already disenchanted with his bride. She was "palpably ignorant . . . without whimsy, inordinate-ly well-bred . . . with that Gentile passion for knowing a lot about a little bit." He made her cry by saying that he wouldn't "be true to her forever."

By the end of April, they left San Francisco for Los Angeles, where his father had another wholesale neckwear outlet, and where Greenberg was soon gawking at other women. The neckwear business was slow, so Greenberg tried to get a job at RKO. When that proved unsuccessful, he spewed venom on the movie studios. All you needed to know about them, he wrote to Harold, is that they are "a Jewish business." Inside, they look like "big bathhouses" with "a lot of sporty looking little Jews and fairy scenario writers and high school girls." As for Los Angeles, it was "nothing but cheapness . . . cheap shit, cheap goods . . . a nickel buys a dime if you have the nickel and you can piss on the sidewalk."

Early in June, the necktie business failed, leaving Greenberg stranded without an income. The newlyweds moved into the three-room cottage "bordering the wilderness" in Carmel, where Toady's mother was nursing a sprained back. "Haven't a cent and we're living on the mother," he told Harold. Among the others who made their home in this pastel West Coast version of an Italian hill town were the poet Robinson Jeffers, the muckraking journalist Lincoln Steffens, and the photographer Ansel Adams— "California Bohemia," as Greenberg described it. He found a job at a newspaper in nearby Monterey, which published his interview with Charles Laughton under a byline. The actor was "a dud," he wrote Harold, "and carried his wife with him to prove he wasn't a fairy." After a week Greenberg was fired; not enough experience, he was told. Much later, Greenberg admitted to an interviewer that he "was incompetent. I was too screwed up. I wasn't grown up yet." He then started writing short stories: "send them out and get them back." He was now twenty-five years old and "too young," he wrote, "to be married."

Early in August, Greenberg's father offered him money for only one purpose: to come home. So, although he felt "like a skunk," he would soon leave Carmel and Toady, who was pregnant. Greenberg wrote that he was "as unconcerned about my seed as if I'd used it to water the burnt grass here . . . I'm ashamed of being a father and I'm too young to be one." In fact, he was exactly the same age his father was when Greenberg was born.

On the way home, Greenberg spent a few days in Syracuse with Harold, who then came to New York for a week's visit in October. Soon after Harold left, Greenberg learned that *Esquire* magazine had bought his short story "Mutiny in Jalisco" for $50. He had submitted it under a pseudonym, R. H. Torres, and was pleased to send the magazine a bit of biographical data: his full name was Robert Herman Torres; he lived in Carmel, California, and knew seven languages. *Esquire* was one of the most successful magazines launched in the 1930s; its blend of provocative female flesh, salty tales of derring-do, and literary fiction was designed to appeal to a male audience. On the cover during 1935 alone, it featured such prominent contributors as Thomas Mann, F. Scott Fitzgerald, Langston Hughes, Erskine Caldwell, Thomas Wolfe, William Saroyan, John Dos Passos, Maxim Gorky, and Georges Simenon. Greenberg's pseudonym, however, was not on the cover, but mentioned on the contents page under the rubric "Semi-Fiction."

Ostensibly the recollections of its author, the story described a bloody firefight during Pancho Villa's rebellion in Mexico in 1912. A band of rebels refuses to obey their colonel's order to charge into a machine-gun nest. After the opponents are routed, the officer selects five men to execute for disobeying orders. A comrade kills the colonel with a single blow from a machete, but is himself killed and later found still clutching the colonel's severed head. Without ever having been there, Greenberg vividly described the parched shrubs and the dearth of shelter in that unforgiving desert, but his soldiers sound more like Boy Scouts or summer campers than hard-bitten followers of a Mexican revolutionary. Nevertheless, after Greenberg's success with *Esquire*, his father would roust him out of bed in the morning, saying, "Get to work. The typewriter is out."

Among the interested readers of "Mutiny in Jalisco" was an editor at the publishing house of Doubleday, Doran. He asked to see any book-length manuscripts Greenberg might have or a proposal for any book he might be planning to write. The National Rifle Association also was interested in Greenberg's further shoot-'em-up fiction, and was even willing to pay a premium—one and one-half cents per word instead of the usual one cent—for anything it could publish in *The American Rifleman*. Soon, the London *Evening Standard* offered to distribute the story to newspapers all over the world, translating it into other languages. Eventually,

Greenberg netted another $51.60 from this endeavor. In 1936, the WPA Writers Project asked "Torres" to provide biographical data for a compilation about "all writers of Spanish descent." Greenberg apparently never replied; the return envelope with its three-cent stamp remained in his files.

While his family was impressed by his writing success, Greenberg was well aware that such Hemingwayesque yarns about gun battles in Mexico were potboilers. When interviewed years later about when he started writing for publication, he ignored this early success and pushed his earliest writing forward by several years to a time when he was producing more serious work.

In the euphoria over getting his writing published, regret over his marriage and impending fatherhood went by the board. In his letters to Harold, Greenberg dwelled on his success as a writer, while conveniently forgetting that his wife would face motherhood without his support. When he received news in mid-November of almost perfect scores in a civil service exam, he expected to find a government job soon, possibly in Washington, D.C. In the meantime, his father sent him to St. Louis to wind up the unprofitable necktie business there and, perhaps, go on to California to await the birth of his child. He stayed at the St. Louis YMCA (an echo of his year at the Marquand School) because it was inexpensive enough to let him send Toady $2 every week. Although he told Harold that he felt "low and cheap," he did not go back to California.

Greenberg was not present when his son was born on February 1, 1935; indeed, he claimed that he forgot most of the time that he was a father. Instead, he lengthily described to Harold his excitement over publication of his second short story in *Esquire*. Impressed by that success, Greenberg's father bought him a typewriter and promised to pay him $25 a week if he would go back to Carmel and continue with his writing. Near the end of August

1935, Greenberg was on his way west, piecing together a journey by train and car, plus a circuitous ride on the Great Northern Railroad to Portland, then south to San Francisco. There was no particular rush to see his wife and son; he was traveling light, having shipped books and clothing to Carmel by boat in a wooden crate. As it turned out, Greenberg probably left Carmel before that baggage arrived. His mother-in-law, Mrs. Ewing, made it clear that she "wanted no part of him," he told an interviewer more than fifty years later. To Harold, he said that he found little Danny "as big and healthy as all the cherubs ever painted"; the baby "smiled the first time he saw me." But the marriage to Toady was over. He boarded a bus for New York after only six days.

At about this time, Greenberg wrote two connected and ambiguous poems that were never published but remained in his files for the rest of his life. The first was called "For My Wife":

> What can I praise but you who are, always
> Whom I have praised already?
> Shall I praise these commonplaces,
> Each cell, the flesh so tried and true
> And all five senses?
> Shall I praise them?
> You are the death of all I write,
> The book, that is, and every page.

The second, "For My Son," ends:

> Thus all things leap and fall to flame
> Even your birth was such.
> I made of something nothing
> And you of that nothing, much.

The confused, contradictory messages in these poems reflect Greenberg's inner conflicts over the marital mess he had left behind. He did not write to Harold for more than three months, explaining that he had been "in awful dumps." In New York, he tried in vain to write more fiction. Meanwhile, an acquaintance who had gone into publishing paid him $125 to translate a German anti-Nazi book, *The Brown Network*. He considered his marriage to Toady "all off," and his efforts to persuade her to divorce him had boiled down to "a dirty question of money." As for Danny, he vacillated between the "torture" of not seeing the boy and indignation over requests from Toady and her mother, who, "full of vulgar Gentile notions about 'safeguarding Danny's future,' wants me to have life insurance [and] so forth." Greenberg also was eager for money but his goals clashed: he wanted enough money to go back to California "to play with the little bastard," and also enough to divorce Toady. He turned once again to poetry, its tone more maudlin than ever:

> If you ruin your life at 26, can you every pick it up again
> Will you ever find someone to love you
> Time isn't big enough. It takes years to find a loving heart
> For yourself. Love's Pilgrim. Oh weary road.

In February 1936, Greenberg was hired for a two-month job at the Federal Civil Service Commission; he would process simple papers and be paid $30 a week. In the evenings he translated from the German "a junky novel" based on the life of Goya, for $200 plus royalties. He found the two jobs enervating, but was glad to send Toady $100 to set the divorce in motion. Although he soon landed a job with the Veterans Bureau at $31.50 a week, the divorce negotiations dragged on, with Toady demanding $10 in monthly alimony plus $15 support for Danny. Greenberg wanted to pay nothing for his child, because Toady and her mother "will otherwise pull my pants off some day," he wrote to Harold. He discerned in them "a mean Gentile quality . . . so cold, so just, so sensible. They'd just as soon draw & quarter me." At the same time, he bragged about how tall his thirteen-month-old son was and wrote that he was "dying for the little stinker."

While still living at home, Greenberg started renting a horse from a nearby stable and went riding in Prospect Park several times a week. It was a pastime that "keeps me alive," he wrote Harold. "I canter through the park and sing 'A Melody from the sky' from the 'The Trail of the Lonesome Pine.'" He galloped so fast that the riding master "bawls me out for sweating the horse." The reins in his hand gave Greenberg a transient illusion of being in charge, a diversion from the divorce and Danny, situations that had spiraled out of control. Nor was it reassuring that at age twenty-seven he was still at home (although now paying $35 a month for room and board) and had yet to embark on a career.

In September 1936, he drove north in his father's new Buick to vacation in Quebec. He relished seeing shrines and churches in that pious Canadian province. He also enjoyed speaking French and proudly reported to Harold that the cashier at a cinema had complimented him on his accent. At his hotel, he spent an evening chatting up the hotel owner's two daughters; the following night, he got drunk and "stayed up till 3, making love to [twenty-year-old] Clotilde in French and exchanging soul kisses."

So far, he had demonstrated a brilliant mind eager to devour a vast array of literature, a gift for learning languages, a rush to making harsh judgments of all his experiences, and a desire to express himself verbally and graphically. But just as the black-and-white yardstick he used to measure the creative work of others lacked modulation, his acute judgment failed to apply a realistic gray scale to his own drawings, poetry, and fiction. He described himself as an artistic prodigy, but was unable to see the mediocrity of his own attempts at art. His youthful behavior demonstrated a certain laziness, a self-indulgence, a callousness that would never disappear. He responded to challenge, like his impulsive marriage and unplanned fatherhood, with anger, childish regression, evasion, flight, and even acute mental breakdown. These would be his reactions to many crises in his life. But he also had a reserve of determination and an assortment of genuine talents that would finally launch him, at almost thirty years old, into a meteoric, influential, and, eventually, even lucrative career. After his return from Canada, Greenberg took the first halting steps in that direction by getting acquainted with Greenwich Village, not too far from where he worked.

During the Depression, the artistic heritage of the Village had merged with the radicalism characteristic of much of New York at the time. Its blend of artists, writers, and musicians mingled with the organizers and hangers-on of various revolutionary sects. First among these was the Communist Party, which garnered its support from Stalin's Soviet Union, a few wealthy American heirs of capitalist fortunes who thrilled at mingling with the proletariat, and a considerable number of idealistic New Yorkers who saw the lingering Depression at home and the rise of nationalist dictatorships in Europe as the death throes of capitalism. The Communist Party struck many as the speediest vehicle for achieving the paradise promised by Marx and Lenin.

To that end, mimeograph machines in Greenwich Village and other lower-Manhattan neighborhoods worked overtime, their operators largely unpaid, churning out agitprop papers. Greenberg, along with many visitors to the Village, soon became aware of fund-raising parties, marches, protests, and rallies, mostly built around the perceived crisis of capitalism. The Communist Party was a major instigator of such events, as it attempted to embrace all leftists, including more moderate reformers, under a United Front policy.

In 1934, the party's John Reed Club had launched a new magazine, less stridently political and more literary than its long-established *New Masses*, and named it *Partisan Review*. William Phillips, an editor of the new publication, wrote under a pseudonym urging a scientific approach to literary criticism, with Marxist theory at its core. He was certain that "the most talented and those who always showed the greatest clarity in their writings are identifying themselves with the struggle of the workers."

Clement Greenberg had been acquainted with *New Masses* as early as June 1928, the end of his sophomore year at Syracuse, and he had instantly offered Harold a slashing critique. Perhaps it had once been a respectable literary and artistic publication, he wrote, but now it was a skimpy sheet "of heavy black type, coarse paper, and a general atmosphere . . . representative of the workman in his naked unassumingness." Instead of "pink radicals proud of their intelligence and collegiate expression," the contributors struck him as "heavy-handed coal-heavers, lumberjacks, and garbage collectors."

Apart from considering *New Masses* as a possible outlet for his poetry and fiction, Greenberg had shown little interest in politics. In 1933, to cheer himself up while enduring the loneliness of San Francisco, he had attended a Communist-sponsored rally on behalf of a bitter strike by San Joaquin Valley farm workers. To Harold, he mocked a Mexican speaker's urging support for the fight against "de capitalistic classes." Near the end of that year, he sent Harold a gruesome postcard showing two stripped corpses hanging from a tree in San Jose. Neither the photo, sold in San Francisco two days after the actual event, nor Greenberg's message indicated why these two had been lynched.

However, as he mingled with the Village radicals in 1937,

Greenberg found himself "very easily influenced . . . about politics and literature." He sympathized with Americans fighting alongside the Spanish Loyalists against the fascists led by Franco, and was familiar with the deadly Stalinist putsch of the anti-Franco forces. He blamed Stalin also for the deplorable content of the current *New Masses*: he had "never read worse," observing that Stalin's "darkness affects the mind more thoroughly than syphilis infects the blood." The behavior of the Russian dictator's disciples would often send him "into a froth," he wrote Harold. These emotions were encouraged by an unnamed "intelligent Marxist" he had recently met.

Greenberg was not alone in searching for a radical alternative to a Communist Party tarnished by its authoritarian Soviet sponsor. His contemporary, Irving Howe, who would spend much of his life seeking a way to humanize Marxism, was as dazzled by this "scientific" philosophy's vitality as he was disappointed by the Stalinists' crude appropriation of it. To him, Marxism not only provided a framework for understanding current events, but also a "profoundly dramatic view of human experience . . . inevitable conflicts, apocalyptic climaxes, ultimate moments, hours of doom, and shining tomorrows." Only later would he see the factional political battles of the thirties as "charades of struggle, substitute rituals for the battles we could not join."

A similar "line" was being developed by the founding editors of *Partisan Review* as they broke with the Communist Party in October 1936, two years after the magazine's debut. The editors, William Phillips and Philip Rahv, were furious over the party's meddling with their literary judgments and decided to publish *Partisan Review* independently. After an industrious search for a non-Communist angel, they revived the magazine in 1937, subsidized by a $1,500 per year grant from the artist George L. K. Morris, brother of the New York civic and cultural figure Newbold Morris.

The Communist Party continued to vilify the magazine, its editors and authors, and even published a competing "Literary Supplement" to *New Masses*, even though *Partisan Review* was able to distribute a scant six hundred copies of its first issue. The Communists were sensitive about new happenings in the Soviet Union that galvanized the "oppositional" left in New York and elsewhere. On top of the Stalinist murders of non-Communist volunteers in Spain, the Soviet regime began a dismal series of trials, accusing Communist Party functionaries of high crimes and executing them as soon as they had abjectly confessed. Such Stalinist atrocities, however, did not persuade the editors of *Partisan Review* that Marxist theory was to blame; Philip Rahv in 1938 affirmed his faith in Marxism, "the marriage of science and humanism," in a *Partisan Review* article. And when the leading accused, Leon Trotsky, managed to escape arrest and flee, first to France and then to Mexico City, he was soon in touch with the revived *Partisan Review*. He would remain an influential figure, both as a writer and as the subject of other writers, even after he was murdered with an ice axe by a Stalinist agent in 1940.

Defections to the Trotsky camp infuriated the Communist Party. When the dissidents tried to distribute a fortnightly paper after being summarily expelled from the party, they were attacked by "a mob of their good comrades of yesterday," recalled Max Shachtman, a founder of the American Communist Party at the age of sixteen and now organizer of a splinter Trotskyite faction. The Communist bullies, he wrote, "ripped the papers out of [the dissenters'] hands and threatened to beat them to the ground." The Trotskyite group's first public meeting was disrupted when "the doors were forced open by a Communist gang . . . armed with lead pipes, blackjacks, clubs, and knives."

The literature purveyed by any of the radical factions hardly consisted of carefully weighed statements of principle; rather it was designed to inflame the reader. Shachtman's passionate 142-page tirade against Bolshevism typified the extreme partisanship of the radical writings of the time. For twenty-five cents, a reader received a roughly printed pamphlet whose twenty-seven chapters unrelentingly eviscerated Stalinists. By contrast, it portrayed Leon Trotsky as a meek, persecuted soul, certainly not the fiery polemicist or the military leader who, during the Russian Civil War, sent armored trains crisscrossing the country, leaving swaths of hunger, disease, and death in their wake.

Clement Greenberg became aware of these battles during frequent visits to a Sunday afternoon open house at the Greenwich Village apartment of his cousin Sonja and her husband, Otto Rosahn. There, he met Harold Rosenberg, the son of Jewish immigrants in Brooklyn, who had graduated from an obscure Brooklyn law school and was already a published poet. He was six feet four inches tall and, said Greenberg many years later, "looked like a Sumerian prince." Just three years older than Greenberg, Rosenberg was firmly established as a facile writer and a fiery talker. Legend had it that he once concocted proof for his friend Lionel Abel that "Helen of Troy was really a loaf of bread." But then, Abel himself had fancifully speculated that a Marxist good deed would be to develop a detective "who could solve crimes by calling upon dialectical materialism."

In January 1933, Rosenberg and a partner, H. R. Hays, published the *New Act*, a little magazine that lasted for just three sporadic issues before expiring in April 1934. The first contained an article by Rosenberg on class-consciousness and literature, as well as several poems and book reviews. Most significant was an essay attacking the esteemed American literary critic Van Wyck Brooks for his decades-long crusade to establish a literature redolent of American values, writings more Emersonian, more Whitmanesque than what he termed the decadence of Marcel Proust, André Gide, James

Joyce, and Franz Kafka. The essay in the *New Act* foreshadowed many blows that would topple Brooks from the cultural summit to irrelevance. The next issue contained, among other tidbits, a fourteen-page Surrealist prose work, "Clavicules," by René Daumal, "leader of a group of young French writers who publish almost exclusively in their own magazine, *Le Grand Jeu.*" The third issue dwindled to a roughly translated article on art and social life by Georgi Plekhanov, a Russian nonconforming radical who died in 1918, and an essay by Ezra Pound on Arthur Rimbaud.

Meanwhile, Rosenberg had found work at the federal relief project for writers, the WPA American Guide series, sponsored by the Works Progress Administration. In 1938, some months after meeting Greenberg, Rosenberg became art editor of the series, a job that would take him and his wife, May Tabak, to Washington. Rosenberg had provided Greenberg's first contact with *Partisan Review*, but the two men's relationship rapidly cooled. Just a few months after their first meeting, Greenberg was writing Harold Lazarus, who was then working in Washington, that Rosenberg would contact him, but to beware of Rosenberg's wife, "a nasty customer."

Two months later, in a revealing projection of his own weaknesses, Greenberg granted that the Rosenbergs were replete "with justice and accuracy" but suffered from a "desire always to be right"; if they showed "more error and less childishness, [Harold] Rosenberg would be a forest-fire success." Two weeks later, Greenberg told Lazarus that Rosenberg "has it in him to be greedy like a child, to grab without waiting to decide whether he wants what he's grabbing." After he saw the Rosenbergs again during their summertime visit to New York, Greenberg wrote Harold that Rosenberg "annoyed me to death." For the rest of his life, Greenberg would demean and denounce Rosenberg, who would reply in kind, a monumental feud that provided decades of amusement to all in the art world except the protagonists themselves.

Before the Rosenbergs left New York, they had introduced Greenberg to Lionel Abel, who had found some success as a playwright and theater critic, and who could have been Greenberg's early guide to the intricacies of dialectical materialism. It was Abel who later called New York the only American city in the early 1930s that believed it was actually in Russia. The city was so radicalized, he said, that a mass meeting of six thousand cheered as Max Shachtman read aloud the full text of Trotsky's speech defending himself against Stalin's slanders.

In some ways, Trotsky's American followers were just as destructive as the Communists. When several hundred members of the Trotskyite faction joined the American Socialist Party in 1936, their doctrinaire squabbling ravaged that long-established left-wing organization: from attracting nine hundred thousand votes in the 1932 presidential election, the Socialists won fewer than two hundred thousand in 1936. Irving Howe described the Trotskyites as "virtuosos of ideology" who practiced "a mixture of intellectual rigor and destructive quarrelsomeness."

Clement Greenberg continued to drift lazily within this overheated radical realm: after all, preaching violent overthrow of the same government that issued his weekly paycheck seemed a bit illogical, if not self-destructive. Yet he lingered strikingly on the fringe; in the memoirs of many players on that turbulent stage, articles and books written many years later, his name appears frequently in the index, but the text mentions him almost always in passing—a bystander, a figure in a group, a face glimpsed in a crowded room. Greenberg would eventually find within this cauldron the germ of theories that lent conviction to his art criticism, but not quite yet. In the meantime, he attended many of the radicals' social events, like many others less in search of ideology than of a few drinks, a good time, and, if lucky, a willing sexual partner.

In truth, he resembled many of those who filled out Trotskyite fund-raisers or rallies. They may have been "heroic," as one participant described them, but most were "proletarians-by-proxy only," including a tea-leaf reader, a hefty husband and wife who were ex-gymnasts, a table tennis champion who broke his hand hitting the table instead of the ball, and an abortionist trolling for work. "Arrivistes and activists" crowded parties funded by well-off dentists and doctors. At one such event, at Irving Plaza, two fetching Vassar graduates and aspiring writers gyrated suggestively in black leotards. Eleanor Clark and Mary McCarthy, wrote one observer, were "both going through a Cultural Transference for Truth and Trotskyism." McCarthy, who was then living with *Partisan Review* editor Philip Rahv, would soon turn up as Greenberg's frequent sexual partner, identified in his date books only as M.M.

Among the contentious radicals were young men who would later pummel and shape American society and culture, while also substantially tailoring their extreme views into garments more suitable for a centrist nation. They also included names that would later be prominent: the sociologist Daniel Bell, the essayist Norman Podhoretz, the literary critics Irving Howe and Alfred Kazin, and the political polemicists Sidney Hook and Irving Kristol. At City College in the late 1930s, Kristol recalled some four decades later, he would read every *Partisan Review* article at least twice, "in a state of awe and exasperation," impressed by "such elegance of style and profundity of mind, depressed . . . that a commoner like myself" could never attain entry into "that intellectual aristocracy."

Among those Kristol faced was Daniel Bell. In 1932, at age thirteen, Bell had joined the Young People's Socialist League and spent Sundays studying dialectical materialism at the radical Rand School at Fifteenth Street and Union Square. Ironically, in 1960 he would publish a key work "on the exhaustion of political ideas in the Fifties," *The End of Ideology.* The literary critic Alfred Kazin recalled that "all the cleverest and most dynamic people . . . gave authority to Marxist opinion . . . When the iron laws of history were pronounced in upper-class accents, it was hard not to be impressed." As a student, Irving Howe had been impressed by the size of the Communist faction at City College: "They must have had four or five-hundred members, including many professors." His Trotskyite bloc included no professors, but when Max Shachtman "demolished" the Communist Morris Schappes in a debate, Howe had "never heard such a barrage of rhetoric, invective, wit, humor, polemical annihilation."

On the fringe of those figures whom Irving Howe would later label "the New York Intellectuals," Greenberg wavered and weighed his prospects as a literary critic. But these talented strivers clearly demonstrated that he was not the sole owner of a persuasive rhetorical style that hammered personal opinion into the sword of certitude. Among these outspoken intellects, the magna cum laude graduate of Syracuse University found himself surrounded by crafty, well-educated veterans of torrid political debates at the City College of New York.

Though they constituted a minuscule urbanized minority in the context of twentieth-century America, the audience for their views even then was considerably larger than Clement Greenberg's single loyal follower, Harold Lazarus. Most of the others had built a secular version of an age-old Jewish religious tradition: noisy disputation over the true meaning of often obscure passages in the Old Testament. Indeed, echoes of that disputatious style would also lurk in Greenberg's rhetoric. Still, in this contentious milieu of the late 1930s, Greenberg was not the self-assured letter-writer who spouted strong views on everything from the trashiness of Los Angeles to the poetry of Rainer Maria Rilke. Rather, he was still the befuddled swain caught up in a hopeless dilemma—an unwilling father who sometimes tried to love his son at a distance, and himself a son still extending the no-man's-land separating him from his own father.

In the spring of 1937, Greenberg lost his government job. The country was going through another trough in the seemingly endless Depression; after a brief recovery, the unemployment rate was again approaching 20 percent. Now, there was plenty of time to write lachrymose letters to Harold: Greenberg had the grippe, he was on a bland diet for pre-ulcer stomach trouble and depressed over the downward spiral of the Spanish Loyalists. The final divorce from Toady came through on June 26; the grounds were desertion and monthly child support was set at $5, considerably less than the $15 she had demanded.

Leaving Danny with her mother in Carmel, Toady moved to Washington, where she contacted Harold Lazarus. Greenberg immediately asked Harold, "What do you think of the cracked ice that is my ex-wifekin?" But he was enraged, six months later, when Harold informed him that Toady was again engaged to be married. "It's no light thing, to have given your life to somebody," Greenberg fumed. "The worst thing is when they take that piece of your life to throw, toss, drop it as they're walking in the street and forget immediately all about it . . . To think that I produced no effect."

In his mind, Greenberg had become the aggrieved party, exploited by Toady and especially her mother, "one of those villainesses in the silken cord plays they used to have . . . years ago." In September 1938, he was outraged that Toady's new husband had agreed to adopt Danny. "Why should my life suddenly have a property judgment on it?" he asked Harold, when Toady's and Mrs. Ewing's "aberrations" were to blame. By November, Greenberg was miffed that Danny was now living with Toady and her husband in Washington: "Only 250 miles away, and, myself, dying to see him," he wrote to Harold, "but somewhat afraid." A week later, he was "bitter sore" that Toady had "made a black villain out of me." He claimed that the only reason he refused to send child support for Danny was that "I wanted old lady Ewing to bear the brunt herself." He was "willing to take the lad any time," he told Harold."

In August 1937, Greenberg had started work at a new job as a clerk with the U. S. Customs Service, Appraiser's Division at the Port of New York; he would be paid $1,700 per year, with a $100 annual raise to a maximum of $2,100. "Some luck!" he wrote to Harold. Greenberg worked in a private office. Mornings he did paperwork there, and he spent afternoons in a warehouse, checking cases of liquor ("so well made and neat") and measuring the contents of wine bottles ("before lunch, the smell of the opened wine drives me nuts"). Reading the invoices, he enjoyed using his French, German, Italian, Portuguese, Greek, and Spanish. His office colleagues were all "nice farts, old farts, still farts," while the warehouse laborers were "real nice proletarians" who had been on the job for at least ten years.

Greenberg's letters now referred increasingly to the dire world situation; he wrote to Harold that he was touched by "lots of 1st hand letters from Spain." Influenced by his new contacts among the Trotskyites, he delved more deeply than ever into the philosophy that underpinned dialectical materialism. Earlier, he had read Oswald Spengler's grimly pessimistic tome, *The Decline of the West*, which anticipated the imminent end of Western civilization. In the crisis-hued world in which Greenberg now circulated, dialectical materialism seemed to offer a way out of inevitable decline. But "if you were not somewhere within the [Communist] Party's wide orbit," wrote Robert Warshow, who would later become a colleague of Greenberg's, "much of your thought and energy had to be devoted to maintaining yourself in opposition." The result, he believed, was "a disastrous vulgarization of intellectual life." The level of culture was depressed, perhaps even more than the economy, as the educated public sank into what would later be excoriated as "middlebrow culture."

In March 1938, at long last, Greenberg moved out of the family home in Brooklyn to a single room with shared bath at 48 West Seventeenth Street in lower Manhattan. It was a neighborhood of factory lofts but it was close to Greenwich Village. The following October, he migrated to a small apartment in a five-story building at 9 Minetta Street in the heart of the Village. The building's faux Oriental doorway opened onto a tiny, tree-lined curving lane off Sixth Avenue. The rent was $36 a month.

Now that he was a full-time Village resident, Greenberg engaged more vigorously in the Trotskyite debates, especially concerning the decline of "high culture." The crisis showed him a chance to carve out a unique position for himself in the cultural debate. Based on his formal education, wide-ranging reading, and strongly developed opinions, he seemed to be heading for a career as a literary critic. However, he was also taking life-drawing classes with the artist Igor Pantukhov, then a close friend of Lee Krasner, another aspiring artist. Krasner spoke highly of Hans Hofmann, an abstract painter who had fled Nazi Germany and founded an art school just east of Greenwich Village. Greenberg made a point of attending his lectures on abstract art in 1938 and 1939.

After a brief flourish during the teens and early twenties, abstract art in America had fallen into obscurity. Its patronage was sparse and those who were interested in modernist art preferred works by Europeans. But in 1936, soon after the government began to fund art projects and the Museum of Modern Art began to champion European artists like Piet Mondrian, a small band in New York organized as Abstract American Artists. The group's first exhibition was held in 1936 in the Squibb Building, near the venue at Fifty-seventh Street and Fifth Avenue where MoMA had presented its earliest shows. Without much encouragement from press or patrons, this group would continue to exhibit into the 1960s. The 1936 show itself attracted little media attention. But the following year an entirely unrelated happening, the founding of the Guggenheim Museum of Nonobjective Art, triggered an extensive, often bitter debate over abstract art in the pages of the *New York Times*. Reviewing the AAA show in April 1937, the sole art critic at the *Times*, Edward Alden Jewell, gingerly tiptoed through that prickly space between the artists' desire for a decent review and his readers' desire for art that conveyed something recognizable. His review highlighted his own bewilderment over modern art of any kind. Each of the AAA's thirty-nine exhibitors, he wrote, was "arguing to some degree his endowment as a raconteur of tales from over yonder on the Rive Gauche." He praised precisely what the abstract artists disdained: the show's "colorful and often resounding mass demonstration of decorative design."

Such marginalizing of new art was hardly a tactful move; it followed by just a few months a front-page story in the *New York Times* announcing a new foundation whose central purpose was "promotion of the abstract type of modern painting." Its president and founder was a "copper man," Solomon R. Guggenheim, who was seeking to "blaze a new trail in popular art appreciation." The nucleus of the collection was already hanging in his luxury apartment at the Plaza Hotel and was shown to the press late in June 1937. Among representational works by Seurat, Chagall, Picasso, and Feininger, the Guggenheim collection also included many works by the pioneer of abstract painting Wassily Kandinsky. There were also many paintings by the unknown Rudolph Bauer, who happened to be the lover of the collection's curator, the formidable Baroness Hilla Rebay; she would become curator of the proposed museum. Rebay was also the mistress of Guggenheim, whom she called "Guggi" in their more intimate moments.

Solomon Guggenheim was one of five brothers who had made their fortune in the American West by developing copper mines and smelters, founding the powerful American Smelting and Refining Corporation. The daughter of another of the brothers, Peggy Guggenheim, was then in Europe amassing her own collection of modern art. She would soon appear in New York to open an art gallery and help launch Clement Greenberg on his life's career.

In an editorial shortly after the Guggenheim foundation was organized, the *Times* lauded plans for the new museum. Such an institution, it said, showed "how the natural wealth of America and the adventurous genius of the American business man are transmuted—steel, aluminum, oil, and now copper—into art, to become the possession of all the people." Jewell was galvanized by such esteem for a kind of art he had just recently called "decoration," and devoted almost his entire Sunday page three days later to abstract art. He now found that some of it was "moving . . . fresh, lyric, emotional," but that much of it seemed to "confront the baffled spectator with a series of statistical charts." A "melee" was brewing, he wrote, and all of modern art could be called into question. He may have been a bit flummoxed reading his own paper the very next day when a widely read editorial column, "Topics of the Times," strongly approved of abstraction, asserting that readers' homes already featured "excellent examples of abstract art," including Oriental carpets whose "designs are nearest . . . to that other abstract art, music."

During the next five weeks, Jewell would preside over the liveliest discussion yet to take place in those somnolent pages. The entire *Sunday Times* art page was devoted to the ruckus between abstract and representational art. It is difficult to imagine that Clement Greenberg, a frequent museum and gallery visitor who had earlier expressed strong opinions about the art he viewed, was unaware of this fiery debate in the city's leading newspaper. In art as in politics, polarization was the keynote of the day; as Jewell attempted to calm the storm, his own feeble knowledge of art and resistance to abstraction were exposed, leaving him dangling between abstraction that his bosses at the *Times* obviously admired and the irate conservatives taking pen in hand.

By mid-July, the New York art world traditionally fled the sweltering city for the beaches of Cape Cod or Long Island, the Adirondacks, or even Europe. But in 1937, the fray over abstraction was "the No. 1 theme for debate," Jewell wrote — "July heat notwithstanding." Jewell himself verbally threw up his hands, admitting that the meaning of abstraction was "slippery . . . sometimes maddeningly subtle." The public was less ambivalent. One reader charged that Baroness Rebay "must be in some kind of trance state" for insisting that abstract art was "transcendent." Another called "Cubistic paintings . . . essentially trivial." On the other side, Merle Armitage, an art director who would drastically modernize graphic design at a number of magazines, cheered the Guggenheim effort on behalf of abstract art, as did the members of AAA.

This inelegant wrangling in the nation's leading newspaper of record was typical of the abysmal late 1930s art discourse. Like Van Wyck Brooks's glorification of New England as the source of uniquely stirring American literature, writers on art overvalued the homely depictions of the American scene by artists like Grant Wood, John Steuart Curry, and Thomas Hart Benton. Back in 1925, Benton's close friend Thomas Craven had lavishly praised him in the *Nation* as "a painter . . . who has extracted from the virgin soul of the Southwest a graphic message of two-fold significance": i.e., that the French have no monopoly on painting and that "continental mannerisms are [no] indication of modernity." Ironically, both Craven and Benton were considered liberals in their day, summering on Cape Cod with a self-styled Bohemian crowd that included Max Eastman, the editor of *New Masses*; the unswerving Communist supporter Corliss Lamont, son of the chairman of the J. P. Morgan investment bank; the perennial Socialist Party candidate Eugene V. Debs; and the writers Julian Huxley and Bernard DeVoto. If they talked about art at all, they tended to distrust European modernism. Benton, for example, found modern art after the First World War lacking in "social value," wrote his biographer.

Thomas Craven had built a lucrative career by scolding American artists for "groveling in the emasculated tradition of French modernists." Doing so, he wrote in H. L. Mencken's influential *American Mercury*, had turned them into "failures and outcasts" comparable to "the whore and the bum." He especially commended his bosom-friend Benton: "He knows his politics, his America, and his technical history of art." In 1935, the prestigious *Harper's Magazine* published Craven's lengthy love letter to the American Scene painters Charles Burchfield, Grant Wood, and John Steuart Curry—all models for "the end of American subservience to foreign cultural fashions"—commending them for being on "the only track that can produce art."

Craven was by no means the only champion of American Scene painters. Typical of the nationalist—and anti-New York—glow they enjoyed was a long *North American Review* article in 1935 about Grant Wood. He was among the artists "painting pictures that their neighbors can understand," artists who "avoid high-sounding talk about art," itself a European import that devalued the work of Americans "to the profit . . . of dealers in foreign art." Even the editor of the respected *Magazine of Art*, Alfred Frankenstein, commended the American Scene artists' "desire to expose the plain, unvarnished facts of American life . . . an art of the people."

Those around *Partisan Review*, meanwhile, expressed a sharply different view of American culture. In Vermont, William Phillips saw all around him "the idiocy of the village" and claimed to have acquired a sense of the "farmer's oxcart indifference." He feared "losing that sense of event and situation that comes from talking to people in New York." Near Chicago, one of the magazine's writers found local people "crude, dull, ignorant, and complacent." Philip Rahv bemoaned a practically deserted summertime New York; he missed normal "intellectual fraternization." It was a stark sketch of a divided country: the city offered information, sophistication, and intellectuality, while the hinterland was sunk in isolation, narrowness, and ignorance.

*　　*　　*

During this time, Greenberg was moving closer to the people connected with *Partisan Review*, as their journal began its trajectory from a Communist mouthpiece to an independent leftist voice in politics and arts. Irving Howe recalled that in the late 1930s the Communist Party "had approached the status of a mass movement," not only in New York but also in California and perhaps in Detroit and Chicago as well. Two of the party's leaders had been elected to New York's City Council and Communists had also seized control of several powerful labor unions, including the ones governing West Coast longshoremen and New York transit workers.

However, the Moscow Trials in the winter of 1937–38 were a watershed, severely damaging the Communist Party's United Front pose and making clear Stalin's relentless prosecution of the exiled Trotsky. Trotsky loyalists, including the crowd around *Partisan Review*, rallied to his cause. They formed an American Committee for the Defense of Leon Trotsky and even dispatched America's most prominent philosopher, John Dewey, to head an investigative panel that would interview Trotsky at his home in Mexico City. In the face of the panel's findings that Stalin's accusations of treason were "a frame-up," the Communist Party even tried to pick off prominent individuals on the other side. In one case, the party dispatched perhaps its wealthiest supporter, Corliss Lamont, to pry the *Partisan Review*'s most respected contributor, Columbia University professor Lionel Trilling, loose from the Trotsky defenders. Lamont sent Trilling a *Saturday Evening Post* article by an American engineer who had spent ten years in the Soviet Union and gave "concrete evidence" concerning "the wrecking activities" of Trotsky and the others accused during the Moscow Trials. Trilling took a month to reply that the author's political views were "not likely to lead him to objectivity." Lamont pressed his case in several subsequent letters, but to no avail.

As these events were unfolding, Clement Greenberg became more involved with both Trotsky's defenders and the Russian exile's writings, especially his views on the role of art in a socialist revolution. *Partisan Review* published them at eye-glazing length in the late summer and fall of 1938. In a seven-page article in the August–September issue, Trotsky argued that while "every new tendency in art has to begin with rebellion," bourgeois society co-opted the rebels by giving them official recognition. As a result of that society's final crisis, he wrote, all of the recent avant-garde movements—Cubism, Futurism, Dada, and Surrealism—had been cut short "without reaching a complete development." He saw art as the most wounded victim of "the decline and decay of bourgeois society" and insisted that only the overthrow of the bour-geoisie would allow art to go forward.

This article was translated by Dwight Macdonald and his wife, Nancy, who were among the most ardent Trotskyites at *Partisan Review* and also in a distinct minority of WASPs among the maga-zine's mostly Jewish staff and contributors. Macdonald's biogra-pher called him "a distinguished goy among the Partisanskis." Educated at Exeter and Yale, Macdonald had quickly found work as a writer in New York. By the mid-1930s his byline often appeared in Henry Luce's luxurious business magazine *Fortune*, founded in 1930 as the first offspring of *Time* magazine. Early in 1936, the last of his series of articles about the steel industry indicted its leadership as "bereft of both the social intelligence of Communism and the dynamic individualist drive of capitalism." His editors slashed this line and many others from the manuscript, and Macdonald wrathfully quit. He stormed out of a job paying $10,000 a year, at a time when the average college professor's annual salary was $2,732, and Greenberg was barely making $1,900 on his government job. Macdonald expected to subsist on the income from stock dividends plus his wife's trust fund of about $2,000 a year.

In Macdonald, Greenberg would find a powerful connection to *Partisan Review*, even though the buttery tweeds and blue work shirt that the Ivy League patrician affected to underline his proletarian leanings made him look slightly ludicrous. "Nature and man had conspired," recalled one colleague, "to give Macdonald the voice of a North American screech owl, the beard of a Russian revolutionist, and the iconoclastic mind of a *Fortune* magazine writer." After a debate between Macdonald and Trotsky on whether the Soviet Union was a worker's state, the exiled revolutionary said, "Everyone has the right to be stupid now and then, but Comrade Macdonald abuses that privilege." However, to the *Partisan Review* editors, Macdonald had his virtues: his blue blood diluted the staff's overwhelming preponderance of Jewish sons of immigrants, and, perhaps more important, his wife, Nancy, worked zealously as the magazine's bookkeeper.

While developing a friendship with Macdonald, Greenberg had been assiduously studying the works of this Leon Trotsky that the magazine's editors esteemed so highly. In their fall 1938 issue, they had published yet another of his essays; the byline read André Breton and Diego Rivera, but it was an open secret that the real author of "Manifesto: Towards a Free Revolutionary Art" was Leon Trotsky, with substantial contributions by Breton. As again translated by the Macdonalds, the manifesto asserted that the artist was "the natural ally of revolution," that "all avenues of communication [were] choked with the debris of capitalist collapse," and that "independent revolutionary art must now . . . struggle against reactionary persecution." To that end, the manifesto called for an "International Federation of Independent Revolutionary Art."

If he had read further, as seems extremely likely considering Greenberg's thorough reading habits, he would also have perused Trotsky's writings on art going back to 1923. They were the only writings by a Marxist thinker that dealt at great length with the importance of art and the central role of artists in the inevitable revolution to come. Here Greenberg acquired a theoretical framework for his own analysis of American culture, as well as an articulate, prestigious friend within *Partisan Review*'s inner circle. He was almost ready to produce a "manifesto" of his own: a polemic on the clash between popular culture and artistic innovation that would engage thoughtful readers in his own time and provide grist for scholarly mills into the next century.

Chapter III

AN OPENING ON THE LEFT

IN ONE OF THE FORTY-SEVEN boxes of Clement Greenberg Papers at the Getty Research Institute in Los Angeles is a folder titled simply "Notes." It contains a set of half-size flimsy sheets, the first four pages covered with careful pencil penmanship, an early draft of Greenberg's most powerful essay, "Avant-Garde and Kitsch." In the remaining thirty-two pages, the precise left margins move further left and the handwriting continues in ink.

Not the first, and certainly not the last, this draft dashes off in many directions. Like an academic paper, it rehearses Marxist theory about that much-flogged "ruling class," the bourgeoisie. Veering toward literature, it cites Daniel Defoe and Samuel Richardson, author of the eighteenth-century novel *Pamela*. Feinting toward music, it suddenly dashes toward the sad fate of Spanish Loyalists, driven from their homeland by Franco's Falangists. In the midst of attempting a history of Bohemia, it suddenly blurts out, "Kitsch is art that exists for its own sake, leaving advertising aside."

Though at this point maddeningly cryptic, the key word has been uttered. The 1987 supplement to the *Oxford English Dictionary* cites only one use prior to Greenberg's, by the Englishman Brian Howard, who in 1926 mentioned "listening to Kitsch on his wireless." Greenberg's own first use of the word seems to have come in his initial letter to Dwight Macdonald in February 1939, critiquing a piece Macdonald had written about Soviet cinema for *Partisan Review*. In the letter, Greenberg referred to "constant seepage from top to bottom, and Kitsch (a wonderful German word that covers all this crap) is the common sewer."

"Avant-Garde and Kitsch" condemned all popular culture, but focused primarily on its media manifestations. Before Greenberg, any number of social critics had deplored the low drama of the movies, which had already decimated the legitimate stage; the bastardized sound of popular recordings arriving in the wake of Caruso's operatic voice; the laugh-track-riddled entertainment invading the home via a box in the parlor; and the cheesy magazine images selling Post Toasties and cigarettes. Many critics observed how the privations of the Depression conspired with the assault of mass media to marginalize the traditional high culture of the concert, serious theater, and classic literature. Only a few years earlier, Greenberg himself had dabbled with writing for popular media, but warily; his short story in *Esquire* had been published under a pseudonym.

Greenberg's most immediate contribution to the critique was the word *kitsch* itself. Its harsh, Germanic tone conveys derision and contempt, while its strident plosive syllable sticks in the brain like an irritating burr. A creative work tarred with "kitsch" can scarcely defend itself; the word is so charged with toxic effluvia that its single syllable can still unfairly condemn an entire artistic movement to a sleazy grave, no further explanation needed. And the person who so much as murmured an occasional fondness for kitsch, perhaps a sentimental song, especially among the high-minded New York intellectuals, could be summarily expelled.

Greenberg's article grew out of a letter on the subject that he had written to the editors of *Partisan Review*, with Dwight Macdonald's encouragement. While he feared his own "flights of spun theory," as he told Lazarus, the writing was so addictive he expected to finish it in a week. Two weeks later, he submitted it to the review, fearful that it was "not ample enough. They'll probably turn it down, and my *oeuvres inédites* will mount," he told his friend. In fact, at the very moment Greenberg was writing to Harold, Macdonald phoned to say the piece was "very good, but had to be recast in form." Although the Macdonalds came over that same evening to provide advice, acting on it would have to wait: Greenberg was sailing to Europe the following morning. The notion of boarding the *Ile de France* on April 20, 1939, as "German battleships are cruising the coast," may have provided Greenberg a frisson of anxiety, but the voyage itself was uneventful: seven days of "deck tennis and ping-pong, drink and chatter." To his family, he reported a "perpetual state of hysteria . . . my emotion is not equal to the occasion"—the prospect of traveling in Europe— before he disembarked by tender at Plymouth. In Wales, he would look up a girl he had met in a life-drawing class, then visit Stratford, Oxford, London, Paris, southern France, Rome, and Florence. He was also hoping to see "a bit of Switzerland" during his five-week journey. Greenberg described his first three days in England in a twenty-four-page letter to his family. Walking alone in the rain along the banks of the Avon in Stratford, "a quiet, shady little stream you can almost jump across," he encountered a flotilla of "disagreeable, greedy and beautiful swans . . . begging for something to eat." In a courtyard at Oxford, he was invited to his rooms by a student "for a smoke." The man "was as beautiful as it is possible for a man to be," Greenberg wrote, concluding, "no wonder so many Englishmen are homos." Arriving in London late in the evening, he discovered "the most beautiful city I'd ever seen . . . haphazard 'natural' streets, the signs, the squares, the clear lights and the neatness. And most of all, the architectural vanity." Over his long life, Greenberg would spend a good deal of time in London, developing a dense web of art contacts.

He found Paris "wonderful . . . it's old, it's gray, it's shabby, very shabby." Like any tourist, he delighted in the "sidewalk cafes, movement, talk, food, theatres, and gayety . . . exactly as it's advertised." His report gives no hint of anxiety in the French capital just months before the outbreak of the Second World War. He also spent time with his grandparents and an aunt's family. They were living in a fine house, with two cars, two dogs, and a maid, so Greenberg wondered why his father was sending $50 every month for the grandparents' support. Greenberg also met Georges Hugnet, "the Surrealist poet whose stuff I like," and planned to see the composer Virgil Thomson, as well as the Surrealist poet Paul Eluard. He had no trouble giving the youthful Jean-Paul Sartre his view of Sartre's just-published novel *La Nausée*. "We agreed about Faulkner," Greenberg told an interviewer many years later, "and I said Faulkner was more important than [Sartre's preference, John] Dos Passos."

After just eight days, Greenberg concluded he'd "stayed in Paris too long," and left for Avignon. Having met more Surrealists—Man Ray and Hans Arp—he formed a lifelong disdain for that movement: "They're all crackpots, every one of them," he wrote his family. A postcard from Avignon to the Greenberg clan described it as "the most wonderful place I've ever been in." Shown on the reverse were the famous bridge, the text of the famous song, and the music for the famous refrain. Such naïveté attracted Mary McCarthy's sharp mockery back home. "My God! It's so beautiful," she aped his postcard style to dinner guests. "Did you know they have water in the streets of Venice? . . . In Rome, I discovered the Spanish Steps and I discovered that place that is called the Sistine Chapel." Greenberg's final letter from Europe bears out McCarthy's burlesque. He raves about his family over Florence, "all the genius that was born in this small space"; he left after fewer than three days, "saturated. The earth has no wonders left." Along with Greenberg's accounts of what he did and saw in Europe, the long letters to his family convey a sense of loneliness, a figure hunched over a sidewalk table obsessively scribbling to divert a dark sense of alienation. The letters sound like those of a bright sixteen-year-old away from home for the first time, rather than of a thirty-year-old who had traveled a great deal in the United States and was the father of a son.

Greenberg returned to turmoil in Washington, where Toady wanted him to take charge of his son; her relationship with her new husband was fraying. Appalled that he might have to move to a larger apartment and hire a nanny, Greenberg spluttered his rage to Harold. He was also livid about Dwight Macdonald's complaint of "unsupported and large generalizations" in "Avant-Garde and Kitsch." To Harold, he fumed that "these people with the best of intentions do as much to smother American culture as the Roman church." As he described it many years later, he then tore up the whole manuscript and, in one sitting, rewrote the entire essay. In his introduction to "Avant-Garde and Kitsch," Greenberg focused on the new twentieth-century media as the villains feeding an innocent public empty cultural calories: Tin Pan Alley songs on records and radio, *Saturday Evening Post* covers, and the rest of mass-media culture were undermining the authenticity of a T. S. Eliot poem, a Braque painting, or a Greek vase. The tide of trash was proof to Greenberg that current bourgeois society was in the final stages of a decay that had actually begun in the mid nineteenth century. It was then, he argued, that an artistic avant-garde, "unheard-of heretofore," began to develop; its "true and most important function" was not to experiment but "to find a path" that would "keep culture moving in the midst of ideological confusion and violence." Perhaps by osmosis, these artistic pioneers acquired "a superior consciousness of history . . . even if unconsciously, for the most part." Of necessity, the avant-garde artists attached themselves to the "rich and cultivated" of the ruling class "by an umbilical cord of gold," which throttled their development.

Despite its veneer of revolutionary radicalism and its portrayal of the ordinary citizen as a hapless victim, the thrust of "Avant-Garde and Kitsch" is adamantly retrograde and elitist. Seizing upon theoretically "iron laws of history," the text flogs technology in all its modern cultural manifestations—recordings, films, radio, and high-speed presses—and looks longingly back to the folk art now pressed to the margins by modernity. In its rage, it echoes Friedrich Nietzsche's contempt for "the herd." The very idea that technology gives the ordinary person an inexpensive entry to "high culture" remained unexplored as Greenberg poured brimstone on the commercial culture of the day. It "is mechanical and operates by formulas." It provides only "vicarious experience and faked sensations." It is "the epitome of all that is spurious in the life of our times." It appropriates the riches of "a fully matured tradition," and "borrows from it devices, tricks, stratagems, rules of thumb, themes, converts them into a system and discards the rest."

Looked at in retrospect, "Avant-Garde and Kitsch" signaled an about-face for 1930s radicals, perhaps resonating with their profound disappointment in "the masses." The workers had not risen up as expected against a capitalist system, even when this system had left 30 percent of them unemployed. They had not joined radical parties in any numbers, instead relying on union organizing to better their conditions. "Avant-Garde and Kitsch" could be read as an indictment of the masses for their affection for kitsch and for their spineless submission to media manipulation. The essay ends on a surly, pessimistic note: "Today we look to socialism *simply* for the preservation of whatever living culture we have right now."

The much-revised version of "Avant-Garde and Kitsch" that was finally published in the fall 1939 *Partisan Review* provoked as much discussion as could be expected from a publication with a mere two thousand subscribers. By including the word "avant-garde" in the title, Greenberg hooked onto its double meaning at that time, referring not just to a pioneering cultural movement in art, but also to the political "advance guard" that Marx, Lenin, and Trotsky deemed central to their revolution. Many an argument among the various factions of New York radicals dwelled upon the social composition, commitment, reliability, and effectiveness of this theoretical vanguard in overthrowing a capitalist system they deemed in extremis.

The article received widespread recognition. Beyond the editors of *Partisan Review*, Van Wyck Brooks called it "very fine," as did the poets Louise Bogan and Delmore Schwartz. Even Harold Rosenberg told Macdonald he liked the piece but, Greenberg carped to Harold, "he can't afford to give me the little salve of a compliment." However, Macdonald told Greenberg that no *Partisan Review* article had ever attracted so much comment; the editors asked Greenberg for more. By mid-March 1940, he was hard at work on his next piece.

*　*　*

While Greenberg's rage was inflamed by the cheap technology that had eroded the influence of elite cultural arbiters, the repellent middle-class values and behaviors expressed by Toady and Mrs. Ewing no doubt played their part in setting off his tirade. Early in July, he had rushed to Washington to try to sort out the crisis surrounding Danny. In a long letter to Harold, who was on a trip to New Orleans, he rambled bitterly about Toady, her "white-trash, imbecile hope of marrying me again" (which might have been a complete invention on Greenberg's part); her husband, Buddy, who "presented, so to speak, a bill for Buster's [Danny's] transportation east"; and meddling Mrs. Ewing, who was preparing to come East. In August, as Greenberg was putting the finishing touches on "Avant-Garde and Kitsch," Mrs. Ewing had sent him "a vicious letter" in response to one of his own criticizing the

boy's diet. As for Danny, he told Harold, "I myself am not as bothered as I should be."

In late September, Greenberg located new lodgings, a fourth-
floor walkup at 6 Jones Street, a six-story stucco and brick building
on a quiet street lined with yellow-flowering trees. He still had only
a single room, but it was two and one-half times larger, newer, and
better kept than the apartment on Minetta Lane, and included "a
tremendous closet" and a modern bathroom. The rent was $37.
Greenberg also bought his first set of furniture, he told Harold,
"vulgar sugar maple, self-effacing enough not to bother me." The
strong opinions Greenberg lavished, first on Harold, then on the
readers of various publications, would hardly change over the
years. Having made up his mind about how and why art evolves
over time, he clung rigidly to those views, ramping up his rhetoric
whenever opposition loomed, and sometimes even when it did
not. Having by now amassed a huge backlog of unpublished poetry and prose, Greenberg in his thirtieth year had finally pulled
himself together and embarked on his critical career.

The criticism extended to his own work, as shown by the many
drafts of articles and speeches in his papers at the Getty. His prose
often takes a desperately abusive tone that leaves a careful reader
wondering who is being so ruthlessly converted, the reader or the
author. He took a dim view of "Avant-Garde and Kitsch" as first
published, telling an interviewer near the end of his life that he
hated how it was written; his argument was full of holes, he said,
but no one picked up on them. When it was reprinted in the first
volume of Greenberg's writings, *Art and Culture*, in 1961, it had
been heavily edited. And when Dwight Macdonald's seminal role
in the writing came up in conversation, Greenberg puffed defen-
sively: "So? So what? It was all my ideas, of course."

Unlike "Avant-Garde and Kitsch," which assaulted all aspects of
mass culture, Greenberg's next article would concentrate on visu-

al art, a cultural domain bereft, it seems in retrospect, of a single intelligent, articulate critical observer. While abstract art was on the agenda, the dialogue about it rested on the lowest possible level. The Abstract American Artists' exhibition in April 1939, for example, had attracted only unfriendly grumblings. As Greenberg recalled in 1957, the New York art scene of the late thirties and early forties clustered around the modest set of galleries near Manhattan's Fifty-seventh Street, while the Museum of Modern Art on nearby Fifty-third Street was "as far away as property" during the Depression. Even the *Partisan Review*'s angel George L. K. Morris, an artist who lived uptown and bought art, found himself alienated from the MoMA milieu. "Everybody learned a lot at the Museum," Greenberg wrote, "especially about Matisse and Picasso, but you did not feel at home in it." He faulted the museum's founding director, Alfred H. Barr, for declining to exhibit the Abstract American Artists' annual, while favoring European modernists. Aside from a few museum publications, serious art criticism was nowhere to be found in print. When Edward Alden Jewell reviewed new WPA-funded murals at the city's radio station, WNYC, in the summer of 1939, he tried to waltz gingerly between the vociferous pro- and anti-abstract art factions. He found the murals by Stuart Davis, Byron Browne, Louis Schanker, and Hans Wicht "soothing," a quality desirable in a broadcasting studio, and praised the artists' "technical adroitness" and their grasp of "the temper and the maturing philosophy of our era." In response, Davis angrily rejected having his work described as "a type of decorative fantasy," something like "old-fashioned German Rathskeller decoration, elves, gnomes, toadstools and mushrooms." He insisted that modern artists "don't want an art that means nothing and that is not for the masses."

A week later, Jewell was again tiptoeing through the abstract art reefs, following a provocative article from the testy mother hen of "nonobjective" art, Hilla Rebay. She had tried to draw a barrier between abstract and nonobjective art: abstraction is relative, she argued, since it needs an object from which to abstract, while nonobjective is absolute. That such hairsplitting could exercise intelligent New Yorkers at a time when Europeans were poised days away from the outbreak of the Second World War indicates how remote those distant events seemed. The following week, with European war a reality, Jewell wrote another meandering disquisition upon abstract versus nonobjective art, while readers littered the page with pithy comments: "Abstraction is drawing something to make you think you are looking at nothing," wrote one, "while non-objectivity is drawing nothing to make you feel you are looking at something." Meanwhile, Peyton Boswell, in an expensive coffee-table book partially underwritten by Time-Life, gloated over the recent emergence of "a true native art" in America, the anecdotal works of Thomas Hart Benton and other American Scene painters. Thomas Craven prepared a revised edition of his *Modern Art*, a glibly written funeral oration for modernism, sanctioned by the Metropolitan Museum of Art. In it, he denounced Amedeo Modigliani as "a symbol of the multitudes of young men who go to the dogs in the slums of Paris . . . Art begins at home," he asserted. "The inevitable sign of great art is . . . the mark of a specific environment, the impress of a special civilization." And a reviewer of American art exhibitions for *North American Review* devoted six pages to cataloging the superior American paintings being shown in museums, recommending the Boswell and Craven books and denouncing the "so-called European schools."

Greenberg's "Towards a Newer Laocoon" was on an entirely different level. It was not purely descriptive, but rather ranged (though perhaps too broadly) over the previous 150 years. It proposed a complex theory of modernism, arguing that each of the arts—music, literature, painting, and sculpture—strives to purify itself of residue from other art forms. He contended that literature had been most intrusive upon other art forms, leading to the pollution of music and visual art by storytelling. In support, Greenberg looked back to the mid-seventeenth century, when "the pictorial arts had been relegated into the hands of the [royal] courts, where they eventually degenerated into trivial interior decoration." Such sweeping statements alienated people more familiar than Greenberg with the history of art, including the Columbia University art historian and sometime *Partisan Review* contributor Meyer Schapiro. It would be difficult to prove that the art of such prized seventeenth-century painters as Vermeer, Rembrandt, and Rubens was, as Greenberg asserted, "trivial interior decoration." Reflecting on this essay shortly after Greenberg's death in 1994, the art critic John Russell admired much of Greenberg's art writing, but saw his purification theory as "some sort of Germanic nonsense that he fostered and thought up for himself."

The text for "Towards a Newer Laocoon" went through multiple revisions by Greenberg and by others. The material in the Getty's folder for this article shows many versions: one was more than twenty-five pages long; another was slashed by an anonymous editor, perhaps Dwight Macdonald, with such stern comments as "out" and "might omit—merely one more example," as well as complaints about too many pages referring to the German eighteenth-century philosopher and dramatist Gotthold Ephraim Lessing and the author's vagueness regarding dates. To Harold, Greenberg complained that the *Partisan Review*'s editors "make me sick. Preserve culture from the Jews. Hitler's almost right." They had forced him to cut his article "outrageously."

The reference to Lessing was only one of Greenberg's frequent citations of erudite and somewhat recherché thinkers. The title, "Towards a Newer Laocoon" was built upon a nearly forgotten book, *For a New Laokoön*, published in 1910 by the Harvard professor Irving Babbitt. Babbitt was the leader of an innovative school of literary criticism, the "new humanism," which criticized confusion that romanticism had instigated in the arts. In Greenberg's subsequent writings, the eighteenth-century German philosopher Immanuel Kant would also often be rolled out as the big gun to settle arguments.

At college and in Greenberg's reading afterward, German literature and philosophy were central concerns. He read German fluently and, even though he did not visit Nazi Germany during his European tour, he felt most at home in German culture. Many Americans at this time considered German culture superior, especially in philosophy, music, and scholarship, and saw the Nazis merely as a temporary overlay. In Greenberg's case, he might have been seduced not only by the prestige of the culture, but also by the *heimlich* quality of the German language—as a more refined, more literary version of the colloquial Yiddish that he had heard at home and learned as his first words.

*   *   *

As Greenberg's essay was published in the midst of a typically torrid New York summer, *Partisan Review* was roiled by more than its usual disarray over deadlines, funding, and political squabbling. Dwight Macdonald was "titivating himself," Greenberg wrote to Harold, "as to whether the historical moment is right" to replace the editors of *Partisan Review* with himself and Greenberg. The editors had been "strongly opposed" to publishing "Towards a Newer Laocoon," perhaps because its message was so opaque, or because they were even more ignorant about the history of art than the author. Greenberg believed the essay was "a success," while simultaneously fearful that the editors were so demoralized that the magazine would have to fold.

Despite the heavy editing that Greenberg resented, his essay reveals an uncertain command of cultural history, though it is buttressed by muscular rhetoric and encapsulated in a Marxist universe of history's "laws" as inevitable, unchallengeable, ironclad. It concentrates on the visual arts, principally painting, as they struggle to purify themselves from the baleful influence of literature. Further intimidating the reader, Greenberg cites and then disposes of lesser-known nineteenth-century artists—Vernet, Leighton, Watts, Böcklin—whose "real talent only made their influence the more pernicious." Their crime, he said, was to accept the fatal embrace of storytelling in their highly marketable paintings.

But Greenberg discerned a fresh wind in the mid-nineteenth century, strangely concurrent with Marx's *Communist Manifesto* of 1848. He seized upon Gustave Courbet as "the first real avant-garde painter" because "he painted only what the eye could see as a machine unaided by the mind." Greenberg purported to discern "a new flatness . . . and an equally new attention to every inch of the canvas, regardless of its relation to the 'centers of interest.'" To Greenberg, these were key issues. He reiterated them frequently and insistently, citing "flatness" as the central criterion for choosing artists and works he admired.

From a biographical standpoint, the most interesting feature of "Towards a Newer Laocoon" was how strongly oriented it was to visual art, mostly at the expense of literature. While this tack may have put off the literary-minded editors of *Partisan Review*, it staked Greenberg's claim on art criticism. Only an aside in the essay refers equivocally to the nineteenth-century literary figures— Zola, the Goncourts, and poets like Verhaeren—whom he saw as "trying to get rid of ideas and 'literature' . . . to establish their art on a more stable basis than the crumbling bourgeois oecumene." The use of twenty-five-cent words such as "oecumene" would become a sort of verbal uppercut in Greenberg's prose, a blow directly to the reader's sense of himself as a cultivated being.

In addition, his ability to persuade the *Partisan Review's* editors to publish "Towards a Newer Laocoon" reinforced a decision toward which Greenberg had been slowly drifting. By "simply thinking about it," he wrote to Harold on June 24, he had "become . . . extraordinarily sensitive to painting. It's wonderful to have sureness of taste . . . in such a fluid element." He had already discovered the modernist artist Maurice Vlaminck, whose recent work he found "extraordinarily good." Interviewed decades later, Greenberg said that from the mid-1930s onward he had "pointedly avoided the company of artists," whom he considered generally "dumb and boring." His interviewers, the authors of a Pulitzer Prize-winning biography of Jackson Pollock, saw him as "an exile" from the world of literary criticism swirling around *Partisan Review.* Delmore Schwartz and Philip Rahv considered him "pompous and intellectually mediocre," so that "he soon began casting his critical eye in other directions." For a while, though, he remained ambivalent, hesitating to abandon literary criticism, which he had practiced so diligently on Harold, as he was feeling his way into writing about art for a wider public. While struggling with an extensive article on Bertolt Brecht's poetry, to be published in *Partisan Review* in March 1941, Greenberg wrote to Harold that he still found it "much easier to write about writing than about non-writing, like painting." Still, he wanted to exercise his newfound knowledge of painting ("what a shame to waste it"), even though, as he later told an interviewer, writing art criticism was "way tougher . . . When it comes to literature, you can quote . . . and you can mix the subject up with the form." Perhaps Greenberg's ultimate choice of art criticism was reinforced by the striking surplus of literary critics circulating within the vortex of *Partisan Review*, as well as the decline of the literary avant-garde in the 1930s. Philip Rahv, at a symposium on American writing, lamented that only "the academicians, the time-servers, the experts in accommodation, the vulgarizers, and the big-money adepts [were] ruling the literary roost." As Leslie Fiedler observed some time later, *Partisan Review* came into existence at the end of a literary period, not at the beginning, a time when "experimentalism in literature was being consolidated and academicized all over the world." Indeed, the writers *Partisan Review* championed, such as W. B. Yeats, Marcel Proust, André Gide, James Joyce, and Franz Kafka, had written their groundbreaking works during the first decades of the twentieth century.

As the 1930s were ending, *Partisan Review* fostered the New Critics, who insisted on the centrality of the creative act while dismissing considerations of the author's social and biographical background. This group, among them Kenneth Burke, Cleanth Brooks, John Crowe Ransom, and R. P. Blackmur, saw criticism itself as a creative endeavor. Formalism, as it was soon named, would quickly occupy the center of American literary studies.

Clement Greenberg gradually abandoned literature to this determined band of critics, but not without cribbing one word from their multifaceted armamentarium. "Formalism" was how he identified his own judgments of art, based, as he often admitted, on the aesthetic theories expounded by Hans Hofmann in the lectures Greenberg attended in the winter of 1938–39. In heavily accented English, the artist who had fled from Nazi persecution spoke about the importance of the surface upon which the artist painted and of the central role of the artist's medium, the painting's form. Hofmann prevented his students from imitating his own work by not showing it to them, but he resolutely pursued abstract art at a time when such work had few followers or patrons. So affected was Greenberg by what Hofmann had to say (as well as what he did) that he footnoted the artist in "Avant-Garde and Kitsch" and endorsed Hofmann's kind of abstraction in "Towards a Newer Laocoon."

As the latter essay was appearing in *Partisan Review*, Greenberg was "in the throes of a slightly strange affair," he told Harold. Jean Bakewell Connolly was the American-born wife of Cyril Connolly, the editor of the new London magazine *Horizon*, which had just reprinted "Avant-Garde and Kitsch" for a European audience. Wanting to shelter his wife from the London blitz, not to mention his dalliances with other women, Connolly sent Jean to New York, recommending she look up Greenberg while there.

Raised in a wealthy Baltimore family, Jean Bakewell had met Connolly while supposedly studying art in Paris, but mostly socializing in the Latin Quarter. At their wedding in Baltimore, Connolly was amazed to discover that the family home had "more bathrooms than bedrooms and more cars than there are people." Jean's mother gave her daughter an allowance of at least £1,000 a year. In the early 1930s, the couple rented a spacious London flat on King's Road with two servants and assorted exotic pets—ferrets, lemurs, and an African genet. Their dinner parties included John Betjeman, Elizabeth Bowen, Nancy Mitford, Anthony Powell, and Evelyn Waugh. But by the end of the decade the marriage was troubled and both partners sought other relationships. Jean spent increasing time in Paris, mostly with gay men such as Denham Fouts and Peter Watson, the son of one of England's wealthiest families. In 1939, Watson agreed to fund *Horizon* with Connolly (then in the south of France with his latest love) as editor. Although they would never again live together after this point, Jean continued to correspond with Connolly and to send him a generous allowance.

Soon after meeting Greenberg, Jean reported to Connolly that he was "nice and intelligent, but shamingly plain, gauche and inarticulate." Greenberg, for his part, was impressed that she seemed to know everyone worth knowing, "all the English writers . . . lords & ladies, high ministers of state . . . from all of which I receive a thrill," he wrote to Harold. After about a week's acquaintance, he continued, "we took to sleeping together furiously." Two days they spent together in the country, in mid-July 1940, left Greenberg "most thoroughly fucked-out and emptied—she takes her sex like a man." Then Greenberg dropped her off for a visit in Massachusetts with W. H. Auden and his companion, Chester Kallman.

Back in New York in mid-August, she and Greenberg spent ten frenzied days in bed, he wrote to Harold, doing "inconceivable things. What pushing & pulling, what flipping & flaming, what jumbling & tumbling, rummying & tummying, fricking & fracking, whipping & whacking." However, Greenberg noted that she resembled Toady, "pleasure greedy and somewhat childish," but could afford to be so, as her income was close to $400 a month. She appeared to be unsentimental; "it's simply that she loves fucking more than anything else." And then she was off to catch up with "Denny" Fouts, a gay American who had been her traveling companion from London and would drive her to California. Jean Connolly had inflamed not only Greenberg's sexuality, but also his ambition. "I must become a great man," he told Harold. "A great man will find other Jean Connollys around, a succession of them. A great man can be lonely with impunity, and not become . . . dependent upon an attractive woman . . . A great man can dazzle instead of being dazzled."

Greenberg's lunge toward greatness did lead to more of his words being published in *Horizon*, but they also brought a swift rebuke from Connolly himself. As London was being pummeled by German bombers in September 1940, Greenberg presented "An American View" in response to Connolly's offer to publish anything Greenberg cared to write. The article rehearsed a crude Marxist argument against the war already under way and included the usual jargon about ruling classes, masses, crisis of capitalism, and historical forces. It suggested that "the European masses are not satisfied enough with the status quo to die for it" and then cited Leon Trotsky's views that saving democracy requires a socialist revolution, that Britain and France could no longer dominate Europe and therefore must submit to fascist Germany. A socialist Britain, Greenberg ventured, would attract the allegiance of German workers, thus undermining Nazi Germany. In an unsigned disclaimer immediately following the article, Connolly roundly rejected these views as "simple and violent," oversimplified, and "if put into practice would lead to disaster."

"An American View" appears to have been propelled by Dwight Macdonald, who was Trotsky's fervent acolyte and "the dominant architect" of *Partisan Review*'s political position since its breakaway from Communist sponsorship. Having come late to radicalism, he urged the editors of *Partisan Review* to more extreme views, and wrote (as one contemporary put it) "enormous searching tracts about the nature of the Soviet state, party discipline and theory, and bureaucratic collectivism, most of them unpublished." Greenberg's first communication with Macdonald had been a long letter mercilessly dissecting one such article. Macdonald, recognizing in it the kind of aggressive frankness that the age demanded, had responded by taking Greenberg under his wing and propelling him toward a sharp-tongued critical career.

It was Greenberg's evident debt to Macdonald that also drew him into coauthoring "10 Propositions on the War," published in *Partisan Review* in July 1941. With London enduring a second year of nightly bombing, France already occupied by Nazi troops, and the Soviet Union woefully unprepared for the Nazi onslaught, many radicals, including the *Partisan Review*'s editors, were rethinking their positions. Like the ill-timed essay in *Horizon*, "10 Propositions" insisted that the Second World War was a conflict among capitalist nations and should not be supported by right-thinking socialists. While the Communist Party had abruptly abandoned its pacifist line after Germany's attack on the Soviet Union, Greenberg and Macdonald argued that nothing had changed. "All support of whatever kind must be withheld from Churchill and Roosevelt," they wrote. "They can only lead us to disaster" and should be subject to "constant and radical criticism."

Such extreme left-wing views mirrored widespread right-wing isolationism in the United States. Just a year earlier, in September 1940, the Selective Service Act establishing a peacetime military draft had passed by a single vote in the House of Representatives. To a twenty-first-century reader, Greenberg and Macdonald's article appears ludicrous, if not reckless. However, many 1930s radicals of both left and right questioned the war. Alfred Kazin later noted, a bit sheepishly, that he had "found it possible to believe that . . . Socialists stayed out of capitalist wars." Irving Howe later confessed that "we underestimated the ferocious urge to total domination characterizing Nazism." On the other hand, Philip Rahv published a blistering repudiation of the Greenberg–Macdonald essay, "10 Propositions and 8 Errors," in the November–December issue of *Partisan Review*. The article appeared just days before the Japanese attack on Pearl Harbor on December 7, 1941, followed by Nazi Germany's declaration of war on the United States.

Taking the long view some twenty years later, the historian Arthur M. Schlesinger, Jr., discounted the New York agitation for and against the war. At a 1959 symposium on 1930s radicals, he insisted that the only significant political activity in the 1930s took place in Washington, D.C: "All the radical chatter . . . in New York, whether Stalinist, Trotskyist, Socialist, or some other sectarian variant," said this historian of the New Deal, "amounted to just that: chatter, none of it of any influence or significance. It was liberalism that had counted." Sidney Hook, a fellow Trotskyite who later joined the mainstream as a professor of political science at New York University, reminisced many years later over those turbulent times. He recalled "something truly comic" about his colleagues' "self-conscious role as political revolutionaries and cultural radicals . . . they were peripheral and parasitic . . . They led a safe life in the culture they decried, made no sacrifices, endured no discomforts, all the while playing the role of radicals." Possibly, Greenberg and Macdonald were aware at the time of what minimal influence their essay would have on national policy, hence expressed their views more shrilly than if they really expected to be heard in Washington. Many years later, Macdonald told an interviewer that he was not as "involved psychologically" with Marxism as William Phillips and Philip Rahv. "I was always a tourist," he said. "I knew I could get out any time." After getting out of *Partisan Review* in 1943, he spent five years publishing *Politics*, a radical sheet of uncertain leftist ideology. His chief support and business manager remained his wife, Nancy, "the Unknown Soldier," as he described her, "of the little magazine world." Macdonald went on to a successful career as a freelance writer for the *New Yorker*, *Harper's* and other middlebrow podiums, vigorously denouncing the evils of middlebrow culture as Greenberg had revealed them to him in "Avant-Garde and Kitsch." But all this happened long after Macdonald and Greenberg had stopped speaking to each other.

Greenberg was chastened by his brief stint as a coauthor; he would never again collaborate on any writing, and never wrote strictly on politics again. He had trouble collaborating with anyone and was quickly finding that the political stage, like the literary scene, was already covered by many others. Instead, he threw himself into getting published on cultural matters. His essays and reviews appeared fairly regularly in *Partisan Review*, where he had become an editor in January 1940. He also had impressed Margaret Marshall, literary editor of the *Nation*, whom he had met in 1940 at one of the Macdonalds' parties. He had found her "too snotty and too unattractive," he wrote to Harold, but when she asked him to call her he said he would. "Hay must be made," he told Harold. "If I don't pursue my career it won't pursue me." His first work for the *Nation*, a rather heavy-handed dicing of Carl Thurston's *The Structure of Art*, appeared in February 1941. Greenberg was still veering between art and literature; still struggling to purify his own writings about art from the siren-call of literature.

Margaret Marshall was an unlikely candidate to serve as literary editor of a left-wing weekly. She had been raised as a Mormon and suffered from frequent, debilitating bouts of depression. At such times, she could spend an entire evening at the homes of people like Diana and Lionel Trilling without uttering a word. But when her mental balance was intact, she was lively and adventuresome; she had hired Mary McCarthy to write theater reviews, and, of course, Greenberg to write about art. In 1941, when he first wrote for the *Nation*, reading the magazine, along with the *New Republic*, was "an obligation of intelligence," recalled Diana Trilling. During the Roosevelt years, she wrote, "what appeared in its pages today was government policy tomorrow."

Getting into print emboldened Greenberg to hone his rhetoric into what soon became his take-no-prisoners style: unambiguous verdicts from which there was no appeal. In a review of little magazines, he noted that "the shades of the 20s are abroad" in *New Directions*, while he deemed the Surrealist-oriented *View* "putrescent," a roundhouse backlash against editor Nicolas Calas, who, in the magazine's second issue, had disparaged not only Greenberg's ideas but also his talent as a painter. It was also in this article that Greenberg rolled out Kant for the first time in print, citing the philosopher's observation that "you only find what you look for."

In its April 1941 issue, *Partisan Review* published Greenberg's longest essay to date, an intense analysis and appreciation of the poetry of Bertolt Brecht, whom he lauded as "the most original literary temperament to have appeared anywhere in the last twenty years." The essay is a detailed review of modern poetry, revealing Greenberg's wide-ranging reading over the previous fifteen years and providing a glimpse, perhaps, of his own failed ambitions to become a poet. Greenberg included not only generous samples of Brecht's German verse and his own free translations as extended footnotes, but a sensitive survey of all recent German literature.

Greenberg's sophistication as a writer contrasts sharply with his immature emotional turmoil over Jean Connolly. Her absence made his life "almost unendurable. I wondered how I was able to live from one moment to the next," he confided to Harold, but only a few paragraphs later he fantasized that if Jean Connolly were to appear, "I'd immediately recognize her for the infantile slut she is." He suggested that her promiscuous behavior (but not his own) was "infantile from top to bottom." Just six days later, he exulted that a long-awaited letter from her indicates that "my glamour girl has come back." That prospect led to a litany of desires: "gossip, sexual intrigue, back-biting and hard undoing . . . women, confidences, confessions & broken hearts. Dissipation, indiscretions, glitter, dash, sparkle, sin. La Connolly has a lot of all that . . . I adore it. Yes, I adore it. Feeling is all. The end of all is to feel deeply."

Less than a month later, Greenberg was falling in love with "a rabbi's daughter"—her identity is not known—"a high-school teacher, an art expert in a fashion, a girl who's been around, is 28 years old, Titian-haired & a knock-out." In between typing the article about Brecht's poetry, he was bedding her in a Tudor City room, "piled high with clothes, notes for a doctor's thesis that was never written, cigarette ashes, suitcases & blankets . . . La Connolly has faded away into the West." But a month later the affair had "gone aground," and "La Connolly threatens to be back at any moment." The letters ends with a heartfelt realization: "Oh, it takes me so long to grow up."

While still maintaining his job with the customs service and now serving as an editor at *Partisan Review*, Greenberg continued to waver between writing on art or on literature. While they were together, the rabbi's daughter introduced Greenberg to collections he had never known about; he decided that "when you've heard of the artist's name," he told Harold, "he is almost always sure to be good." He boasted that his eye had "become as delicate & fastidious as my ear," surely a boon to the artists—Joan Miró, Fernand Léger, and Wassily Kandinsky, Paul Klee—he would review in print just a few short months later. Writing about art, he told Harold, he felt "as though I were spouting horseshit." He feared he was "turning into a snob & prig." To reassure himself, he was reading Baudelaire's *Salons*.

On the last day of 1940, Jean Connolly was, indeed, back, Greenberg telling Harold that she had been "astoundingly faithful" while traveling to California with her gay friend Denham Fouts. By mid-March 1941, Greenberg sounded impatient with "her constant desire . . . I need my seed sometimes." By May she had moved to Greenwich Village, near his apartment, and the two were spending most of their time together. Greenberg reported that his father looked shocked and curious when he unexpectedly dropped in on his son, who was ill, and found Jean giving him lunch. Greenberg did not "relish the curiosity," he wrote to Harold. He felt "a little ashamed."

Greenberg's ambition, by contrast, knew no limits. He still wanted to write poetry, but also he wanted "the profound . . . the bottom, final explanations . . . to prophesy the future," he wrote to Harold, "the worthiest task for those who, like me, think there's no outlet adequate to their opinion of themselves." While the editors of *Partisan Review* appreciated Greenberg's efforts as an editor, he was no match for them in the raucous debate they favored. They "could put me down," he noted many years later, "they could out-talk me, and how." While the *Partisan Review* insiders favored a wry, caustic, Groucho Marx style of debate, Greenberg's rhetoric was drier and harsher, not as spontaneous as theirs. Uneasy among these verbal gymnasts, Greenberg compensated for his faltering verbal style and lack of humor with heavy judgments and pompous lectures. Philip Rahv much later claimed that Greenberg decided to concentrate on art because competition was too intense in literary criticism. Greenberg suggested that disappointment with avant-garde writing had turned him away, but the low level of writing on art at the time did offer a juicy target for his vaulting opinion of himself.

However, a dark cloud hung over Greenberg, as over all his contemporaries: the military draft that had begun in September 1940. From the first, Greenberg had been aware of the threat, asking Harold whether the fact of having a son could perhaps "save" him from it. To make matters worse, Greenberg's younger brother, Martin, had been inducted into the army in March 1941. "His reconciliation to his fate," Greenberg wrote to Harold, "was a process as horrible as the fate."

The long arm of the Selective Service System did not reach Greenberg until August 1942, when he filled out a questionnaire from the draft board, asserting that Danny was his dependent. In October, he quit his job at the Customs Service; he would rely on a part-time job at the Dial Press and his new position as art critic for the *Nation*. *Partisan Review* paid mostly in prestige; even the respected Columbia University professor Lionel Trilling received only $18 for a nine-page article.

Although Greenberg was classified as 1A, the possibility of being drafted seemed "remote," he wrote Harold in December 1942. "They may find that I have chronic trench mouth." However, while he did get a brief deferment, his appeal against the 1A classification was turned down. By mid-February 1943, he was Air Force Private Clement Greenberg, stationed in Miami Beach, Florida.

Chapter IV

WAR

At the age of thirty-two, Clement Greenberg was the second-oldest person in his flight unit as he underwent basic training for what was then the air corps, a branch of the U.S. Army. He bunked in a Miami Beach hotel room with five other recruits and quickly fell into depression: "Words cannot say the miseries of the first week," he wrote to Harold in mid-February 1943, then described the unit's daily routine in painful detail: reveille at 4:45; breakfast at 5; barracks cleaning till 7; march, drill, and exercise until 11:30; lunch at 11:45, then more drilling and exercise until dinner at 5:30; a brief interlude of freedom until lights out at 9. "There are usually two or three moments a week when you feel you can't go on another second, but you do."

By March 10, Greenberg was sick. After he told the doctor treating him for a sore throat about his aspirin allergy, he was given capsules that were basically aspirin. His face swelled to three times its normal size and his body burned and itched; he was rushed to the hospital by ambulance and spent two days there. To the "*Partisan Review* boys" he sent a postcard: "Save yourselves."

In April, Greenberg was promoted to private first class and shipped to Tishomingo, Oklahoma, for training as a clerk. Oddly, the small town in "poor, withered dusty country" struck Greenberg as less provincial than a small town in the East: "You have a feeling of access to the rest of the world," he told Harold. He was billeted at an agricultural junior college, sharing a dorm room with two others. While Greenberg isolated himself from the military comrades sharing his meals, bedroom, and plight, he sought out a camp for German prisoners of war near Tishomingo and wrote a sympathetic article for the *Nation* about it. "God help the fugitive who tries to hide himself in the unsubstantial foliage of . . . [the camp's] gullies," he wrote, "or to slip past the squinting eyes of the Bible-pounding natives." Greenberg also expressed considerable sympathy for the more than two hundred thousand prisoners of war, mostly "boys or hardly more than that," captured in North Africa after the Allied landings in Morocco and Algeria in November 1942.

It is difficult to believe that the man who wrote this cogent, compassionate report would, just six weeks later, plunge into hopeless depression, followed by a violent psychotic episode. Shortly after writing about the German POWs, Greenberg had been sent to Kellogg Field in Battle Creek, Michigan, to await his next assignment. There, he could sleep until 10 A.M. and spend the rest of the day reading novels from the camp's library. His breakdown began in June when he discovered that he would not get a desk job, but would be sent into combat, probably into the looming assault on "Fortress Europe" in 1943. A five-day furlough in New York made him jittery, a condition that worsened on his return to Kellogg Field. To Harold, he described "a week of the blackest depression, and then blooey, I shook and shouted and wanted to cry." After six days in the hospital, he was diagnosed as "maladjusted, slightly neurotic." His own conclusion was that "living in an enormous barracks for the first time did me in."

But something darker than slight neurosis emerges from an unmailed letter to Jeannie Connolly, found by his widow, Janice Van Horne, in a 1930 German edition of Goethe's *Faust*, after Greenberg's death in 1994. "The very sight of the base," Greenberg wrote, "poured awful blackness into me, awful, awful." After skipping lunch, he "cried without tears all alone in the library." When he arrived at the Fort Custer hospital, his clothes were taken and he marched in pajamas and robe "down corridor after corridor connecting the long bungalows which are the hospital's wards." The doctor had written that Greenberg might "do something desperate," so he was placed in a locked ward, with "the loonies parading about." His 10 x 6 foot room contained nothing but a bed, a barred window and a door that could not be closed from the inside. "I protested madly but the three big orderlies excused themselves by saying they were in . . ." Here the letter tantalizingly ends.

When Greenberg was allowed to leave the hospital, he was put to work writing the base's history. "But it's no good," he wrote to Harold. He awakened in the morning to nausea, had "jitters at noon," and felt normal only toward evening; the day was punctuated by "fits of despair" and crying jags. At the time, Greenberg argued that "something physical" had caused his problems, although later he insisted that the army was the sole cause of his depression, and that he "felt trapped."

On August 24, 1943, Greenberg appeared before a board of army officers where a psychiatrist recommended he be discharged. Afterward, he lived alone in a staff room, awaiting his final dismissal. By September 11, when his discharge was imminent, his symptoms appear to have vanished, and he was already contemplating a job offer to become an editor of *Contemporary Jewish Record* at $100 a week. "Of course, it's not my sort of thing," he grumbled to Harold, but "$100 is too tempting." In less than three months, Greenberg had evolved from a bawling baby in a locked mental ward to boasting that "of course I don't know how to be an editor but I found out on *Partisan Review* you can learn how in a week." Some forty years later he told the editor of his writings, John O'Brian: "I certainly was unmoored . . . but not that much, not enough to think I had a vocation in contradistinction to my fellow soldiers' lack of any."

More likely, Greenberg shrank from intimacy with his comrades, the very fabric of "the masses," whose socialist devotion had seemed so certain to him in 1940 and 1941. In the barracks, on the drill ground, and in the mess hall, he could only quail at being confronted by the avid consumers of Tin Pan Alley songs, Edgar A. Guest's verse, even John Steinbeck's novels—all that he had consigned to kitsch back in 1940. Greenberg's letters, mailed and unmailed, highlight his utter contempt for his fellow soldiers; he names not a single buddy and pours venom on the entire experience of military life. Postwar accounts of the military experience offer ample evidence of the crudity and intrusiveness unavoidable among draftees. Inevitably, someone ridiculed his age and his baldness, his New York Jewishness and his intellectual bent. Others perhaps mocked his arrogant bluster and sissified interest in fine art.

Also in August, Jean Connolly borrowed $100 from Greenberg's father to pay for a trip to see her ailing lover, but she left after two weeks when the money ran out. Soon she informed Greenberg that she had fallen in love with Laurence Vail, a sometime painter and poet who had previously been married to the writer Kay Boyle and the heiress Peggy Guggenheim, and that they planned to marry in Mexico as soon as her Reno divorce from husband Cyril was final. Ironically, Greenberg had written a brief, mixed review of Vail's collaged bottles in December 1942, calling him a greatly gifted artist.

Despite this, Greenberg hoped to stay with Jean at her house in western Connecticut when he was discharged. But Jean refused to house him, as she was already involved with Laurence Vail, who lived nearby. Not that Greenberg wanted to continue his affair with Jean; he just "wanted to name the time and place" for their breakup, he told Harold. But he abandoned the plan, and by the end of September he had located a room at the Murray Hill Hotel in New York City.

His first writing after the army ordeal was published in the *Nation*, a review of Piet Mondrian's "Broadway Boogie Woogie" which had just been acquired by the Museum of Modern Art. He tempered his verdict of the artist's "sudden originality" with criticisms: new and "slightly impure" colors, lack of "neat and precise mechanical execution, weak yellow and purple hues . . . color wandering off in all directions." A week later, Greenberg issued a rare "reconsideration." His memory had played tricks on him, he wrote; there were "no orange, purple or impure colors." On a second visit (possibly prompted by MoMA complaints), he found the work enormously improved and suggested that "perhaps after an aging of six months or so it will seem completely successful."

For the rest of 1943, Greenberg published eight reviews in the *Nation*; all except one dealt with art. He took on Alexander Calder, whose world, he said, "lacks history. Lots of things go on in it, but nothing happens." He found Calder inferior to David Smith, another sculptor of welded steel, whom Greenberg would champion for the rest of his life. He faulted Giorgio de Chirico for creating "a parody of Renaissance composition" and color like "stale Florentine sugar." Reviewing a large exhibition of Van Gogh, he chose wording that could well have described his own emotional commotions: Van Gogh's work failed because of "his failure to react upon and discipline his temperament." In mid-November, a season when New York art sales peaked in anticipation of the gift-giving season, Greenberg planted (or tried to plant) the kiss of death on Eugene Berman: his pictures were "too overpowering, too decadent, too spurious, and, really, too well done to be dealt with in measured words. If this is art, the age is doomed."

Even in these early reviews, Greenberg displayed a cocksure writing style, sometimes prescribing that the artist start or stop doing a particular thing and flinging a moralistic rhetoric at the reader, implying that disagreeing with his views was a spiritual lapse. It was a rhetorical style incubated among the intellectuals clustered around *Partisan Review*. Irving Howe recalled that this "style of brilliance" was often hard to accept: "free-lance dash, peacock strut, knockout synthesis." These writers cultivated an image of "the intellectual as anti-specialist . . . as roamer among theories, as dilettante connoisseur, as *luftmensch* of the mind." Howe attributed this fragile persona to these intellectuals' "roots loosed in Jewish soil, but still not torn out, lowered into American soil but still not fixed," giving "a seemingly endless range of possibilities."

Many of Greenberg's early writings demonstrated this sort of restless ambivalence toward his Jewish heritage. His affectionate review of *The World of Sholom Aleichem* finds the Eastern European ghetto chronicler deeper than Dickens and his Yiddish writings impossible to translate. The aggressively secular Greenberg suggested that "the shop talk of Talmudic scholarship" had seeped into every Jew's bones "without [his] ever having read the Talmud." Certainly Greenberg's own writings reflected Talmudic prescriptions and disputations.

This ambivalence contributed to Greenberg's conflicted engagement with his family, especially his father. Until September 1943, he was still paying a dutiful weekly visit to Flatbush, even as he resented that regular pilgrimage. "Brooklyn would invariably depress me," he wrote to Harold. "In a way it depressed me more than the army." He appeared delighted when his father's growing fortune allowed the family to move to 360 Central Park West, a short subway ride away. As Greenberg was attempting to separate from his family, he also cut himself loose from Harold. After mid-November 1943, Greenberg wrote to Harold only sporadically; the letters became "increasingly formal and distant," wrote Greenberg's widow and editor of *The Harold Letters*, Janice Van Horne. She believed that the absence of any letters for three years after 1943 seemed "unlikely and remains unexplained."

However, in January 1945, Greenberg attended a party organized by Harold Lazarus and his friend Maurice English. Seeing the two together for the first time may have confirmed for Greenberg what he had surely suspected but no doubt repressed, that Harold was homosexual. Greenberg had on many occasions expressed contempt for homosexuals—he had found Jeannie's gay friends intolerable—and would continue to denigrate them, as he frequently denigrated women.

While Greenberg's break with his college friend and confidante seems abrupt and somewhat cruel, it can also be explained by major changes in Greenberg's life. For one thing, the kinds of critical writings he had practiced on Harold for almost fifteen years were now being published in the *Nation*, *Partisan Review*, and other periodicals: quite simply, he no longer needed his audience of one. For another, his social life, which had previously been narrow and difficult, was blossoming. In the mid 1940s, Greenberg often dined with Margaret Marshall, his ostensible boss at the *Nation*, and spent time with the writers Djuna Barnes and Walter Mehring, the art historian Kenneth Clark, the sociologist Lewis Coser, the philosopher Hannah Arendt, and the anthropologist Selden Rodman. Mixed in with multiple dental appointments in Greenberg's datebooks were lunches with "Pa," down to one a month, and frequent evenings with Edna and William Phillips of *Partisan Review*. At one of Margaret Marshall's parties, Lionel Trilling complained about an article Greenberg had edited for *Contemporary Jewish Record* that dwelled on Henry Adams's anti-Semitic bias. Trilling, who had just been appointed the only Jewish full professor in Columbia University's English department, insisted that Adams had many other virtues, while Greenberg accused Trilling of Jewish self-hatred. "Blows were averted only by the intervention of cooler heads," wrote one interviewer.

Greenberg's datebooks for 1944 and 1945 are peppered with appointments with "M.M." This was Mary McCarthy, then still married to Edmund Wilson and living on Cape Cod. She would leave her son Reuel with a nanny and spend the week in New York, as she wrote later to friends, "to see a lover, then to see a psychoanalyst, then an editor or publisher, then a lawyer, and finally the dentist." The analyst was Dr. Abraham Kardiner, himself analyzed by Sigmund Freud, and one of many refugee psychiatrists who popularized Freudian analysis in the United States. Later McCarthy told a biographer that her affair with Greenberg was "lengthy and not very enjoyable . . . When you have an affair with some man you don't like, somehow they're the hardest to break with." There were rumors that she was having a concurrent affair with John Dos Passos. For his part, Greenberg told another McCarthy biographer many years later that though at first "intimidated," he found her "fun to be with. If you had something to say, she'd toss the ball back . . . Mary would correct your diction and pronunciation . . . She was a bit of a prig at times. Prigs tend to go by the book." In a letter to Bowden Broadwater, who would become her third husband, she wrote that Greenberg couldn't forgive her "for the fact that he hadn't fallen in love with me." She refrained from suggesting that there could be a contrary interpretation "and went on cooking his scrambled eggs."

McCarthy told another biographer that she was uninterested in Greenberg's formalist theory of art and, many decades later, found it difficult to say what about him *did* interest her. She described him as a "very sadistic" and overbearing man who would volunteer to "spank Reuel," her six-year-old son by Wilson. McCarthy was bitter over Greenberg's behavior when she invited him to visit her and Wilson on Cape Cod in the summer of 1944. He was "perfectly odious all the time he was here," she wrote to Broadwater. "He did nothing but criticize me, not help with the dishes, sleep until one and want both breakfast and lunch, fleck imaginary specks off my face and costume, and flirt with my worst enemies." As McCarthy often did, she retaliated by creating a fictional Greenberg knockoff, Martin Samuels, in an unpublished novelette. This writer and critic "never entered a friend's apartment without making some criticism of the lighting, décor, or ventilation; he rearranged books on people's bookshelves, turned out the gas under dishes the cook had left simmering on the stove, took the knitting out of old ladies' hands to criticize the stitch they were using, and once went to so far in his usurpation of someone else's domesticity as to spank a lively child while he was waiting for his mother."

Greenberg retaliated in kind, even many decades after he had had any contact with McCarthy. He told a biographer that he once observed that Mary was more than one-quarter Jewish. "Her eyes blazed," he recalled. "She took me seriously." He confessed that for just a week he wanted to marry Mary, "when she was in between men. I didn't know enough to listen to my entrails." However, he was sure that McCarthy wouldn't have married him: "She wasn't going to marry a Jew."

Soon after McCarthy flounced out of his life, Greenberg was again reminded of his own problematic son, Danny. In 1943, while still in the army, he had stopped writing to the boy's grandmother, Mrs. Ewing; he told Harold that Danny "doesn't need me and is much more well-adjusted than the old lady gave me to understand." Three years later, the grandmother delivered the boy, now eleven years old, to Greenberg's Greenwich Village apartment at 248 West Eleventh Street and "stole out at daybreak." Greenberg was awakened by the boy "crying for granny, granny . . . and wailing when he found she was long gone, leaving only a note behind." Greenberg had (in his estimation) more important tasks than caring for an eleven-year-old and quickly shipped him on, like a troublesome parcel, for a week at William and Edna Phillips's summer home. When the boy returned, Greenberg had hired a nanny; he would continue to distance himself from the troubled boy throughout his life.

At the time, Greenberg was having an affair with Jean Connolly's sister Annie Bakewell, and when Danny unexpectedly arrived at his house he summoned Annie to take care of the boy until he found a nanny. He was still seeing Annie a year later, when an argument between them erupted while visiting the Phillipses' country house. On that occasion, he "slapped Annie soundly," he wrote Harold, and had not seen her since. Another one of Greenberg's dates during that time was Phyllis Fleiss, who told Jackson Pollock biographers that she was "awed by the man and thrilled by the company he kept," but that "he was always terrorizing me." She described Greenberg finding a half-dead mouse in the gutter one night on Park Avenue. "He picked it up and dangled it in front of my face. I screamed, of course, and ran, but he chased after me with this mouse. He had a sadistic streak a mile wide."

In his first letter to Harold after a two-and-a-half-year silence, Greenberg described a "socially hectic" life, with visitors dropping in most evenings, including the young film critic Manny Farber and John Farrelly, who persuaded Greenberg to read some of his early poetry. "I was surprised how good some of it was," he told Harold, "underived . . . absolutely underived." He wrote that he no longer felt "alone and aimless as I used to in my twenties . . . No more dawdling and reading and sweating and yearning and thinking about myself." He thought it "strange, how little self-confidence I had and the conviction that the opposition was invincible."

To beat back that perceived opposition, Greenberg developed aggressive mechanisms. At a party in 1946 at the home of Lionel Abel, he accused Abel's friend, the philosopher Jean Wahl, of being an anti-Semite. When Abel objected, Greenberg suggested they settle the dispute downstairs in the street. Abel was frail, just recovering from a lung infection, but Greenberg nevertheless "knocked him around." The following year, he was holding forth at length during Peggy Guggenheim's party when Max Ernst irritably dumped a butt-laden ashtray on his head. The critic leaped up to throttle Ernst, who was "overcome with laughter." Then the youthful Surrealist Nicolas Calas "took a roundhouse swing at Greenberg and, to everyone's surprise, connected. The crowd clustered around Greenberg, sitting on the floor, practically under the piano." His date rushed to press two aspirins and water on Greenberg, who gratefully swallowed the pills. However, seconds later, he remembered his aspirin allergy and roared that he had been poisoned. To an interviewer, much later, he explained that "the three fights I got into . . . have all been with Surrealists, or ex-would-be Surrealists, who make a practice of courting violence by abuse."

✳   ✳   ✳

In his writings, both early and late, as well as in his many speeches, Greenberg expressed his views on art with the same kind of bull's-eye certainty that he used in reminiscing about Mary McCarthy years later. As one of many reviewers observed, his published writings contained "not a drop of fat . . . the appetite for content, relevance and appraisal is relentless . . . Clement Greenberg is a born, almost helpless seeker-out of distinctions and maker of comparisons." Having absorbed from Hans Hofmann the notion of "aesthetic logic" and from Trotsky "the idea of historical logic," Greenberg personalized these unverifiable insights by adding the concept of the critic's "eye," a mystical quality that few possessed and many trusted. Another analyst of Greenberg's writings found "astonishing" consistency in its "repetitive and assertive dogmatism." Once he had decreed early on that Cubism was the seminal impulse in modern art, he never reexamined that view; he resembled a rabbi who sets forth certain immutable moral parameters. He was proud of such dogmatism, telling Jackson Pollock's biographers that "to be attacked personally is a favorable sign . . . if you are not against most opinion, something is off."

While Greenberg sometimes sounded as though he were handing down commandments engraved on stone tablets, his theory about how art evolves, his wide-ranging curiosity, and his polished prose presented a beacon of enlightenment to the growing art audience of the 1940s. As the end of the Second World War was in sight and the economy was beginning to look rosy, ten million veterans were guaranteed a college education. Many of them valued an art critic who could tell them what was so great about, say, Wassily Kandinsky, the Russian painter whose puzzling abstracts were generously represented in New York's Museum of Nonobjective Art (the future Guggenheim). In an obituary published in the *Nation* in 1945, Greenberg incisively told his readers just what made Kandinsky great and what did not: "One of the first . . . to get an intellectual purchase on post-Cubist painting yet he failed in the end to understand it in practice." This statement alone could send readers to the museum to see for themselves, to agree or quibble. Greenberg sent them off with another judgment: "For a relatively short time, Kandinsky was a great painter; he was and will remain a large and revolutionary phenomenon . . . yet he stays apart from the mainstream and in the last analysis remains a provincial." Then a final thunderclap: "The example of his work is dangerous to younger painters."

The confident way Greenberg expressed his views was not only a function of his intelligence and tendency to intimidate, but was also thrown into high relief by the disarray of others writing about art. The opening of Peggy Guggenheim's Art of This Century in March 1943, for example, had received a scant, anonymous paragraph in the *New York Times*. And the *Times* had given three anonymous, rather lukewarm, paragraphs to the gallery's first juried show two months later, even though the high-profile jurors included Duchamp, Mondrian, Guggenheim, James Thrall Soby, and James Johnson Sweeney.

Greenberg never directly attacked the *Times*, despite its patently wispy feints at modernism, but his statements did much to undermine the waxen example set by the paper and by other antimodernists. It took just a single unsigned paragraph in the *Nation* to annihilate the self-appointed "dean of American painting," Thomas Craven. Reviewing Craven's latest revision of *The Story of Painting*, Greenberg noted that Craven wrote "less brazenly than usual. Something has taken the wind and vinegar out of him and he seems to be addressing himself to children." And he pointed to such "egregious errors" as stating that Leonardo "invented chiaroscuro."

In reality, Greenberg's rhetorical tone was hardly more prescriptive than that of the political or literary critics published by *Partisan Review*, though it seemed strident in comparison with the *Times* and other mainstream venues. Irving Howe observed that America's first "intelligentsia," not intellectuals but a class that functioned both culturally and politically, savored rudeness. Such a tone was "a spear . . . to break the skin of complacency." In its early years, he observed, *Partisan Review*'s harsh tone "was not only the weapon of cultural underdogs but also a sign that intellectual Jews had become sufficiently self-assured to stop playing by Gentile rules."

In that spirit, Philip Rahv pilloried the Harvard historian Bernard DeVoto for *The Literary Fallacy*, "as vicious and mindless a tract as any so far produced by those who have set themselves the task of subverting the critical spirit of modern art and thought." When Sinclair Lewis sprang to DeVoto's defense, Rahv called him "a fugitive from an earlier self," before again belaboring DeVoto as a brash purveyor of "bourgeois philistine values," and "a terrible show-off besides." Along the way, Rahv also flayed Van Wyck Brooks as even more "archaic" than DeVoto. Greenberg considered Rahv and his coeditor William Phillips "two of the most intelligent people in the country," while also warning William Barrett, another Gentile Yale graduate attracted to the *Partisan Review* circle, of "the limits, the peculiar twists and turns of that intelligence."

Right after Pearl Harbor blasted the United States into the Second World War, Rahv and Phillips had persuaded other staffers that further discussion of the war would be fruitless, and the magazine had emphasized cultural issues. The two editors papered over their differences, a task eased by the departure of Dwight Macdonald to start his own magazine, *Politics*. Macdonald's magazine lasted for five years, although circulation never rose above five thousand. It drummed an anti-Stalinist ultraradical line and published many emerging thinkers, such as C. Wright Mills, Paul Goodman, Oscar Handlin, James Agee, Nathan Glazer, Irving Kristol, Marshall McLuhan, and Bruno Bettelheim before grinding to a halt in 1949.

Greenberg's relations with Macdonald continued, before eventually coming to a halt as well. He later told John O'Brian that he had been "on the outs" with Macdonald for twenty years before he died in 1982: "He saved all his morality for public affairs." Macdonald was equally tart. In a 1979 interview with Diana Trilling, he boasted of having connected Greenberg with *Partisan Review*: "In fact, I invented Clem Greenberg," he said. "I'm not so sure that he did know anything about art," but he pushed his views on a "worried, jumped-up wartime-educated public."

Nor were relations much more pacific at *Partisan Review*. By the time Greenberg returned from his military tour in September 1943, differences between the two remaining editors were resurfacing. In addition, now that the *Nation* was paying him $15 for each of his frequent, brief reviews, Greenberg may have been reluctant to spend a great deal of time preparing a much longer, more complex *Partisan Review* essay for a similar amount. After publishing five pieces there in 1941, he published just two in 1942, nothing in 1943, and just three essays in 1944.

Of the two editors, Philip Rahv was the more striking, a saturnine presence that William Barrett found "dark and faintly menacing," his gaze "heavy-lidded, exotic," the persona possibly "a mysterious agent on the Orient Express." Phillips "was pushed into the shadow by Rahv's more aggressive and blustering personality," Barrett recalled. The poet Delmore Schwartz called him Philip Slav behind his back. Mary McCarthy, who had lived for some years with Rahv during the late 1930s, lampooned him in her acidic novel *The Oasis* as Will Taub, a Russian-born New York intellectual for whom the only reality was "the Movement, Bohemian women, the anti-movement, downtown bars, argument, discussion, subways, newsstands, the office."

Meanwhile, Greenberg's reviews in the *Nation* and his occasional essays in *Partisan Review* were becoming more dogmatic and his tone, according to Barrett, "more solemn." At *Partisan Review*, "some questioning murmurs began to arise." Greenberg believed that they originated with Rahv, whose ignorance of and contempt for art were common knowledge; he had never even visited the Metropolitan. At a staff meeting called by Phillips in 1945, the antagonisms boiled over, leading to Rahv's departure from the magazine. Greenberg replaced Rahv as William Phillips's best friend, a relationship that would flourish for many years. On many occasions, Phillips replaced Harold Lazarus as Greenberg's wailing wall.

The young Leslie Fiedler noticed that the *Partisan Review* writers were "characteristically unhappy with each other and with the magazine itself, and they would resent to a man being spoken of as a group," but while they asserted their independence and inhabited a spectrum of political beliefs from anarchist to Republican, they were all marked by their onetime proximity to the Communist movement. Alfred Kazin observed that as the Second World War was ending, the *Partisan Review* editors, accustomed as they were to leaving tradition behind, "put all their zeal for social revolution into the purer and perhaps more lasting revolution of modern literature and art." Sidney Hook much later decided that *Partisan Review* was never serious about revolution or about politics, but "simply against things as they were."

Like the magazine's editors, Greenberg was drifting away from politics and toward culture. In 1944, he wrote forty-four pieces; twenty-seven of them were published in the *Nation*, only three in *Partisan Review* and two each in *Politics* and *Contemporary Jewish Record*, where he became managing editor in the fall. Twenty-one of these dealt with art exhibitions; he also reviewed six art-related books and seven more literary books. This concentrated array established Greenberg as a force in the lively modern art market. One biographer asserts that his writing appeared so easy and fluid that readers assumed they practically wrote themselves. In fact, the forty-seven boxes of Greenberg's papers reveal pieces painstakingly edited, revised, and edited again.

These boxes also reveal other articles, also revised and polished, but never published. One article deplores the English-speaking world's neglect of Goethe; he was a modern man, wrote Greenberg, again challenging wartime anti-German attitudes. He devoted a fourteen-page manuscript to Thomas Mann's four Joseph novels, the last of which had been published in 1943. The brief draft for a history of easel painting had a thin Marxist glaze, arguing that "painting begins with bourgeoisie in N. Italy," and moves on to a complex analysis that rushes from Giotto in the fourteenth century and Flemish art in the fifteenth to Ingres and Delacroix in the nineteenth. The conclusion was that the abstract art of the twentieth century was a reaction to all that had gone before. Greenberg based his comments on what few Old Masters he had crammed into his single six-week European journey. As there is no evidence that they were ever submitted to any periodical, these essays may not have been intended for publication, but rather to act as mental exercises on the history of art. While Greenberg read selectively on the art of Old Masters, his command of art history before the mid-nineteenth century remained distinctly shaky. Discussing his own early writings, Greenberg told an interviewer that the art criticism he read in the early 1940s was unhelpful, mostly "poor stuff," and that he had no regrets over "educating myself in public." He had read very little about art, he said. "I was so sure of my eye at that time . . . I thought I'd bet my eye against whatever."

One of the artists that caught his eye sealed his reputation for discerning new talent. Late in 1943, Greenberg wrote his first review of Jackson Pollock, to whom Lee Krasner had introduced him a year earlier. He tied the works in the young artist's first one-man show, at Art of This Century, to "that American chiaroscuro which dominated Melville, Hawthorne, and Poe, a peculiar but apt linking of art and literature. While he deemed "pretentious" some of Pollock's titles, such as *Guardians of the Secret* and *Male and Female*, the Greenberg oracle offered a veiled prediction that this artist might "relapse into an influence, but . . . not for long."

Through 1944, Greenberg was giving Pollock the benefit of the doubt. In May, he argued that Pollock's pastel and gouache works, "for all their shortcomings . . . deserve attention." In November, he complimented Peggy Guggenheim for "her enterprise in presenting young and unrecognized artists at Art of This Century, singling out William Baziotes and Pollock as "among the six or seven best young artists we possess." It was no exaggeration, Greenberg wrote, "to say that the future of American painting depends on what . . . Baziotes, Pollock, and only a comparatively few others do from now on."

While Greenberg credited Peggy Guggenheim for the liveliness of her gallery, it was her assistant, Howard Putzel, who located, promoted, and babysat many of the new artists shown at Art of This Century. Putzel was born in San Francisco in 1898, and in May 1934 organized the first exhibition in California of any Surrealist art, showing works of Joan Miró at a San Francisco gallery. In September, he organized the first West Coast exhibition of Salvador Dalí in the back rooms of a San Francisco bookstore, and in October he showed Max Ernst. In 1936 he opened the Putzel Gallery in Los Angeles with a show of Miró, Yves Tanguy, Dalí, and Klee. A butterball in round glasses, Putzel suffered from heart problems, a thyroid condition, and frequent epileptic seizures; he was shy yet combative, nervous, temperamental, and sometimes inarticulate. His tenacious support for the artists he appreciated overcame his offbeat appearance and personality, but could not prevent endemic financial disasters. In 1938 he fled to Paris, where he met Guggenheim and began dragging her to the studios of artists he favored. She had expected to meet "a little black hunchback," she later recalled, but instead encountered "a big fat blond." He at first struck her as "nearly incoherent," but she soon discovered that "behind his incomprehensible conversation and behavior" lurked not only a passion for modern art, but a well-schooled eye for new artists. He would arrive at her apartment in the morning with various parcels under his arm and would sulk if she didn't buy; he also sulked when she bought things without his approval.

Putzel returned to New York in 1940, convinced that the next place the new art would appear was the United States. After helping the Surrealist artist Gordon Onslow-Ford get a job teaching a course on Surrealism at the New School for Social Research, Putzel organized concurrent exhibitions, showing works by de Chirico, Ernst, and Miró, René Magritte, and Yves Tanguy; a final exhibition included seven younger Surrealists. Attending the course on Surrealism at the New School were American artists who would later be important Abstract Expressionists: William Baziotes, Tony Smith, and, probably, Jackson Pollock.

Putzel was at the airport when Peggy Guggenheim's chartered airplane landed in New York on July 14, 1941, carrying her soon-to-be husband Max Ernst, the rest of her entourage, and her rich collection of modernist paintings. When she selected a gallery space at 28–30 West Fifty-seventh Street, he advised her to hire the émigré architect Frederick Kiesler to design the interior. Even before Art of This Century opened, Putzel brought potential customers to Guggenheim's Beekman Place apartment and sold many paintings by Ernst. When the doors did open, "Putzel virtually controlled all aspects" of the gallery, his biographer wrote; "essentially the artists who dealt with Peggy Guggenheim in the earlier years of the gallery dealt with Putzel."

Greenberg reviewed the gallery's opening equivocally in January 1943. He generally approved of Kiesler's design and even of how the Surrealist works were displayed, but couldn't resist complaining that the rest of the gallery was "a little crowded and scrappy." Still, he judged a Klee, an Ernst, and a de Chirico in the exhibition "the best examples of these artists' work I have seen in this country." Howard Putzel may have introduced Pollock to Guggenheim, and by the summer of 1943 he had persuaded her to put Pollock under contract, a monthly stipend of $150 in exchange for exclusive rights to exhibit his work. "The whole thing was based on our friendship with Putzel," said Lee Krasner many years later. "He was at our house every night, and he told Jackson what to do and how to behave. Otherwise I doubt it would have happened."

Putzel left Art of This Century before the 1944–45 season to open his own gallery at 67 East Fifty-seventh Street. It was financed by a British intelligence figure, Kenneth McPherson, for whom Putzel had obtained paintings. Among the artists he exhibited in one show, "A Problem for Critics," were European Surrealists like Masson, Matta, and Arp, along with Americans whose style as yet had no name: Adolph Gottlieb, Mark Rothko, Arshile Gorky, Krasner, Pollock, David Smith, Richard Pousette-Dart, and Mark Tobey. Perhaps reflecting the general euphoria following the Allies' defeat of Nazi Germany on May 8, the *Times's* Jewell enthusiastically welcomed the fresh Americans: "Their works indicate genuine talent, enthusiasm, and originality," he wrote. "I believe we see real American painting beginning now." Greenberg grumbled that Putzel was showing too disparate an array of artists, but agreed that "there is no question that Mr. Putzel has hold of something here." As usual, he opposed inclusion of the Surrealists; such artists' continuing use of representation struck him as "a step backward." Soon after this exhibition closed, Putzel died of heart problems at the age of forty-seven. He had lost McPherson's support, and the 67 Gallery, like all his other ventures, was in financial trouble.

However, the fact that the gallery had been located uptown and the timely emergence of the Americans were symptoms of an art boom that had surprised New York while the Second World War was still raging. In July 1944 *Art News* published details collected by Aline B. Louchheim, who as Aline Saarinen (after her marriage to the Finnish architect Eero Saarinen) would become the first woman to write about art for the *New York Times*. She attributed the "picture boom" to the WPA art projects, an overheated wartime economy, enhanced museum education outreach, and sponsorship of art by large corporations like IBM and Pepsi. Most of the buyers were midlevel businessmen or professionals, and under age forty-five. Many were comfortable with abstraction and works by Americans. They bought, but cautiously; rank beginners seldom paid more than $500 for anything. Even as the Nazis were being routed from Stalingrad and the Allies were pummeling German troops in Italy, the New York art auctions saw "high prices and frenzied interest." Louchheim discerned "outstanding sales of important contemporary masters, red-star-studded galleries and sly, pleased smiles of dealers."

The boom continued the following season, as auctions set an all-time record and galleries reported a 37 percent increase in sales over the previous record year. Average volume per gallery rose from 125 pictures to 160; prices were also higher, with about 20 percent of sales above $1,000. However, the merry New York market did not extend across the United States. A 1945 survey of artists by the American Federation for the Arts found that 44 percent lived primarily by teaching and another 32 percent by commercial art. Few of the rest lived on art sales, but survived on investments or inheritances, odd jobs, museum curating, interior decorating, writing, and, for a few women, alimony. Income from art, an average of $1,154 per year, was consumed by expenses—studio rental, supplies and materials. One respondent wrote that "many artists have trained themselves never to tell about their financial failure as artists."

By 1946, *Fortune* magazine lavished more than six of its oversize pages on extending Louchheim's earlier reports and delving more deeply into "57th Street," now home to 150 dealers, "the heart, brain and nervous system of the art business in America." Collecting art had become a status symbol for corporations, and at least one-third of individual buyers were also new. With Europe torn by war, New York became the center of art auctions. Sales at

Parke-Bernet increased from $2.5 million in 1939 to $4 million in 1942, and would swell to more than $6 million in 1945. For the first time, many of the collectors (a full one-third of the individuals named in the article) were Jewish.

Nor was the visibility of American Jews limited to the art world. Horrified by the emerging reports of atrocities in Europe, many were asserting their cultural roots in other domains as well. In February, Greenberg was among such figures as Lionel Trilling, Alfred Kazin, Louis Kronenberger, Delmore Schwartz, and Howard Fast who contributed to a symposium about American literature and the younger Jewish generation published by *Contemporary Jewish Record*. In another striking display of ambivalence toward his own heritage, Greenberg cited his parents' repudiation of the religion, "by becoming free-thinking socialists," yet conversing principally in Yiddish and insisting on identifying themselves as Jews. Even as he was striding forth into the secular world, especially the realm of art where few Jews had ventured, Greenberg declared that "a quality of Jewishness is present in every word I write."

Contemporary Jewish Record was a long-established journal sponsored by the American Jewish Committee. The organizers were largely German-Jewish businessmen and professionals who in the late nineteenth century were perturbed as much by widespread anti-Semitism as by the mass influx of poor and poorly educated Jews from Eastern Europe, a tide that threatened to undermine the hard-won status of American-born Jews of German background. No sooner was the American Jewish Committee organized, in 1906, than members fell into disagreements over its scope and views. The debate intensified after 1933, when East European Jews and their children began exerting strong pressures, some on behalf of Zionism, others toward secularism or even assimilation.

In the fall of 1944, Greenberg took up his post as associate editor of *Contemporary Jewish Record*, which became *Commentary* a year later. The editor, Elliott Cohen, had also edited the *Menorah Journal*, a predecessor of *Contemporary Jewish Record*. He had discovered and encouraged such writers as Lionel Trilling and Clifton Fadiman, and was a sad example of the many doors closed to Jews before the Second World War. The sociologist Daniel Bell described him as "probably one of the brightest students Yale University had had in many years," though also psychologically frail. Bell was devoted to English literature; his chief ambition had been to teach at Yale. But, in the words of a department spokesman, who admired his ability but wishes to remain anonymous, the university found it "hard . . . to imagine a Hebrew teaching the Protestant tradition to young men at Yale." Cohen believed that the debut of *Commentary* "in the shadow of the atomic bomb and the concentration camps represented an 'act of faith' in the redeeming power of the intellect." He saw *Commentary*'s audience as primarily middle-class and Jewish, but not as intellectual as *Partisan Review*. In the wider world, both magazines displayed an unmistakably Jewish mentality. To Elliott Cohen, the chief difference between the two publications was that "we admit to being a Jewish magazine and they don't."

Both publications roosted in run-down spaces in lower Manhattan, *Partisan Review* on Astor Place, south of Union Square, where radical orators still proclaimed some future utopia, and *Commentary* in a loft on the top floor of a small building in the garment district. As the essayist Midge Decter recalled it more than half a century later, the place was "complete with hot- and cold-leaking skylight and no air conditioning." Cohen occupied a corner office with two windows, while the other editors sat two to a cubicle "with a single, basically useless window between them"; Decter, then a secretary, sat under the leaking skylight. "Sometimes in summer," she recalled, "the editors found it necessary to decamp to a nearby air-conditioned bar in order to meet the magazine's deadline." Greenberg shared an office with Robert Warshow, who, perhaps to his elitist office mate's disgust, wrote knowingly and warmly about movies and popular culture. He also attracted many young aspiring writers, another annoying reminder to Greenberg of his unfulfilled literary ambitions. Decter saw Greenberg's job at *Commentary* as "in essence a sinecure . . . [it] did not seem to involve spending a great deal of time in the office."

When a young writer did approach him, Greenberg tended to be gruff. In 1946, Irving Howe brought him an essay reacting to Isaac Rosenfeld's new novel, *Passage from Home*. In it, the author commented on the serious father-son frictions in immigrant Jewish families: the father's effort to fulfill his intellectual ambitions through the son, while the son sees that ambition as "the brand of alienation." Certainly, this was a theme close to Greenberg's experience, but when Howe told Greenberg he wanted to publish the essay because he needed the money, Greenberg growled: "I don't care why you want to print it. All I care is whether it's any good." Howe moved past those brusque words and published many more articles in *Commentary*, "mostly under the guidance of Greenberg, a hard man with a strong mind."

Much like his stern advice to Howe, Greenberg also began in 1944 to advise artists while visiting their studios. Using his favorite form of written communication, the postcard, he notified William Baziotes that he would visit his studio at 9 P.M. of a Sunday evening in June. Baziotes had been included in a Surrealist exhibition two years earlier and continued to follow the movement closely. Greenberg's postcards to him both announced his visits and solicited the artist's opinions of his statements, especially his statements about the Surrealism he despised. After publishing two articles in the *Nation* in August 1944, he asked Baziotes what he'd thought of their harsh critical edge—specifically his statement that Surrealist paintings were not art but "pictorial literature," and that the whole movement "proved a blessing to the restless rich, the expatriates, and aesthete-flaneurs in general who were repelled by the asceticisms of modern art." Their lifestyle, said Greenberg, sanctioned "the sense of chic with which they reject arduous disciplines." Clearly, Greenberg knew that Baziotes and the Surrealists still in New York would be enraged by such a critique, but he blithely wrote that he wasn't "waiting for lightning to descend, or hoping that it will descend, for it may not at all. The Surrealists have probably got too tired."

Greenberg was honing a rhetorical skill capable of shredding an array of targets with a single sentence. Unlike most critics before him, he seemed to have no desire to please or any sense of modulating his critiques to avoid the angry ripostes sure to follow. Ironically, the man who could not bring himself to go to war was eager to do battle, and not just verbally. In his address book for 1943 to 1945, Greenberg translated a quotation from Robespierre as "Virtue without . . . intimidation is disastrous and intimidation without . . . virtue has no power." Greenberg translated Robespierre's *terreur* as "intimidation," when standard French-English dictionaries define it as terror, fright, awe, or dread—a not uncommon reaction to Greenberg's razor-edged prose.

In 1945, Greenberg reviewed an exhibition at the conservative National Academy of Design, only to assert that "a brief glance" sufficed to fill him with "gloom." Then followed a multitargeted tirade: "Van Wyck Brooks's resentment of advanced literature's lack of 'affirmation' would find greater justification if it were directed at backward art." He drubbed "these painters of purple and emerald landscapes, of glazed figurines and wax flowers, these nigglers, these picklers of nudes and bakers of mud pies." He then observed that "it is in the very nature of academicism to be pessimistic for it believes history to be a repetitious and monotonous

decline from a former golden age." In a late echo of Marxist theory, he cited the contrasting view of the avant-garde, which
"believes that history is creative, always evolving novelty out of
itself." In the same review, Greenberg upheld Mondrian and
Kandinsky as models of this creative avant-garde, but reserved the
last half of his article for Jackson Pollock. Greenberg had seen
Pollock's second one-man show at Art of This Century, which, he
said, established him as "the strongest painter of his generation
and perhaps the greatest one to appear since Miró." In a much-
quoted phrase, Greenberg wrote that "he is not afraid to look
ugly—all profoundly original art looks ugly at first."

Surprising as it seems at this distance, Greenberg's review of
this Pollock exhibition reverberated in the small but growing art
world, despite its appearance in a basically political magazine of
limited circulation. Pollock's biographers Steven Naifeh and
Gregory White Smith believed that Greenberg's comments
"turned the world upside down, and Jackson, the complete original, was now on top." Greenberg and Pollock, they added,
"seemed ideally matched: Jackson's energetic, uncouth, ambitious
paintings and Greenberg's earnest, ambitious prose." In April 1946,
Greenberg appended two paragraphs to a longer review of other
artists, stating he was "still learning from Pollock" and reluctant to
"attempt a more thorough analysis of his art." Lee Krasner,
Pollock's wife, encouraged their friendship, although she was
"skeptical of Greenberg's intelligence." According to Krasner's
nephew Ronald Stein, she saw the critic as "a necessary evil . . . a
person to be used and manipulated to get exposure for Jackson."

In July 1946, Greenberg spent the weekend at Krasner and
Pollock's house in The Springs, then a run-down village in the
midst of eastern Long Island's potato fields. The hosts courted
Greenberg from the moment he arrived, humoring his habit of
sleeping late by sitting with him at the kitchen table talking until

three or four in the morning. Greenberg's prematurely bald egg-shaped head made him look older than his thirty-seven years and more pedantic than he really was. Interviewed much later by Naifeh and Smith, Greenberg said that Krasner was "damn significant for me. I was learning from her all the time." She had stressed to him the import of Hans Hofmann's theories "which he then repeated back to her, with the proprietary certitude that marked all his conversation."

During that visit, Greenberg also looked long and hard at the paintings in Pollock's garage studio. He squinted at each work, "with brow furrowed, lips pursed, and fingers pressed beneath his eyes to help them focus," or so another Pollock biography described his behavior. "Sometimes his look was quick, sometimes long. Either way, it was quickly followed by a judgment. The painting was first-rate, or second-rate, or missed altogether." Looking at a new painting lying on the floor, reported one witness, Greenberg "said slowly, his Brooklyn accent thinly disguised by an acquired southern drawl, 'That's interesting. Why don't you do eight or ten of those?'" Despite Greenberg's heavy-handed counsel, Pollock listened carefully. Later, he would advise the artist Fritz Bultman: "Be nice to Clem . . . if he likes your work he'll help you."

⁂   ⁂   ⁂

Partisan Review published not a single one of the twenty-four articles Greenberg wrote in 1947, but he had found a new outlet, the *New York Times Book Review*, which published four reviews of books about art by Herbert Read, Charles Baudelaire, Lionello Venturi, and Edward T. Chase. At the end of the year, *Commentary* published his sober review of *Röyte Pomeranzen*, a study of Jewish jokes by Immanuel Olsvanger. Unlike Freud, who had spun an entire theory of consciousness from the world of Jewish jokes, Greenberg dourly theorized that for East European

Jews, jokes were "perhaps the only secular culture," and managed to crank out some twenty-six hundred words without once cracking a smile.

Greenberg's most significant—and longest—1947 essay was published in Cyril Connolly's *Horizon*. The article grew out of a desperate request from Connolly for permission to name Greenberg as co respondent in a British divorce from Jeannie. Her Reno divorce of January 7, 1946, was not recognized by British courts, and Connolly was under pressure to marry his current flame, Lys. Greenberg replied with an extraordinary letter calling Jeannie "a kind of praying mantis whom love consumes." Hastening to join Connolly in the abused men's club, Greenberg wrote that she "paralyzed and destroyed the men in her life by playing a bogus motherly role, revenging herself on her [often absent] father" until "they were finally reduced to pulp, helpless, prostrate, and weepy." Greenberg still considered her "one of the most fascinating creatures that ever walked the earth" even though "everyone who is ever in love with Jean contracts a mother neurosis." Connolly conceded that Greenberg had "explained brilliantly the mechanism of Jean's destructive apparatus," but also admitted that he had abused "her sweet side" through "arrogance and selfishness." He then begged Greenberg for "a sacrifice . . . allow me to cite you in my divorce case" (to which Greenberg readily agreed), and accepted, sight unseen, Greenberg's offer of an article.

The article, "The Present Prospects of American Painting and Sculpture," appeared in the October issue of *Horizon*, which was devoted entirely to "Art on the American Horizon." It included pieces by Marshal McLuhan, Ralph Ellison, Wallace Stevens, and W. H. Auden, photos by Walker Evans, and poetry by e.e. cummings and John Berryman. That a prestigious British publication now focused on American culture demonstrated the shattering reversal of cultural dominance wrought by the Second World War.

The mighty British Empire was divesting fractious colonies, while the British population was still rebuilding shattered cities and enduring austere rationing. By contrast, the United States claimed for itself, in the words of *Time* publisher Henry Luce, "the American century."

Greenberg's article opened with a flash roll call of American painters, of whom perhaps only Whistler was known outside the United States, and observed that the U. S. was awakening from a three-hundred-year-long cultural sleep as a colony of European culture. A surge of cosmopolitanism had made "the cultured American . . . more knowing than cultivated, glib in a kind of fashionable *koiné* . . . a compendium of what he (or more usually she) reads in certain knowing magazines—anxious to be right, correct, *au courant*, rather than wise or happy." Greenberg described the cultured few developing "minimal judgment in literature," while 99 percent of the entire art world consisted of "tourists . . . flashing the stickers on their bags, and always on the point of leaving for the equivalent of Mexico or having just returned from there." Among the better informed, discussion of American art was "a kind of travelogue patter," blather that "fills the three or four art magazines that live an endowed existence in New York and whose copy is supplied by permanent college girls, male and female."

Greenberg's erstwhile Marxism was clearly tattered by the reality of the Europeans economy's dependence on the Marshall Plan. He still identified "general middlebrow taste" as "a danger," but also found "the American effort at mass culture . . . an unparalleled venture, one not to be sneered at . . . Only the enormous productivity of American industrialism could have led any society to think it possible to cultivate the *masses*." Far from despising the herd he had so eloquently macerated in "Avant-Garde and Kitsch," he now discovered that the American mania for self-improvement had melded with widespread prosperity to foster an "experiment in mass cultivation [that] makes us in several respects the most historically advanced country on earth."

He also promoted David Smith, "a sculptor and kind of constructivist" whom he found "more fully realized" than Pollock. Greenberg linked Smith's materials, "steel, alloys, the blowtorch," with "American industrialism and engineering." Smith and Pollock struck Greenberg as the only contemporary American artists whose work was "capable of withstanding the test of international scrutiny" and "might justify the term major." He thought so highly of Smith that he had put a down payment on his "Construction, 1937"; two days before Christmas 1947, Smith turned ownership of it over to Greenberg. Despite such support, the artist's sales for the entire year totaled $150.

Greenberg blamed the plight of Smith and other modernists on the past promoters of modernism in America: the early modernist messiah Alfred Stieglitz and the fifteen-year-old Museum of Modern Art "whose *chicté* . . . in the long run is almost an equal liability." In addition, neither MoMA nor Fifty-seventh Street were the wellsprings of new American art; "downtown, below 34th Street . . . the fate of American art is being decided—by young people, few of them over forty, who live in cold water flats and exist from hand to mouth."

He attributed this renaissance of American painting to Hans Hofmann; in the future, Greenberg predicted, he would be seen as "the most important figure in American art since 1935 and one of the most influential forces in its entire history." Indeed, most of the artists Greenberg admired had studied either with Hofmann, as Greenberg himself briefly had, or with Hofmann's disciples. However, the future of art in America, he wrote, depended on "a collection of *peintres maudits*" now eking out an existence in Greenwich Village. "Their isolation is inconceivable, crushing, unbroken, damning. That anyone can produce art on a respectable level in this situation is highly improbable. What can fifty do against a hundred and forty million?"

Evidently, some considered the "fifty" an imminent threat. *Time* devoted an entire column to outrage at Greenberg's admiration for Pollock and David Smith, as well as at "Britain's highbrow magazine" for being "duped into accepting a crank's view of American art." It was another blast in an uproar that had shaken the State Department, Congress, and even President Harry S. Truman for more than a year. In January 1946, a visual arts specialist in the State Department's Office of International Information and Cultural Affairs, LeRoy Davidson, a former curator at the Walker Art Center in Minneapolis, bought new American art for exhibitions to tour outside the United States. This comparatively mild propaganda effort titled "Advancing American Art" set off an angry outburst by the American Artists' Professional League about the exhibition's modernist bias. In November, the National Academy of Design and the Salmagundi Club complained to Secretary of State James Byrnes that the exhibition was "strongly marked with the radicalism of the new trends in European art" and was "not indigenous." In February 1947, the widely read magazine *Look* published pictures of some works in the show under the headline, "Your Money Bought These Paintings"; the captions and two paragraphs of text reinforced the shock. Then a conservative New York congressman, John Taber, wrote to the new Secretary of State, General George Marshall, that the pictures had been selected to "make the U.S. appear ridiculous" and would generate only "ill-will toward the U.S." Since a $31 million budget for the Voice of America was at stake, Marshall promised that no more paintings would be bought.

A counteroffensive began in March 1947, when the American Federation for the Arts urged its members to write to Secretary Marshall in support of the exhibition, and, after a mass meeting in

May, some 350 people signed a petition in support. The American Artists' Professional League ramped up its opposition, spreading rumors that the State Department was "honeycombed with leftists" and that "alien ideologies" were developing "a strangle-hold" in museums and art schools. President Harry S. Truman also weighed in: "If that is art, I'm a Hottentot," he said, and wrote to the State Department that "so-called modern art is merely the vaporings of half-baked lazy people." A prestigious panel was summoned to decide the fate of the paintings, including Grace McCann Morley, the progressive director of the San Francisco Museum of Art; the Washington collector Duncan Phillips; Perry T. Rathbone, director of the St. Louis City Art Museum; Daniel Catton Rich, director of the Chicago Art Institute; and James Johnson Sweeney, former curator of paintings at New York's Museum of Modern Art. Although the panel recommended keeping the paintings, a nervous State Department, already accused of harboring leftists or even Communists, eventually sold the pictures and sponsored no further exhibitions for ten years.

Despite the hullabaloo over the show, the selection truly represented a spectrum of styles in twentieth-century American art. On a budget of $56,600, Davidson had acquired seventy-nine oils and thirty-eight watercolors. The most expensive work was a John Marin oil at $2,500; a Marsden Hartley came in for $250. Artists represented also included Reginald Marsh, Stuart Davis, Georgia O'Keeffe, Walt Kuhn, and William Gropper. Although a two-week preview of the exhibition at the Metropolitan Museum of Art was disavowed by its director, Henry Francis Taylor, the art was shown to enthusiastic crowds in Paris during December 1946 and attracted admiration through 1947 in Prague, Guatemala, Cuba, and Haiti.

The noisy debate over this show ultimately benefited critics like Greenberg, who supported modern art. It bore out his contention that the avant-garde must always counter mainstream opinion. Furthermore, the thrusts and ripostes engaged the already growing audience for modern art, a young crowd better educated, more worldly, and certainly more prosperous than any generation in American history. The circulation of the *Nation* was also growing, and readers of his frequent reviews were eager to learn who and what Clement Greenberg was recommending or denouncing this week.

Not all insiders noticed the changed atmosphere. The art historian Milton W. Brown returned from military service in 1946 and found "business as usual [although] better than usual." The artists famous when he had gone off to war had undergone "only a slight reshuffling of positions." At the Met, contemporary Americans, even those considered conservative, had been removed to the basement; the rest of the collections "still exude that staleness with which museums . . . manage to envelop genius." Even MoMA demonstrated its "inherent timidity," although modern works were "so well presented and so pleasantly displayed that it is difficult to quarrel with the museum's basic inadequacies." As for Art of This Century, it struck Brown as "an anthropological museum exhibiting the embalmed remnants of early modern art."

With the war over and other modernist galleries opening in New York, Peggy Guggenheim was ready to close hers and take the collection back to Europe. She left behind a tell-all memoir, *Out of This Century: Confessions of an Art Addict*; Greenberg had read and critiqued every chapter. Her family considered it so indiscreet that agents were sent to buy up all the copies in bookstores. A joke later claimed that Peggy Guggenheim kept a little book listing all the men she had taken to bed, and Clement Greenberg was said to be the only heterosexual male not in it. Despite the friendship they had developed during her time in New York, Greenberg could not resist acidulous carping when he reviewed the book in

Commentary. Writing under the pseudonym K. Hardesh, perhaps to avert her friends' retaliation, Greenberg remarked that while Gertrude Stein entered international bohemia "on the wings of literature," Guggenheim "flew in on money and a kind of vitality that amounts almost to genius." He zeroed in on the career described in the book "as a martyrology," which left out no humiliation or self-absorbed line. Greenberg perhaps referred to his own agonies when he wondered if this is "how naked and helpless we Jews become once we abandon our 'system' completely and surrender ourselves to a world so utterly Gentile in its lack of prescriptions and prohibitions as bohemia really is."

Only later, having spent considerable time in that bohemia, would Greenberg look back and realize (though not admit) that his views in the late 1940s had been unduly pessimistic. He would see the vitality evident among New York artists clustered on Eighth Street and note that as early as the mid-30s, Willem de Kooning was "already a mature, complete, and independent painter . . . perhaps the strongest and most original one in the country then." He would also realize how seriously the Eighth Street artists had taken Klee, Miró, and the early Kandinsky. As a center of artistic innovation, he would write, Paris had been pushed aside by "a number of relatively obscure American artists already possessed [of] the fullest painting culture of their time."

But for now, none of this seemed clear, and his pessimism remained intact. As he complained in August 1947, at the end of his last surviving letter to Harold, "I have the feeling now that I'm at a turning point—toward what, I don't know." By the time he looked back ten years later, he knew that he had been poised to establish those obscure Americans at the epicenter of contemporary art.

Chapter V

THE GURU EMERGES

THE LIVELY 1947–48 New York art season and the growing support for abstract art had done little to dispel Greenberg's gloom over the plight of contemporary American art. In his article "The Situation at the Moment," he urged artists to bear up under their "isolation . . . the natural condition of high art in America." He saw the best of them struggling in a "shabby studio on the fifth floor of a cold-water, walk-up tenement on Hudson Street; the frantic scrabbling for money; the two or three fellow-painters who admire your work; the neurosis of alienation that makes you such a difficult person to get along with." Describing the crisis of European art "under the suction of events and a declining bourgeois order," he concluded that if Western art had any future at all, it would depend on American artists. Despite this, he said, "most of the best painting done in this country at the moment does not reach the public eye, but remains west of Seventh Avenue, stacked against the wall."

While deploring such conditions, Greenberg also minimized the size of the New York avant-garde art world. All of it—artists, museum workers, and critics—consisted of some fifty people, he told the youthful art critic Irving Sandler in 1948. Greenberg had good reason to minimize the number; it made his position more exclusive. And Sandler had the same good reason ten years later to arrive at barely 250 souls "even remotely connected to the New York School."

Even when the situation seemed to be improving, it wasn't. In

August, in a *Partisan Review* symposium on "The State of American Writing," Greenberg portrayed the avant-garde as increasingly accepted and professionalized. "The avant-garde writer *gets ahead* now," he said, working at a university, magazine, or publishing house, invited to lecture or participate in round-tables, even writing introductions to the classics. However, such public acceptance could be detrimental, for already "the avant-garde has been allowed to freeze itself into . . . a standardized repertory of attitudes," facing "political crisis" on one side and aggressively expanding middlebrow culture on the other. He glumly concluded that, "the situation is not better in painting and music."

While Greenberg would continue his litany of artists' woes, and artists would continue to shiver in unheated studios for some time, a fresh breeze was beginning to stir the American art scene. Less than six weeks after his downbeat report in *Partisan Review*, Greenberg was among fifteen men shown in a double-spread photo around a paper- and ashtray-littered table in the penthouse of the Museum of Modern Art. They had been summoned by *Life* magazine to discuss open-ended questions: Was modern art "a good or a bad development"? Was it "something that responsible people can support"? Or could it be ignored "as a minor and impermanent phase of culture"? In the photo's background was a Picasso signature painting, "Girl Before a Mirror," hauled upstairs from its usual prominent place in the museum's galleries. This work had been selected by the organizer of the panel, Russell Davenport, as "key to the whole discussion" because it was "accepted at every hand as a great modern classic," was not "an *extreme* example of 'modernism,'" and because it continued to challenge the ordinary viewer. The exercise smacked of the Presbyterian outreach vocabulary common to both *Life* publisher Henry Luce, who was born in China to American missionaries, and MoMA founding director Alfred H. Barr, the son of a

Presbyterian minister. (Other panelists included Meyer Schapiro, Paris-based *Transition* editor Georges Duthuit, Aldous Huxley, Met director Henry Francis Taylor, *Art News* editor Alfred Frankfurter, James Johnson Sweeney, James Thrall Soby, and several professors and curators.) Davenport cited the bafflement of "the layman" faced with modern art as a reason for asking whether "a great civilization like ours [could] continue to flourish without the humanizing influence of a living art that is understood and enjoyed by a large public?"

The *Life* roundtable may have been inspired by a *New York Times Magazine* article, published in July, offering readers a guide to understanding abstract art. "We are in new territory," wrote Aline B. Louchheim, "and cannot depend on old charts and maps." She suggested that "the man who can accept, at the same time, the frieze of the Parthenon, ideal and serene, and the sculpture of a Romanesque church, frenzied and distorted, should also be able to understand that the art of our time can be abruptly different from that of the Renaissance." She included, but did not attribute, Greenberg's judgment from his 1947 *Horizon* article that Jackson Pollock was "the most powerful painter in contemporary America, and the only one who promises to be a major one." Readers responded vigorously for several weeks, some calling abstract art "effete escapism" having "no roots in American tradition," merely "fashionable," a product of American neuroses, while others admired it as the product of scientific research: "it is only natural that an artist should experiment."

In fact, the impetus for the Round Table on Modern Art came from the very summit of the Time-Life empire, the founder and publisher Henry R. Luce. While he had supported coverage of art from the beginning of *Life* in 1936, he favored the bucolic American Scene art. He had allowed the color plates for eighty-nine such works first reproduced in *Life* to be used as illustrations for Peyton Boswell's anti-abstract diatribe *Modern American Painting*, published in 1939. In 1943, Luce had told a museum audience in Dayton, Ohio, that he hoped American art would "take a more positive turn" after the war. With the Second World War over and the Cold War heating up, Luce had a change of heart. Now a trustee at the MoMA, he asked the museum's president, Nelson Rockefeller, whether *Life* should denounce modern art as a destructive force. By way of answer, Rockefeller invited Luce to dinner, and later described the outcome: Luce, he said, became "convinced that modern forms of artistic expression were the only area left in democracy where there was true freedom . . . that it was one of the great bastions of freedom and strength in our lives." This was a time when word of arrests and even murder of dissident artists was seeping out of Eastern Europe. In the Soviet Union, the Stalinist persecution of the most innovative artists and writers that had begun during the 1930s was suspended during the Second World War. But now thought police were again muzzling that nation's most creative citizens.

In his heart Luce was unconvinced that abstract art was worthy, but he told *Life*'s editors: "To overcome my skepticism and perhaps the skepticism of quite a few truck drivers, you will have to be sure that each page has beauty or fascination and *Life* thinks it is just about the most wonderful thing it ever did." The editors' response had a profound effect, not only on Greenberg's future, but on the fate of all American art to come. By linking the new art emerging from cold-water flats in lower Manhattan with the Western world's titanic struggle against Soviet tyranny, the critics of abstract art were effectively muzzled, while the artists producing works previously described as baffling, challenging, troubling, ugly, or even insane now stood forth as courageous fighters for artistic freedom.

As spread out over many pages in *Life*, the roundtable discussion was frank and furious. Greenberg challenged the Met's director, Henry Francis Taylor, when he bragged about thousands of new visitors attracted by an exhibition of works by the sentimental mid-nineteenth-century illustrator William S. Mount. They "showed a reprehensible attitude toward art," Greenberg said. "You can't cater to that attitude." Taylor shot back: "Says who?" And Greenberg asked, "Are we going to judge truth by quantity and sheer mass?" He shone, too, in a nuanced discussion of contemporary paintings, illustrated by five large color reproductions. He saw William Baziotes's *The Dwarf* as "bad art . . . academic in color" and "helpless" in drawing. He suggested that Willem de Kooning's *Painting 1948* reminded him of "a Beethoven quartet where you can't specify what the emotion is but are profoundly stirred nevertheless." And he glowed over Jackson Pollock's *Cathedral,* calling it "one of the best paintings recently produced in this country."

While the panel was billed as representing all views on modern art, the report of its deliberations was tailored to please publisher Luce. It concluded that in making modern art, "the artist is engaged in a tremendous individualistic struggle . . . to discover and to assert and to express himself." The freedom enjoyed by such an artist contrasted sharply with the fate of artists in Nazi Germany and Soviet Russia, who were persecuted if they created abstract paintings. Abstract art was "part of the great process of freedom, which is so critical in our time"; therefore "the layman who might otherwise be disposed to throw all modern art in the ash can may think twice—and may on second thought reconsider."

Taylor, Greenberg's sparring partner at the roundtable, was not about to reconsider. The following December, *Atlantic Monthly* published his angry description of the event—"an atmosphere of klieg lights and candid cameras"—and his bleak sermon on the contemporary fate of art. "Even to attempt to associate truth with beauty," he wrote, "brings down the horror and contempt of the intelligentsia today." He, too, referred sympathetically to "the innocent layman . . . suspecting that the chief purpose of American art is to illustrate the Kinsey Report." But Taylor was clinging to a slippery slope; within five years, he abruptly resigned, at age fifty-two, and died two years later.

Greenberg, by contrast, was in the ascendant. He should have taken intense satisfaction at being included among these prominent cultural figures, and seeing his words printed in a magazine boasting a circulation of more than 5.3 million, more than any other publication in America. In retrospect, the *Life* Round Table was a turning point for him, as well as for the artists he championed. For the first time, major publications were taking abstract art seriously and attempting to educate their readers about it. Still, Greenberg was wary of this sudden burst of attention. A powerful motor was now propelling him and the artists he favored toward that fickle spotlight defining celebrity in mid-twentieth-century America.

Greenberg had little time to reflect on—much less write about—the irony of *Life*, a publication devoted to the middlebrow and to outright kitsch, as the agent of his success. Merely six months after he reviewed Pollock's first one-man show at the Betty Parsons Gallery—in which he compared the painter's work with "Picasso's and Braque's masterpieces of the 1912–1915 phase of Cubism"—*Life* ran a lengthy piece about Pollock, illustrated with three large color reproductions of paintings and two black-and-white photos showing the artist's dribble technique. The headline asked, "Is he the greatest living painter in the United States?" The brief text did not name Greenberg, but stated that "a formidably high-brow New York critic" had selected the "brooding, puzzled-looking" artist as "a fine candidate to become the greatest American painter of the 20th century." Granting that some critics found his work "as unpalatable as yesterday's macaroni," Pollock had "burst forth as the shining new phenomenon of American art." The impact of the other twenty-nine articles Greenberg wrote in 1948 paled before such publicity. The Pollock article triggered the biggest reader furor of any *Life* article that year; of 532 letters, only twenty were favorable to Pollock or to the magazine for publishing that spread. However, Greenberg's close connection to the "shining new phenomenon" would vault him from being a relatively obscure downtown art maven to an essential guide to the new American art scene.

Superficially, it is difficult to see any affinity between the fastidiously highbrow critic Clement Greenberg and the churlish, aggressively lowbrow artist Jackson Pollock. The urban middle-class Jewish milieu that spawned Greenberg contrasts strikingly with the hardscrabble itinerant family in which Pollock grew up. Greenberg had never stopped learning and studying after his graduation, magna cum laude, from Syracuse University. Pollock had been expelled from a Los Angeles high school, drifted to New York, where his two brothers were already trying to establish themselves as artists, and survived on handouts during the Depression. But despite this gaping discrepancy, Greenberg was irrevocably drawn to Pollock; he would later tell one interviewer: "I took one look at [Pollock's painting] and . . . I knew that Jackson was the greatest painter this country has produced." For his part, Pollock was awed by Greenberg's education, his refined vocabulary, and his writing ability.

Despite their divergent backgrounds, the two men also shared some telling life experiences. Both their families were uprooted from their origins, Greenberg's fleeing persecution in eastern Europe for a better life in New York, Pollock's migrating from the poor prospects of 1920s Wyoming for the promise, unfulfilled but always on the horizon, of finding gold in California. Both men were late bloomers, dawdling at the margins of life before embark-

today could not become an entire was College cut up

ing on a career. Both were seeking a means of expressing their creative impulses: Greenberg obsessively drawing, trying poetry and fiction, and now art criticism; Pollock assisting with the murals of Thomas Hart Benton and drifting into a relationship with the ambitious painter Lee Krasner. And there was in both men an undercurrent of violence, hardly contained by Greenberg and often breaking into the open in Pollock. Both had a painful tendency to redirect other violent impulses toward themselves, triggering episodes of depression so deep that both were found mentally unfit for military service in the Second World War. Both dealt with those depressed episodes with excessive drinking. An early Pollock biographer described how Greenberg identified with "the Gothic American roughness and brutality" represented by Pollock, and how Greenberg used Pollock to act out his own fantasies "of the frontier" and of "the revolutionary artist." For Pollock, Greenberg may have represented a kind, sensitive surrogate father who knew how to manage "the intricacies of urban life and . . . a world in which Jackson felt inadequate."

Both Greenberg and Pollock had trouble forming friendly one-on-one relationships. Even in his lengthy correspondence with Harold Lazarus, Greenberg browbeat his friend and threw the replies away, whereas Lazarus kept all his letters from Greenberg. While Greenberg's fluent, persuasive rhetoric impressed his readers with subtle insights and fine discrimination, it also pummeled them with its air of certainty and moral superiority. Pollock had little conversational skill; he retreated into sullen brooding, inappropriate taunts, and finally drink and violence; Greenberg found in him an ideal, undemanding listener. In the studio, he would tell Pollock that a picture was good or bad. "That's the only way I talk," he told Pollock biographers. The artist "listened intently and later would lead friends through the studio proudly pointing out, 'Clem likes this, Clem likes that.'"

A strong case can be built for the origin of "Clem's" affection for Pollock by revisiting Greenberg's early career at *Partisan Review*. When the publication had just broken with the Communist Party and regrouped as a radical Trotskyite organ, it published several of Trotsky's manifestos on art. Of all those who led the Russian Revolution, only Trotsky had thought seriously about the subject. As early as 1923, when he was Lenin's likely heir, he had written *Literature and Revolution*, an equivocal work that zigzagged wildly between asserting the freedom of the creative artist and the need to control his or her output to support the revolution. Trotsky argued that while "the proletariat is spiritually . . . very sensitive, it is uneducated aesthetically." The intelligentsia would therefore have to guide the proletariat's aesthetic development until socialism brought the classless society. Before this paradise arrived, wrote Trotsky, art should be addressed to helping the proletariat in "the expression of the new spiritual point of view . . . This is not a state order, but a historic demand. Its strength lies in the objectivity of historic necessity." So impressed with the Russian revolutionary was Greenberg that, after Trotsky was killed by a Stalinist agent in 1940, he drafted an "Ode to Trotsky," which like all his poetry was never published.

By 1945, Greenberg no longer referred to Trotsky, though he continued to cite Marx with particular respect. But while the Russian's name disappeared from his writings, a tantalizing residue remained: admiration for Trotsky's heroic proletarian as the harbinger of a classless society and culture. In 1949, Greenberg wrote ardently on the *art brut* of Jean Dubuffet, who "exposed for the first time to our respectful view the spontaneous graphic effusions, the *lumpen* art, of the urban lower classes. Most of the art we see scrawled on sidewalks is jeering and . . . the obscenity of what gets scribbled on lavatory walls is rather 'anti-social.' But the beauty these things acquire at Dubuffet's transfiguring hands is so social that they become eligible for the museums." The artist had transmuted kitsch into gold.

This potpourri of Marxist theory and aesthetic judgment forms the background for Greenberg's enthusiastic support of Pollock. On the one side, we have a critic nourished in the bosom of the bourgeoisie. His father had made good in business and paid his son's tuition at Syracuse University rather than sending him to New York's free City College, the rough-and-tumble finishing school for the New York intellectuals. Greenberg had circulated among New York Trotskyites, but mainly as a way of establishing himself as an art critic or meeting women. In short, the elitist Clement Greenberg had little more than a theoretical knowledge of proletarian culture and derived his view of its potential from his reading of Marxist and Trotskyite literature. Now, however, he had met an artist with impeccable proletarian credentials. He was sloppy, ungroomed, rude, foul-mouthed, pugnacious, antisocial, and often drunk. His parents were what we now call trailer trash. His education was sketchy and he was poor, relying on his brothers, and later his wife, for sustenance.

Viewing the Greenberg–Pollock relationship from the vantage of more than fifty years, the *New Yorker's* Adam Gopnik found that the "hyper-aggressive, hard-drinking style" they forged was "a marriage of strategic Jewish drinking, just enough to loosen your tongue . . . and all-out Western, three-week hair-raising, Huck Finn's dad-style benders." Gopnik saw Greenberg's ability to persuade *Life* to cover Pollock so favorably as "one of the great winning bets in the history of criticism."

But this judgment fails to consider the prevailing mood of that time: the euphoria of military triumph so quickly eclipsed by Stalinist threat; Americans savoring a burst of prosperity after almost twenty years of depression and war, then confronted almost overnight by a sworn, aggressive, cruel, and heavily armed foe.

The postwar euphoria dwindled quickly in the face of dogged—sometimes hysterical—resistance to a totalitarianism deemed even more insidious than Nazism because unexpected. In that struggle, the freedom of creative people in the West contrasted sharply with the persecution suffered by writers, artists, and composers trapped behind the Iron Curtain.

In New York, a Cultural and Scientific Conference for World Peace, in 1949, featured Dmitri Shostakovich abjectly confessing to composing music "only for the narrow strata of sophisticated musicians," while failing "to meet with approval among the broad masses of listeners." *Life* described the conference's American organizers, among them the playwrights Lillian Hellman, Clifford Odets, and Arthur Miller, as well as the composer Aaron Copland, as a cabal of "hard-working fellow-travelers" and "soft-headed do-gooders" promoting "organizations labeled by the U.S. attorney general as subversive." Countering the conference was an ad hoc group of liberal anti-Communists, Americans for Intellectual Freedom, hastily assembled by Sidney Hook.

At the *Nation*, the political and the private mingled as the magazine's editor and owner, Freda Kirchwey, fell under the influence of her lover, Julio del Vayo, an exile from Franco's Spain and a zealous advocate of the Soviet Union. The magazine's front matter leaned toward the extreme left, while the cultural pages at the back retained their moderate views. As the *Nation* increasingly supported the Soviet takeover of eastern Europe—even the show trials at which moderate leaders and some longtime Communists were summarily tried and executed—a bitter rift developed among the regular contributors, with Greenberg strongly supporting the anti-Communist side. In June 1949 he resigned—albeit quietly to protect Margaret Marshall, the woman who had hired him.

His last regular column, on June 11, surveyed the previous season, pleased that so many new talents were making the United

States "for the first time an equal participant in the dialogue with Europe," while bemoaning a sagging market for the new art. Far from voicing a Marxist interpretation—that the bourgeoisie was philistine to the core—he blamed the public's unwillingness to buy "advanced art" most significantly on "some inner rhythm in the market." Even Jackson Pollock had not been able to cash in on the *Life* publicity: at his one-man show at the Betty Parsons Gallery in the 1949–50 season, prices remained below $500.

This was the end of regular Greenberg reviews in any publication. His hand-picked successor the following season, Weldon Kees, was a critic, poet, and painter who greatly valued Greenberg's opinion of his paintings. Instead of a biweekly column, Kees's reviews would be published monthly. His controversial debut blasted the right-wing Michigan congressman George Dondero, who denounced abstract art as a Communist plot: he had obviously not heard the news that abstract art was now viewed as an anti-Communist blow for artistic freedom. Kees's sarcastic article depicted the congressman as "something of a Dadaist" and associated him with Hitler and Stalin. Although Kees staunchly backed the anti-Stalinists on the *Nation*'s cultural staff, he became disenchanted with New York and went West after less than a year. He disappeared on July 18, 1955, his car found parked at the north end of the Golden Gate Bridge with no trace of its driver.

Greenberg returned to the *Nation* in November 1950 to lament European critics' treatment of the abstract American artists shown at the previous summer's Venice Biennale. He cited the Europeans' habitual condescension toward American cultural barbarians, aggravated by resentment of their continuing military and economic dependence on the United States. Greenberg particularly attacked the English critic David Sylvester, who had on November 9 described much of the American work at the Biennale as "ham-fisted, paint-curdling illustration." That Sylvester had included Arshile Gorky among the "ham-fisted" enraged Greenberg, and he accused the Englishman of "still looking forward to the Picasso of 1928, even if it is only an academicized pastiche of him." Sylvester's reply followed in the same issue. He accused Greenberg of "a tendency to romanticize things American," and insisted that he found "the brand of romanticism" displayed by the likes of Pollock, de Kooning, and Gorky "repellent and contemptible . . . incoherent, modernistic, mucoid, earnest, and onanistic . . . it gets hot and bothered over nothing."

That the *Nation* had published Sylvester's criticism in the first place may have aggravated Greenberg's anger at its continuing pro-Soviet stance. Early in 1951, Greenberg had joined the American Committee for Cultural Freedom, an offshoot of the Congress for Cultural Freedom, organized in Berlin the previous year to counter the Soviet-sponsored cultural offensive. The Congress was sponsored by an international A-list, including Eleanor Roosevelt, Upton Sinclair, Walter Reuther, Arthur Koestler, James T. Farrell, and Arthur Schlesinger, Jr. The American group also included Sidney Hook, Daniel Bell, Diana Trilling, Irving Kristol, Norman Thomas, and Ralph Ellison.

When the committee asked former staffers at the *Nation* to complain to Kirchwey about the magazine's leftward drift, Greenberg submitted a long letter accusing foreign editor del Vayo of consistently supporting Soviet foreign policy, undermining American foreign policy, and even failing to condemn Communist North Korea's invasion of South Korea the previous June. Greenberg's letter was rejected, so he submitted it to the *New Leader*, which published it on March 19.

Less than three weeks later, the *Nation* announced a $200,000 suit against Greenberg and the *New Leader* for "false, defamatory, and scurrilous" statements. The dispute reverberated through New York's intellectual universe: Arthur Schlesinger, Jr., wrote to support Greenberg; the *Nation's* contributing editor, the theologian Reinhold Niebuhr, resigned, "sick of Del Vayo's animadversions on foreign affairs," as did two members of the *Nation's* editorial board; the perennial Socialist candidate for president Norman Thomas called the libel case "an enormous mistake"; and the American Committee for Cultural Freedom announced that it would contribute money for the *New Leader's* defense.

By 1955, when the lawsuit petered out without a judgment for either side, abstract art was firmly established as a Cold War weapon for the West. Soon after the Second World War ended, the MoMA had begun assembling international exhibitions that were encouraged by Nelson Rockefeller and significantly funded, it was later learned, by the CIA. The museum's director, Alfred H. Barr, also promoted modern art as a symbol of artistic freedom. In 1952, the *New York Times Magazine* published his article "Is Modern Art Communistic?" Barr argued that totalitarian systems could not tolerate abstract art and had denounced it as decadent.

The *Times* continued to feature news articles about Soviet persecution of modernist artists. In January 1954, the *New York Times Magazine* published Aline Louchheim's article promoting "cultural diplomacy," including exhibitions abroad of new American art. The following August, she was surprised to find her name in the headline of an article in the house organ of the Soviet Ministry of Culture. It decried her notion of cultural diplomacy, calling it "dollar diplomacy," and condemned modern art as a capitalist plot, "carefully diverting the masses from . . . capitalistic reality." The *Times* so frequently published reports by its Moscow reporters on the government's heavy-handed persecution of deviant artists that the contemporary reader suspects a direct phone line between the harried artist and the sympathetic correspondent. The published stories were factual, but the headlines conveyed the desired message: "Soviet Artists Pledge to Reflect Communism's Ideals in

Works," went one, while another proclaimed, "'Bourgeois' Art Shocks Russians."

When modern art was drafted as a soldier in the Cold War, the critical dialogue took a sharp turn away from puzzlement and disdain to curiosity, acceptance, and affection. By 1946, the artistic movement supported principally by Greenberg had acquired a name: in a lukewarm review of works by Hans Hofmann, Robert Coates, the *New Yorker's* art critic, had referred to "what some people call the spatter-and-daub school of painting and I, more politely, have christened Abstract Expressionism." By 1950, this style's association with artistic freedom silenced many of its critics. Jackson Pollock's second exhibition at Betty Parsons Gallery the previous November, unlike the first, had attracted not only the usual well-wishers among fellow-artists, but well-off collectors and museum curators. Although some balked at paying as much as $1,000 for a Pollock, a record number of his works were sold before the show closed on December 10.

In the spring of 1950, a group of Abstract Expressionist artists sent a letter to the president of the Metropolitan, protesting the director's "contempt for modern paintings" and accusing the jurors for a forthcoming exhibition of prejudice against advanced art. On May 22, that letter appeared on the front page of the *New York Times* with a headline: "18 Painters Boycott Metropolitan; Charge 'Hostility to Advanced Art.'" The *Herald-Tribune's* editorial the next day censured "The Irascible Eighteen," and the epithet stuck. Six months later, photographer Nina Leen posed fourteen of the eighteen for a group portrait published in *Life* the following January captioned "Irascible Group of Advanced artists Led Fight Against Show." At the very center of that solemn group stood Jackson Pollock, wearing a suit like the others, and looking angry.

Greenberg took no notice of these events, at least in print. Liberated from biweekly deadline pressure at the *Nation*, he wrote elsewhere about Paul Klee, Van Gogh, Renoir, Chinese art, Marsden Hartley, and T. S. Eliot. He expressed more qualms about the sudden acceptance of new art and artists than about discrimination against them. Ever since "Towards a Newer Laocoon," he had been arguing that avant-gardes flourish only on the margins of society, that acceptance would destroy their creative impetus. Pollock's triumphant show and The Irascibles' splash indicated that the mainstream was lapping at his chosen pioneers. Furthermore, Greenberg may have been skeptical about the quality of lesser artists in the Abstract Expressionist mode. Of the abstract painters in the 1940s and 1950s, he told an interviewer some four decades later, "Unless you were great you were lousy."

* * *

It was not merely a surge of indifferent art that distracted Greenberg from his critical writings but also a hectic social life. In 1948, he spent time with an eclectic array of notables: the psychoanalysts Ernest Jones and Bruno Bettelheim; the literary critics Harvey Swados and Anatole Broyard, the art historian Robert Goldwater; the novelist Arthur Koestler; the art dealers Charles Egan, Samuel Kootz, Sidney Janis, Julien Levy, and Pierre Matisse; the sociologist Daniel Bell, Aline Louchheim; and the columnist Dorothy Norman. Greenberg's desk calendar listed drinks, dinners, and parties on Manhattan's fashionable East Side. Also listed were many appointments with dentists and physicians, more than one would expect for an active thirty-nine-year-old man.

When the Abstract American Artists were organizing their spring show, Greenberg submitted one of his own paintings, the first he had ever shown publicly in the twenty years he had been painting. Weldon Kees reported to a friend that "he is nervous as hell about it, naturally." Kees had just seen Greenberg's most recent works and said, "They show a strong influence of Jackson

Pollock." However, Greenberg's art never went beyond these slight attempts. While he often boasted of his early drawing talent, and indeed his youthful letters to Harold Lazarus also include charming sketches, his art never developed further.

The same might be said of his love affairs at the time. Early in 1949, Greenberg began seeing a good deal of Marjorie Ferguson, who was on temporary leave from the State Department's United States Information Service in Italy. After she returned to Florence in late February, she was writing him almost daily, wondering whether she was in love with him and urging him to visit her in September. Greenberg did not see her again until 1954 and rarely thereafter, but the correspondence continued for more than thirty years, until 1983, when Ferguson, elderly and suffering from a crippling disease, dictated a short note to him, to which he briefly replied. Greenberg kept all her letters in a separate folder, tantalizing messages from a faraway love that went nowhere.

In May 1950, however, he became involved with the woman who in all likelihood was the great love of his life. Helen Frankenthaler was twenty-one years old, educated at private New York City schools, where Rufino Tamayo was among her art instructors. Her parents came from long-established German Jewish families; her father was a New York Superior Court judge. Sophisticated for her age, and determined to find a place in an increasingly crowded art universe still skeptical of talented women, Frankenthaler soon captivated Greenberg as no other woman had. Greenberg introduced her to the artists that interested him, among them David Smith and Franz Kline, and took her along on weekends at the Pollock-Krasner house.

Frankenthaler had invited Greenberg to a show at the Seligmann Gallery of recent works by Bennington graduates, including her own. He sharply criticized her painting, "Woman on a Horse," a Cubist work influenced by her teacher Paul Feeley.

However, when Frankenthaler phoned him a few days later, he invited her to his apartment for drinks. The story was outlined in the detailed accounts of his daily life that he was entering in English-made, leather-bound date books, with a 2 1/2 x 3 1/2 inch page for each day. He wrote in minuscule script, as though he felt undeserving of such refined paper bound with buttery leather—not a strapping, influential critic but a timid, frightened fellow. Much later, he called them his "fact books," and indeed, they recorded appointments, hours of arising and bedtime, medications taken, and, often, important events and moods. Soon, the pages were filled with "dinner with Helen," and "drinks with Helen." In the heat of the relationship, he may have fallen behind on the entries, recording on June 19, "the night I think I first laid H." By October, he was having dinner with Frankenthaler every other evening. He steered the gallery director John Bernard Myers to her studio and saw to it that one of her paintings was included in a group show that opened at Myers's Tibor de Nagy Gallery in May 1951. In November, the same gallery exhibited her first one-person show.

Greenberg advised Frankenthaler to enroll in Hans Hofmann's summer school in Provincetown, Massachusetts, while he fulfilled a commitment to teach at Black Mountain College, near Asheville, North Carolina. For a while, before they parted, Helen wsa able to distract Greenberg from the dark and depressing mood that fell on him when he learned that his ex-lover Jean Connolly had suffered a stroke. But soon afterward his gloom deepened, when the news of Jeannie's death coincided with his separation from Helen. "Got drunk before dinner and continued afterward," he wrote in his date book. Greenberg was teaching two character-istically broad-brush courses at Black Mountain: "The Development of Modern Painting and Sculpture from their Origins to the Present Time," and a seminar in art criticism organized around Kant's *Critique of Judgment*. Meanwhile, Frankenthaler was running to the mailbox every day, eager to find a letter from her absent lover.

When they reunited in the fall, she was his partner in the hectic social round he had developed. He relished entering in his datebook appointments for dinner or drinks, "*chez moi*" or at prestigious addresses elsewhere. Frankenthaler had become aware of New York intellectual life while still a student, "always interested in bantering and ideas," she told an interviewer many years later. Participating in that world with Greenberg "was very exciting to me, if not rather glamorous." Frankenthaler found it "heart-pounding" to meet "people that had been heroes or enigmas to me, to see the Trillings, to see Saul Bellow, to see Jackson Pollock."

Frankenthaler's career quickly blossomed as she produced a steady stream of canvases, more stained than painted, in strict conformity with Greenberg's dicta on flatness. Certainly, her rapid acceptance as a rising young artist was related to her connection with Greenberg. However, as Hilton Kramer noted, "It was Miss Frankenthaler's uncommon gifts that enabled her to take such prompt artistic advantage of them."

Greenberg's intense relationship with Frankenthaler and his many other social obligations, not to mention his ostensibly full-time job as associate editor of *Commentary*, apparently left him little time for writing. Aside from his blast at the *Nation*, he produced only four pieces in 1951: two book reviews for the *New York Times* and two long articles for *Partisan Review*. The first favorably reassessed Chaim Soutine, a late arrival in Paris from Eastern Europe and one of the few Jewish artists to emerge from the School of Paris during the 1920s. The second reinforced Paul Cézanne's standing as "the most copious source of what we know as modern art," while it launched fresh darts at the false avant-gardes he wanted "consigned to the outer darkness of academicism": Surrealism, Neue Sachlichkeit, Neo-Romanticism, Magic

Realism, and, of course, Social Realism—all of them figural in one form or another, as opposed to the total abstraction Greenberg favored. He considered both articles important enough to include them in the first anthology of his writings, *Art and Culture*, but he found the original versions so flawed that he substantially rewrote them before publishing the volume in 1961.

Greenberg's romance with Frankenthaler may have inspired the title of his first review article of 1952, "Feeling Is All." This essay begins with a sunny account of a comprehensive Matisse show at the MoMA and includes friendly reviews of Barnett Newman and Franz Kline exhibitions, capped by a rave for Pollock: "No one in this period realizes as much as strongly and as truly." In France, he asserted, "people would already be calling him *maître* and speculating in his pictures." He chided the American museum directors, collectors, and newspaper critics who refused to believe that "we have at last produced the best painter of a whole generation." He was unusually lighthearted, even though his datebooks record a long series of weekly "shots"—probably treatments for depression, as he hinted with various comments along the lines of "came out of a low period."

On July 25, 1952, Greenberg and Frankenthaler headed north from New York on an idyllic driving trip through Nova Scotia to Cape Breton, Canada, sightseeing, swimming, painting, and sketching. When they returned on August 22, they had covered almost four thousand miles in a 1951 Ford with a troublesome radiator. Frankenthaler recorded feeling "low around mid-day" and taking antihistamines to control hay fever. Sometimes they camped and sometimes they stayed in a cheap cabin or motel. Frequently, they had trouble buying liquor in communities where prohibition still prevailed. "Whiskey down to nothing, Woe," she wrote two weeks before they returned to New York. "No liquor at all. Can get bootleg in town, but won't bother."

While Greenberg and Frankenthaler were traveling, the fiftieth anniversary issue of *Art News* published Greenberg's essay "Cross-Breeding of Modern Sculpture," among contributions from such notable writers on art as Bernard Berenson, Siegfried Giedion, Arnold Hauser, and Herbert Read. Greenberg's ambitious essay attempts, in a few pages, to educate the reader in the entire history of sculpture in the West, from the ancient Greeks to the mid-twentieth century, while also offering a comparison of sculpture and painting and critiquing modern architects for ignoring these two media in their building designs. Published in *American Mercury* at about the same time was his "Cézanne: Gateway to Contemporary Painting," a wide-ranging discussion of the seminal modernist painter. In both essays, Greenberg shows off his knowledge of arts outside the modernist canon, but he also offers the reader interested in appreciating modern art a capsule education on where this often baffling work came from and a hint as to where it might be going. In each case, the format implies a seamless connection between the transparent art of the past and the difficult art of the present, and concludes that the passage from past to present was somehow inevitable.

As his published pieces dwindled, Greenberg worked on a large number of projects that ultimately went nowhere: a six-page article arguing that Manet was more "advanced" than previously thought; three pages on Fernand Léger's ability to flatten the image in his paintings; five pages on how the Postimpressionists Cézanne, Seurat, Van Gogh, and Gauguin represented the second turning point in the development of modern art; twelve pages titled "The Decline of Art," and twenty-seven pages titled "The Agony of Painting." All were carefully stored in folders, but never came to fruition, largely because the topics he chose were unsuitable for magazine publication: some were too narrow or technical to interest the average reader, and others were too broad to be covered in an article of reasonable length. Greenberg also created a wide-ranging reading list for himself. Among the forthcoming books he check-marked in a catalog were Alan Bullock's biography of Adolf Hitler, a history of the Middle East from 1939 to 1946, an account of the laws and charities of Spanish and Portuguese Jews in London, a study of the Roman middle class, and Hugh Seton-Watson's *Decline of Imperial Russia*. The obsessive revising and eclectic reading would be lifelong habits.

Greenberg wrote little further in 1952, except two paragraphs for Jackson Pollock's first retrospective exhibition, a monument to the painter's meteoric rise, in less than nine years, from his first participation in a group show at Art of This Century. The retrospective exhibition, in November and December, was jointly sponsored by the Lawrence Museum at Williams College and Helen Frankenthaler's alma mater, Bennington. Greenberg's central role in Pollock's success dominates this exhibition. He not only selected the eight paintings in the show but composed the brief wording of the exhibition catalog, in which he stressed the "telling evidence of the magnitude of [Pollock's] achievement over the past decade." He deemed the paintings he had selected "major works, major in a way that very little in American art has been up to now," setting the standard for the current "main tradition of painting." He then congratulated Bennington for sponsoring "such a well-chosen and representative exhibition," and suggested that it demonstrated "why the most adventurous painters" in Paris were beginning "to look to this country with apprehensive rivalry."

At the party after the opening, Lee Krasner took charge of the bar, effectively blocking her husband from imbibing. When a stranger offered Pollock a drink, Greenberg told the artist, "Jackson, lay off." Pollock replied: "Nothing doing," and added, "You fool." Greenberg later recalled feeling outrage, denied that he had urged Pollock not to drink, "but Jackson sensed it . . . I was off of him for a couple of years."

Nevertheless, Greenberg's seeming favoritism to Pollock and his own rise as an art guru were raising hackles in New York's burgeoning community of advanced artists. Since 1949, many of them had gathered regularly in a loft at 39 East Eighth Street, in Greenwich Village. Among the twelve founders of what they called The Club were Willem de Kooning, Milton Resnick, Ad Reinhardt, and Franz Kline; according to one observer, Philip Pavia was "the principal nuts-and-bolts organizer." The weekly panel discussions on Fridays and roundtables on Wednesdays that he organized attracted not only many younger artists, but some members of the pioneering Abstract American Artists, veterans of the modernist art wars of the 1930s, as well as writers, musicians, and assorted intellectuals who came for the talk but stayed for the drinking and dancing that followed. "When the party mood was on," recalled William Barrett, "an old hand-crank phonograph would turn up with some borrowed records." Greenberg "disdained to socialize at The Club," but Barrett had a single memory of him dancing the jitterbug late one night, and concluded that this "was part of his program for becoming the well-rounded highbrow."

Greenberg and Frankenthaler had attended some of the early Friday night lectures at The Club, and gone on afterward to the nearby Cedar Tavern for more drinking and discussion. But Greenberg lost interest when an unexpectedly large crowd attended the opening of a group exhibition, in May 1951, of sixty-one artists organized by The Club in a vacant furniture store a block away on East Ninth Street. By 1952, Greenberg and Frankenthaler were no longer welcome at The Club, as the younger artists favored de Kooning over Pollock. Even Friedel Dzubas, one of those younger artists who remained Greenberg's friend, told an interviewer that his colleagues found Pollock's work uneven while de Kooning "could not paint a bad picture." Greenberg's standing within that group, said Dzubas, "deteriorated . . . he became the enemy . . . a very feared, very respected enemy . . . but certainly the enemy."

The polarization within the art community intensified after *Art News* published Harold Rosenberg's essay, "The American Action Painters," late in 1952. Rosenberg rhapsodized over the vanguard American painter engaging "the white expanse of the canvas as Melville's Ishmael took to the sea . . . he gesticulated upon the canvas and watched for what each novelty would declare him and his art to be." He described the result of this encounter as a private myth, a secular version of "a religious conversion." Such a pattern may have applied to Abstract Expressionist artists like Mark Rothko or even de Kooning, but seemed to ignore that rough-hewn creator of dancing whirls of paint, Jackson Pollock. Far from following a logical development in the evolution of modernist art, as Greenberg argued, Rosenberg saw artists seeking inspiration from "anything that has to do with action—psychology, philosophy, history, mythology, hero worship." He claimed to discern "a certain moment when the canvas began to appear to one American painter after another as an arena in which to act rather than as a space in which to reproduce, redesign, analyze, or 'express' an object . . . the canvas was not a picture but an event." Thus, any critic who still judges art "in terms of schools, styles, form, as if the painter were still concerned with producing a certain kind of object instead of living on the canvas, is bound to seem a stranger."

The obvious criticism of Greenberg was far from the first blow in a feud that had simmered since the late 1930s, when Greenberg was already sniping at Rosenberg in his letters to Harold Lazarus. The rift had widened in 1942, when Rosenberg objected to Greenberg's introduction to a selection of poems published in

Partisan Review. In a letter, Rosenberg complained of Greenberg's choices as well as his reference to "himself, his tastes, and opinions no less than ten times in 1 3/4 pages." At the time, Greenberg had mildly replied: "Mr. Rosenberg seems to read my stuff rather closely."

The tension between Greenberg and Rosenberg heightened considerably after Thomas B. Hess, Rosenberg's fellow-enthusiast for de Kooning and the newly-named editor of *Art News*, published a scathing review of Greenberg's book about Joan Miró. This work "could not pass the standards set for college freshmen," he wrote. Facts were "shockingly haphazard," Greenberg seemed "blissfully ignorant of art history's methodology or objective approach." He found most irritating Greenberg's "steady machine-gun fire of absolute value judgments." These flaws reflected Greenberg's generalized rage, which Hess sarcastically deemed "one of the most pleasant features of his published reviews," in which "not only specific exhibitions but whole styles and even generations have been marvelously excoriated."

Greenberg was uncharacteristically silent in the face of this assault. Perhaps he was intimidated by the patrician background of Hess, who had been schooled privately in the United States and Switzerland, graduated Phi Beta Kappa and magna cum laude from Yale in 1942, and interned briefly at MoMA before serving overseas as an army air force pilot. Moreover, Hess was in a position to publish Greenberg's writings in *Art News*, and had done so only a few months earlier in the fiftieth anniversary issue.

By contrast, Harold Rosenberg represented a living reproach to Greenberg. He, too, was born of immigrant Jewish parents and raised in Brooklyn. He had left City College after two years, but then received a degree from Brooklyn Law School. During the Depression, he had supported left-wing causes, but also found work editing the New York volume of the WPA American Guide series at a respectable $28 a week. In 1940, he had moved to Washington to work at the Office of War Information, where his bosses lauded his ability to place government propaganda messages onto network radio. In 1943, he was promoted to deputy chief of the Domestic Radio Bureau in New York, at $3,000 a year. He and his wife, May Tabak, moved into a fine apartment at 110 East Eleventh Street, not far from where The Club would meet a few years later.

Irving Howe had never met anyone like Rosenberg, "who could talk with such unflagging manic brilliance, pouring out a Niagara of epigrams . . . He was always available . . . Harold was Harold as granite is granite." Like Greenberg, he relied on "historical crisis" to explain the new American art, but Howe noted that "his ideas could not be bottled, they had a curious way of evaporating into the upper air . . . as if they came alive only through his voice."

Rosenberg's verbal glibness eluded Greenberg, as did the friendships Rosenberg had formed with French intellectuals. Unlike Greenberg, who shunned the Surrealists in New York during the war, Rosenberg had befriended André Breton. After the war, Jean-Paul Sartre, whom Greenberg had sought out in 1939, published several of Rosenberg's essays in *Les Temps modernes* and stayed in Rosenberg's apartment when visiting New York. Simone de Beauvoir also stayed with the Rosenbergs in 1947, writing to Sartre that she had argued with Harold "about politics and philosophy till I was half-dead from exhaustion and exasperation."

Rosenberg was unusually tall, an imposing figure with a shock of black hair, a fierce moustache, and bushy eyebrows. William Barrett recalled a disagreement over art between Rosenberg and Greenberg, with Greenberg, who did not always avoid fisticuffs, saying, "I'm not going to tangle with that guy, he's too big." While Greenberg's talk veered toward the magisterial, Rosenberg's quick wit and ready smile softened his sometimes overbearing torrent of words. In 1950, he was still working for the Advertising Council and was sufficiently highly placed to confer with President Harry S. Truman. In addition to art, he was also writing about poetry, unscrupulous psychiatrists, and politics. An article he had published in *Commentary*, "The Communist: His Mentality and His Morals," attracted attention from the Naval Intelligence School and a publisher suggested he expand it into a book. With an income of nearly $10,000, he could afford summers in The Springs, near the Pollock–Krasner house.

Perhaps what most irked Greenberg was the background they shared: a troubling ambivalence toward their Jewish heritage, veering from an insider's contemptuous anti-Semitism to affection for Jewish values, then to a rush toward full assimilation. Rosenberg tried to convey those dilemmas in an article published in *Commentary* in 1948: "The tension of my experience never belongs to the right time or place . . . it contains all sorts of anachronisms and cultural fragments: the Old Testament and the Gospels, Plato, 18th century music, the notion of freedom as taught in the New York city school system, the fantastic emotional residues of the Jewish family." His experience was "broken and complicated by all sorts of time-lags, symbolic substitutions, decayed absolutes, experimental hypotheses."

Underneath all the bluster, Greenberg and Rosenberg shared memories of a time in America when Jews were routinely mocked, when anti-Semitism was a reflex among the upper class, when universities sparingly hired Jewish professors and set small quotas for Jewish students. The grim fate of millions of European Jews was a fresh memory, as was the Nazis' murder of so many of Germany's respected Jewish intellectuals. Within the Jewish community, the fledgling state of Israel posed an uncertain refuge for the survivors.

Furthermore, Greenberg and Rosenberg shared a background of left-wing politics followed by a postwar anti-Communist bias, a disdain for mass culture and a fear that middlebrow culture would devour the highbrow, a tilt toward the modernist literature of Kafka and T. S. Eliot, a frustrated desire for acclaim as poets, and a stubborn resistance to changing their minds when confronted with new information. Nevertheless, they took positive pleasure in pummeling each other. When the artist Paul Brach suggested that Rosenberg had written "The American Action Painters" just to denigrate Jackson Pollock, Rosenberg flashed "an inscrutable smile and a gangster-like snarl, 'You're a smart kid.'"

Greenberg and Rosenberg developed coteries among the New York intellectuals. Norman Podhoretz, no friend of Greenberg, also faulted Rosenberg: "Harold never looked at a picture." While he was "not exactly agreeable," Podhoretz admired his verbal fireworks. At the *New Yorker*, editor William Shawn read the Action Painters piece and told Rosenberg, "I don't know what you're talking about." Even Hannah Arendt, who had been Rosenberg's lover, questioned his verbal gymnastics. He sounded like Greenberg, she wrote to her close friend Mary McCarthy, when he "talked for hours with great assurance an astounding amount of nonsense about art." McCarthy, however, was enthusiastic as she reviewed Rosenberg's first essay collection, *The Tradition of the New*, in *Partisan Review*. She admired his ability to embrace the twentieth century's love affair with technology and new ideas. Rosenberg was clearly a complex person, perhaps more messianic than he would have liked to be, a secular rabbi carrying on the Hassidic tradition of scholarly infighting in an assimilated world.

Most of these retrospective evaluations ignore the tenuous position still occupied by modern art into the mid-1950s. Despite Rosenberg and Greenberg's support, despite the many galleries showing abstract expressionists, those genuinely enthusiastic about the new art comprised a tiny fraction of Americans, and those willing to buy this art were just a handful. In a 1951 article, Aline

Louchheim noted that "a comment about abstract art is still guaranteed to jolt any dinner party conversation out of desultory amiability." Even though abstractions accounted for 40 percent of all New York art exhibitions in the 1951–52 season, most of the public, she wrote, was "confused or belligerent, or resistant."

Moreover, despite *Life* magazine's attention and Greenberg's steady admiration, Pollock had earned only $3,100 in all of 1949. The following year, Parsons was unable to sell any large Pollocks, now priced at $4,000, or any small ones at $300. Pollock's friend Alfonso Ossorio acquired a key painting, *Lavender Mist*, for installments totaling $1,500. Five years later, another key painting, *Blue Poles*, went for $6,000 and in 1956, a shrewd collector bought *Number 31, 1950* for all of $8,000.

In 1953, Greenberg took another searching look at American culture, the first since his early essays "Avant-Garde and Kitsch" and "Towards a Newer Laocoon," in a two-part article published in *Commentary* titled "The Plight of Our Culture." In the first section, subtitled "Industrialism and Class Mobility," he took on a towering figure among the *Partisan Review* intellectuals, the American poet and critic T. S. Eliot. Greenberg dismembered Eliot's widely reviewed 1948 book *Notes Towards the Definition of Culture* by associating its political notions with those of the French collaborationist Charles Maurras, who espoused ultranationalism and anti-Semitism. He then suggested that Eliot's innocence "of the urgent reality" of politics was "as much a deficiency of sensibility as of intelligence." Greenberg took issue with Eliot's elitism as "useless" and "threadbare . . . journalism" and finally expressed alarm "for the author's soul, not his mind." Unlike Eliot, who found all culture in serious decline, Greenberg was now promoting a somewhat more optimistic view than the one he'd offered in the late 1930s.

Behind this article was a massive paper trail, more than 150 typewritten and handwritten pages comprising three surviving drafts and innumerable discarded sections, all filed away for possible future use. This file and many others bear out a picture of the writer as meticulously weighing every word and obsessively recasting every sentence. Sometimes, he would edit already published writings, as he did on the clipping of "Cézanne: Gateway to Contemporary Painting," published only the year before.

As "The Plight of Our Culture" was being published over the course of the summer, Helen Frankenthaler was traveling in Europe. She had asked Greenberg to join her, but he could not leave *Commentary* for the three months she was gone. Furthermore, he was in the throes of eleven appointments with a Dr. Shapiro, a dentist who installed his "final bridge" on August 11, even though it was only the harbinger of serious dental problems to come. He often had dinner out alone and went to the movies alone. On August 26, Frankenthaler telephoned him from aboard the ship bringing her home, and on Wednesday, September 2, Greenberg was at the dock to meet her. Later that fall, they traveled together to New England and Quebec.

The following year, Greenberg managed the necessary time off, and on July 27, he and Frankenthaler flew to Madrid. Upon landing, she napped and he went to the Prado. Later, they dined at the esteemed Jockey Club and danced until 1:30 A.M. The next day, they visited the Prado, indulged in a siesta, then took a city tour and ended the day with champagne in their room. Frankenthaler slept late while Greenberg visited Toledo and returned to the Prado. The next day included another visit to the Prado and dancing at Pavillon, a posh supper club. After more trips to the Prado, a bullfight and dinner at the Ritz, they flew to Rome on August 2, to stay at the Hotel d'Inghilterra.

Like many tourists in Rome, Greenberg and Frankenthaler took an American Express city tour, tackled the gigantic Vatican complex, rode in a horse-drawn carriage, and dropped three coins in the Trevi fountain. Their trip seemed like a leisurely honeymoon, with visits to acquaintances and tours of principal sights and museums. They rented a car for the drive to Naples, where they viewed the antiquities at the museum, lunched at a "gyp joint," and developed "general anger and restlessness because of creepy, starving, make-a-lire Neapolitans." Relief was at hand in glamorous nearby Positano, an enchanting village favored by jet-setters, its pastel houses and terraced lemon and olive groves clinging to cliffs high above the azure Gulf of Salerno. After more sightseeing in Rome, they toured Etruscan sites in Tarquinia, then drove north toward Florence, dodging into churches and soon forming opinions: "We think generally people have over-rated Giotto and Piero. They can't compare to Venetians and Spaniards." Greenberg picked up this judgment in an unpublished lecture, saved in his papers: "Titian, Rubens, Velazquez and Rembrandt are, as I believe, far greater painters than Giotto or Piero della Francesca."

In Florence, they saw Greenberg's old flame Marjorie Ferguson and were invited to tea by the Renaissance art expert Bernard Berenson. As the trip wore on, they took to napping in the afternoons, drank steadily, and arose later, sometimes with morning hangovers. They rushed through Ravenna, apparently without viewing the legendary sixth-century mosaics, toward Venice, where Peggy Guggenheim entertained them for drinks, dinners, and lunches. On September 20, they left for Paris and, after a week, went on to London. After more visits with friends and contacts, they boarded the SS *United States*, landing in New York on October 10.

But despite the seeming harmony of their long voyage, the relationship began to unravel soon afterward. For more than three years, Greenberg and Helen had been close, but not truly a union. She kept her apartment and he kept his, though they had seen each other almost every day. The European trip had put them in closer contact, sharing hotel rooms every night and always touring together. The travel journal at the end of the trip lacked the effervescence of the beginning; the constant social events were taxing, togetherness was wearing, and sheer fun fading. A trial marriage lasting some two months appeared to be enough. Frankenthaler asked for more space and Greenberg sank into depression. "Home all day. Working. Dinner out," was his glum datebook entry for Saturday, November 6, and the next day, "Ditto." Similar entries for the following weekend: "Home working. Movies alone." On the eighteenth, he had dinner with Frankenthaler and spent the night at her apartment; the rest of November included scattered evenings at Frankenthaler's, but the relationship was clearly dwindling toward a mournful entry for New Year's Eve: "Office 11–2:30, home."

Before Greenberg's European trip, he had seven review articles published. Only one was published after his return; it was based on the Ryerson Lecture he had given at Yale University the previous May. While Greenberg's romance with Helen Frankenthaler sputtered on during the early months of 1955, it ended definitively on April 10, with a brief entry in his datebook: "Separation from H final."

Chapter VI

A VIEW FROM THE SUMMIT

As so often happens when an intense relationship ends, the death throes of the Greenberg–Frankenthaler romance dragged agonizingly on and off for many months. In early February 1955, Greenberg was having solitary dinners and walks around his neighborhood, but by later that month he was again dining with Frankenthaler. He sporadically slept over at her apartment until their "final separation" of April, spending many of the following nights alone, but in early May he again dined and stayed at Frankenthaler's. Helen wanted a six-week separation, but after only two weeks Greenberg felt so anxious that he lapsed into depression.

On June 2, he became disoriented; on the sixth, he was seen by Frankenthaler's psychiatrist, Annette Herzman Gill, an orthodox Freudian. He told an interviewer much later that when Dr. Gill saw him the next day, "she decided I was too much for her" and referred him instead to Ralph Klein, a psychologist with no known medical training. On June 15, Greenberg entered into a six-year-long ostensibly therapeutic relationship with Klein that, so he claimed, "changed my life." It also considerably changed Klein's life, giving him access to many prominent art world figures.

At the time he began Greenberg's intensive treatment—daily talk sessions, some running for two or more hours—Ralph Klein was a follower of Harry Stack Sullivan, an American disciple of Sigmund Freud who placed even more emphasis on parent-child relationships than Freud himself. He was associated with the William Alanson White Institute, which continued Sullivan's teachings after the latter's death in 1949. In 1957, Klein would join Saul Newton and Jane Pearce in leaving the White Institute over the American Psychiatric Association's refusal to sanction training of nonmedical psychoanalysts: neither Klein nor Newton held a medical degree. Newton insisted that he had studied with Sullivan himself and was carrying on the master's work. "I loved the man," he later said of Sullivan. "I owed it to him to start up a training institute." However, the institution that he, Klein, and Pearce started veered far away from Sullivan's central notion—the crucial importance of close interpersonal relationships—to its opposite, the pernicious effects of such relationships.

To a patient like Clement Greenberg, a man painfully emerging from the most intimate and extended love affair of his life, such a theory opened a perilous door. Klein, whom he soon started calling "Ralph," reinforced his lifelong fear and avoidance of just such relationships. Beginning with his family and moving on to his close friend Harold Lazarus, his wife Toady, and his son Danny, Greenberg had reflexively distanced himself. His article opposing the Second World War had separated him from the editors of *Partisan Review* and, when published in *Horizon*, from Cyril Connolly. In his art criticism, he recoiled from the emotional baggage borne by Surrealism or Expressionism and wavered between a complicated theory and plain gut reaction, his "eye," to support the cool abstract art to which he was instinctively drawn.

In the breakdown that followed his split with Frankenthaler, Greenberg relied on his younger brother, Martin, who owed his editorial job at *Commentary* to Clement and who was significantly dominated by him. It was Martin who went with his older brother to Helen's apartment on June 16 to collect his belongings, and then to a second session that day with Ralph Klein. Afterward, Martin took him home to Great Neck, where Clement stayed for two or three weeks; each day, Martin would take him to Klein's office and wait outside for the therapeutic hour to pass. "He was kind of sleepwalking," Martin told an interviewer much later. "He wasn't manic in behavior, but manic in thought . . . He was better . . . to be with, more human, more open, than he ever was before or since."

While Greenberg's breakdown has been attributed to his breakup with Helen Frankenthaler, it seems likely that his son Danny's persistent mental problems also contributed to his anxieties and may even have encouraged Frankenthaler to break free. Throughout the two decades since Danny's inconvenient arrival, Greenberg had never been able to forge a fatherly relationship with him. During this time, the youngster drifted in and out of Greenberg's life, usually arriving at an inopportune moment: in the midst of a romance, a difficult writing project, or a busy social calendar. Greenberg tolerated his son's occasional presence but never devoted serious attention to him. Danny's education remained in the control of his mother and grandmother; his schooling varied from extremely permissive to bracingly military. He had already started attending college at Johns Hopkins when, on June 4, 1955, he showed up unannounced at Greenberg's apartment. For the next four days, father and son visited various psychiatrists in an effort to discover what was troubling Danny. It was the beginning of a lengthy process that would eventually include a diagnosis of schizophrenia, various treatments, angry confrontations, and Danny's institutionalization.

Klein practiced "Newtonian" therapy, developed by his colleague Saul Newton, which would have assuaged any guilt Greenberg may have felt over his role in Danny's fate. Unlike most psychotherapeutic approaches, which aim at strengthening the patient's intimate relationships, this treatment considered such relationships the root of the patient's problems. All close ties were to be severed—if necessary by a letter composed by the therapist.

So eager was Greenberg for Klein's treatment that he arose far earlier than his usual 11:30 or noon in order to receive his daily therapy at around 10 A.M. By July 24, he noted in his datebook: "Felt
necessity and capability of taking control of self." As well he might,
since Ralph Klein, though as yet uncertified, adhered to the psy-
choanalytic tradition of vacationing during the month of August.

Before July ended, Greenberg dropped in, uninvited, on the
Pollock ménage in The Springs for a weekend. He was hoping to
see Ralph Klein, who was already vacationing with Newtonian
colleagues in Barnes Landing nearby. He was not exactly welcome: Krasner and Pollock were furious about a review he had
written of Pollock's 1954 show at the Sidney Janis Gallery, his first
uptown venue. Uncharacteristically, Greenberg had written that
some of the works in the show "were forced, pumped, dressed
up"—somewhat different from what the painter wanted to hear.
Nor was the marriage very cordial, as Pollock, drunk, and Krasner,
enraged, were lashing at each other every waking moment. "He
had a sharp sense of how to find someone's sore spot and he was
out to wreck her," Greenberg said many years later. When Pollock
sensed that Greenberg was taking Krasner's side, he became even
more inflamed, calling her a "Jewish cunt" and shouting that he
had never loved her.

Greenberg recommended that Krasner see Ralph Klein's colleague, Jane Pearce, the only physician among the Newtonians
conveniently vacationing nearby. The very next day, Pearce
advised Krasner to start therapy immediately. Pollock at first
balked, but when Krasner insisted he followed her to Pearce's
office and decided that he too would once again enter therapy.
"Jackson couldn't stand the idea of Lee and me in therapy without
him," said Greenberg. "He didn't want to be left out." In
September, Pollock began weekly sessions with Ralph Klein at his
office on West Eighty-sixth Street, a ten-minute subway ride from

his old barroom haunts in Greenwich Village. Greenberg, meanwhile, resumed his own thrice-weekly therapy sessions with Klein.

The Newtonian therapists were just beginning to hone their treatment theories, which were built around a simplistic slogan—if it feels good, just do it—and which eventually led to the abuse and virtual enslavement of their patients. They insisted that patients live communally in several apartment houses on the upper West Side, that they sleep with a different partner every night, that they allow their children to be raised by others and send them to boarding school as soon as possible. By the middle 1970s, as many as six hundred people lived under these conditions, forbidden to leave or stop their "treatment." Saul Newton was the chief therapist; he once told a patient, "I am the spider, and this is my web." A decade later, Jane Pearce was gone, but Ralph Klein was still one of the "Gang of Four," whose typical therapy was to berate patients and accuse them of "murderousness and psychopathy." The attorney for a woman who in 1985 had escaped and kidnapped her child called the Newtonian group "a combination Jonestown, Creedmore State [Mental] Hospital, and *Lord of the Flies*." And the head of the William Alanson White Institute, from which the Newtonians had split, called Newton's use of Harry Stack Sullivan's name "a blasphemy."

*   *   *

In the months before Greenberg's breakdown, when his relationship with Frankenthaler had still appeared salvageable, he wrote a widely reprinted essay for *Partisan Review*, "American-Type Painting." In it, he first offered a relatively flimsy theory as to how and why modernist art evolves. He then evaluated the artists comprising the New York School, a high-minded essay for critics that can also be read by any aspiring artist, dealer, or collector as the morning line of a racing tipster. As though they were horses, Greenberg

Greenberg as he appeared in the Syracuse University yearbook, 1930, and in a group portrait for his fraternity: the future critic is in the front row, far right

OPPOSITE PAGE, TOP: Most of "The Irascible Eighteen" in 1950: William Baziotes, James C. Brooks, Jimmy Ernst, Adolph Gottlieb, Hedda Sterne, Clyfford Still, Willem de Kooning, Bradley Walter Tomlin, Barnett Newman, Jackson Pollock (looking angry), Theodoros Stamos, Richard Pousette-Dart, Robert Motherwell, Ad Reinhardt, and Mark Rothko

OPPOSITE PAGE, BOTTOM: Greenberg's bête noire Harold Rosenberg, with May Tabak and daughter Patia, in Washington Square, 1950

ABOVE: Jackson Pollock in 1953

RIGHT: Pollock's *Troubled Queen* (1945), painted at around the time Greenberg began championing his work

Pollock, Greenberg, unidentified child, Helen Frankenthaler, and Lee Krasner
on the beach, ca. 1952.

Greenberg and Frankenthaler at Bolton's Landing, 1951

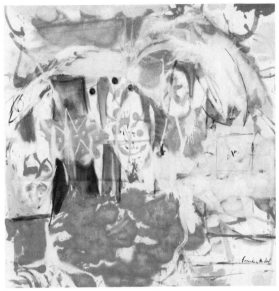

TOP:
Helen Frankenthaler, *Dawn After the Storm* (1957). The influence of her canvas stains could be seen in works such as Morris Louis's 1961 painting *Theta* (overleaf).

BOTTOM:
Philippe Halsman's atmospheric portrait was used to illustrate Greenberg's *Saturday Evening Post* article "The Case for Abstract Art" in 1959

OPPOSITE PAGE, TOP: Greenberg, squinting in judgment and with sempiternal cigarette, by Hans Namuth, 1950

OPPOSITE PAGE, BOTTOM: Morris Louis, *Theta* (1961)

ABOVE: David Smith, *Cubi XVIII* (1964). Controversy over Greenberg's alleged alteration of works by Smith shadowed the last decades of his life.

RIGHT: John O'Brian, the editor of Greenberg's collected writings

The critic at work. TOP: One of Greenberg's favorite activities, a studio critique at the Emma Lake Artists' Workshop in 1962. BOTTOM: Appraising a Kenneth Noland painting at the Guggenheim, early 1970s

identified this one as having early promise and then fading, another who continues to develop, and still another who performs inconsistently but may yet excel. Overall, he was optimistic about the breed, especially compared with its European cousins. For the growing audience of art buffs, this article offered a lexicon of insider terminology: Arshile Gorky "found a way to ease the pressure of Picassoid space," de Kooning "hankers after *terribilità*," Adolph Gottlieb and Robert Motherwell "stay closer to late Cubism," Pollock "cannot build with color," Clyfford Still's painting "is the first really Whitmanesque kind," Barnet Newman "has replaced Pollock as the *enfant terrible* of abstract expressionism," Mark Rothko "makes me think of Matisse." Near the end, Greenberg addressed himself directly to collectors, chiding them for continuing to buy "the pallid French equivalent" of Abstract Expressionist art: "The imported article is handsomer, no doubt," he wrote, "but the handsomeness is too obvious to have staying power."

A respected but more traditional artist, Fairfield Porter, disputed Greenberg's views about the necessary dominance of abstract art as well as his preference for American artists. In replying, Greenberg barely contained his wrath as he questioned or minimized every one of Porter's points and suggested that "he is just juggling words and wants to have them his own way simply for the sake of having them his own way." And the combative tone persisted in Greenberg's other writings during that stressful spring of 1955. In *Commentary* he published "The Jewishness of Franz Kafka: Some Sources of His Particular Vision," suggesting that "the treadmill of routine" faced by Kafka's heroes resembles *Halachah*, a Jewish rule-book for repetitious religious observances. In the process, he assaulted the Cambridge literary critic F. R. Leavis, who had recently developed the so-called New Criticism. Leavis submitted a thoughtful rebuttal, to which Greenberg replied in turn. The squabble continued until Greenberg finally rolled out Kant's *Critique of Aesthetic Judgment* as proof that logical argument has no place in judging art, only "*taste* as exercised through experience of the work of art."

These wounding exchanges perhaps echoed the sort of conversations Greenberg and Frankenthaler were having as their romance fell apart: a strained politeness but charged with anger and, on Greenberg's side, so painful that they ended in depression, disorientation, and (judging from his own date books) a regular diet of alcohol and sleeping pills. In his relationship with Frankenthaler, he was unable to have the last word, so when his assertions in print were questioned he made sure he got the final say. He tried to overwhelm Porter, a relatively weak opponent, by parading his superior knowledge. With Leavis he turned to flattery, as he well might have used it to plead his case with Helen.

Another subtle bid for Frankenthaler's favor in that spring of 1955, even as the relationship breathed its last, consisted of a one-man exhibition at her alma mater, Bennington College, for an artist she admired, Hans Hofmann. Greenberg selected all twenty-two pictures from 1938 to 1955 and wrote an effusive introduction, perhaps partly a sales pitch, since a half dozen of the paintings were for sale. Instead of an assessment of Hofmann's strengths and contributions, Greenberg took a defensive stance, anticipating a criticism not yet expressed. Hofmann's art is not simply an inspiration for new American art, he argued, but admirable "independent of its function as an influence." That "art critics and art bureaucrats" seemed unaware of this "is because their taste cannot solve Hofmann's difficult originality."

In his writings, not to mention his lectures and conversations, Greenberg had taken to belaboring other critics for failing to appreciate his favorite artists. As for his own art education, there is sparse evidence of any formal studies, nor do his datebooks record any visits to the many libraries or archives New York had to offer.

Before 1955, his quick swing through Europe on the eve of the Second World War and his 1954 museum hopping with Frankenthaler appear to be his only firsthand experience of art not available in North America. In defending his finely calibrated ranking of artists, he still alluded to the relentless mills of history that distill the western world's impulses to produce the next new thing. Yet he also fell back on Kant's views about art, that the taste of the viewer is the ultimate judgmental criterion. He cited history as a mechanical process, while handing down the sole verdict of his "eye." But despite the apparent contradictions, Greenberg's assertions about the motivations for art, buttressed by heavy rhetoric and not a few threats to foes, had vaulted him toward the summit of the art-critical world in the United States. In the mid-1950s, that world offered few credible opponents to his dogmatically expressed views. And while other critics may have expressed preferences for different kinds of art, Greenberg alone offered a theory for how new art develops.

Greenberg wielded a particularly keen scalpel in three book reviews, which concluded his writings for 1955. In the *New York Times*, he slashed at his peers by concluding a review of two new works about Toulouse-Lautrec with faint praise: "The short texts . . . are superior to the usual run of art writing." But he also faulted Toulouse-Lautrec for "mistakes on canvas analogous to those of Gauguin, another 'post' and anti-Impressionist, illustrating a derived conception of art rather than one achieved through the processes themselves of oil, canvas, and immediate experience." This demeaning of subject matter and reduction of painting to mere materials foreshadowed Greenberg's next new thing: the Color Field painting of Morris Louis, Kenneth Noland, Jules Olitski, and especially, despite her rejection of him, Helen Frankenthaler.

The next book review prompted an exchange of letters between

Greenberg and James Laughlin, director of the avant-garde publishing house New Directions and editor of *Perspectives USA,* a
highbrow magazine published by the U. S. State Department in
English, French, German, and Italian. Near the end of 1954,
Laughlin had asked Greenberg to review two new Bernard
Berenson books for the Asian market. When Greenberg suggested
he also publish an article about contemporary American painting,
Laughlin had "grave doubts," as he feared it would be "way over
the heads of our Asian readers . . . a very bad advertisement for the
state of American culture, [since most] would find it quite incomprehensible and think our painters were off their heads."

In the review he did turn in of Berenson's *Piero della Francesca*
and *The Arch of Constantine,* Greenberg recalled the venerable
aesthete's history as a youthful Jewish immigrant from Lithuania
and his subsequent transformation as "surprisingly American."
While acknowledging that "hardly any" of Berenson's original
judgments on Italian Renaissance paintings had been "overruled,"
he deplored his subject's "frequent animadversions on modern art"
and instructed the old man in what he should tackle next: "draw
the conclusions from his vast experience of art and shape them
into a coherent intellectual structure." He grudgingly conceded
the value of "the two little books at hand," but ultimately dismissed
Berenson as "a working critic, not a philosopher of art." In another article, his last of that year, Greenberg went on to slash at
Wyndham Lewis, the *Times's* art critic Howard Devree, and the
venerable English critic Herbert Read—perhaps because of Read's
earlier association with the Surrealists.

Greenberg was emboldened in his attacks by the burgeoning
audience and lively market for Abstract Expressionist art. In a foreword to the catalog of the Betty Parsons Gallery's tenth anniversary
exhibition in December 1955, he boasted that the status of
American art had "radically changed" from European tutelage to

radiating influence around the world. It was "a triumph" for which he endorsed Parsons, who had exhibited Pollock, Hofmann, Still, Newman, Rothko, and others "at a time when they could bring her little prestige and even less money." He viewed Parsons as more oriented to "the studio and production side of art," than to "the commercial apparatus of art," and her establishment as "an artist's—and critic's—gallery: a place where art goes on and is not just shown and sold."

While Greenberg deserves due credit for the triumph of American art after the Second World War, American prosperity and access to higher education contributed much, as did two kinds of postwar mobility: upward, into the middle class; and geographic, from rural to urban places. Between 1940 and 1955, the number of college graduates among American adults nearly doubled, from 8 to 15 percent, as did the number of faculty, and spending on higher education more than quadrupled. During those years, average family income tripled, vaulting a majority into the middle or upper class. Another revolution took place in rural areas: the farm population dropped from 23 percent of the total population to just over 11 percent, even as the average farm tripled in size and quadrupled in value.

These profound alterations in American society expressed themselves visibly in the New York art world. In the first in-depth *New York Times* article about the city's art market, Aline Louchheim in 1950 had described the overheated auction scene at Parke-Bernet, then the city's leading salesroom (later taken over by Sotheby's). Both Old Master and modern works attracted standing-room crowds. The sharp-eyed reporter spotted, among others, MoMA director Alfred Barr in the room; he bought little, but raised eyebrows and fingers to cue museum friends who were private collectors. "The indirect effect of this," she wrote, "is the salutary one of keeping up the market in modern art."

Following the trend, between 1947 and 1957 the number of New York galleries multiplied five times, to 180, with the majority selling contemporary art, and total gallery sales rose by 500 percent. Some forty galleries opened new exhibitions every month. Those who bought showed "a descendancy in caste," one gallery owner told an interviewer; they included the businessman with tax considerations and the housewife bearing a swatch of upholstery fabric.

Greenberg's friend Samuel Kootz had opened his gallery in 1949, but quit to become a private dealer in 1955. "There wasn't a hell of a lot of money to be made," he told an interviewer. Big paintings by Hans Hofmann were selling for only $900, when a market for Abstract Expressionists developed quickly around 1955. "People we couldn't convince—museums, critics, collectors— suddenly everybody began to feel something was right," said Kootz. At that point, he lost interest: "All I was doing was dealing in certitudes."

But acute outside observers saw a new and different version of the striving, acquisitive American. To New York intellectuals such as William Barrett, the new collectors appeared ignorant, relying heavily on critics and dealers. Buying new art, Barrett wrote, was not just a financial investment, but also polished the buyer's social status: it betokened "cultural chic," and buying early could be lucrative indeed. One such collector told Barrett, "I never ask myself whether a work is good or not, but only if it has historical importance."

The master of appealing to this sort of buyer was Sidney Janis. He had been active at the Museum of Modern Art since the early 1930s and had bought many works from its exhibitions. In 1935, the museum flouted a longstanding tradition against showing individual collections by exhibiting Janis's property; it included Rousseau's celebrated painting *The Dream*, which the museum's director coveted and which Janis sold to MoMA in 1953 for $125,000. Janis opened his gallery in 1948, with an exhibition of Fernand Léger in a posh suite on West Fifty-seventh Street, just four blocks north of the MoMA. He soon became interested in the Abstract Expressionists, luring Jackson Pollock from the Betty Parsons Gallery in 1952, adding de Kooning and the estate of Arshile Gorky in 1953, and Mark Rothko in 1955. Having started his career as a successful shirt manufacturer who dabbled in collecting art, Janis had developed a feel for how to do business in art. In the mid 1950s, he had unsuccessfully offered to sell the MoMA Pollock's *Autumn Rhythm* for $8,000; after the artist's death in 1956, his widow demanded $30,000 for the same work; when the MoMA failed to meet the new price, Janis had no trouble selling it to the Met.

The pattern of Janis's exhibitions—European modernists shading into Abstract Expressionists—closely followed the interest of the MoMA. After the Second World War, its founding director, Alfred Barr had resumed his annual summer visits to Paris in search of new art, but was disappointed in what he saw. Still, the museum tended to show mostly European masters, many of them in large one-man shows, while Americans were shown more rarely and usually in broad-brush surveys. But by the early 1950s, exhibitions like the Whitney's "Thirty-Five Americans" persuaded many close art observers that the best pictures were abstractions by Americans age thirty-five to fifty-five. Thomas Hess surveyed "ten fat years" in *Art News* and found that the likes of Pollock, de Kooning, Motherwell, Gottlieb and many others were "overwhelmingly superior" to the Europeans still being favored at the MoMA. However, he observed that "our big collectors" were still avoiding Americans; the artists, he wrote, "would be delighted with a chance to become disillusioned with material success."

※　　※　　※

In the fall of 1955, Greenberg was still nursing his wounds over Frankenthaler's rejection when he ran into her at an opening at Tibor de Nagy Gallery. Frankenthaler was there with a new boyfriend, Howard Sackler, a young playwright. Another guest at the party was Janice Van Horne, a twenty-one-year-old who had been in New York for just a few weeks after graduating from Bennington. An English literature major, she had found a job writing program blurbs at a new publication, *TV Guide*, and was sharing a studio apartment in Greenwich Village with her college friend Debby Booth. At the party, Greenberg chatted briefly with the two young women. Van Horne did not remember what they talked about but, as she recalled many years later, "We sat there for some time. We had fun, he put me at ease." Greenberg then disappeared into the crowd, and Van Horne noticed "a commotion, evidently caused by Clem having hit someone." It soon appeared that he had punched the art dealer John Myers for saying how nice it was Frankenthaler had a new friend. Shortly after that, Van Horne heard, Greenberg had gone into the bedroom with Frankenthaler and apparently slapped her, whereupon Sackler knocked Greenberg to the floor.

Van Horne had not witnessed these fisticuffs behind closed doors and might not have been entirely aware of them at the time. Before leaving, she said goodbye to Greenberg and was "pleased when he asked for my phone number," learning only afterward that he was an eminent art critic. Two nights later, he invited her out for a drink. "Before we parted," she recalled, "he said that I might not hear from him for a while because he had some things to straighten out." This was, of course, his relationship with Frankenthaler, which according to his datebook caused him to spend an entire day brooding at home. Apparently this was all it took for him to resolve his lingering feelings about Frankenthaler, for a day or two later he and Van Horne went on what she considered their "first date." Soon, they were seeing each other "pretty much every day," and on November 30, she accompanied Greenberg to Pittsburgh for the opening of the Carnegie International Exhibition. Before Christmas they decided to marry, and in February, Van Horne moved into Greenberg's apartment.

The marriage took place on May 4, 1956, in the chambers of Judge Harvey Breitel. While her old-line German family was "horrified" that their daughter was marrying a Jew, not to mention a man twenty-six years older than she, her mother attended the wedding. So did Greenberg's father and two brothers; longtime friends Sidney and Gertrude Phillips, who were witnesses; the artist Friedel Dzubas with his two children; and Van Horne's friend Nancy Spraker. After lunch at the Vanderbilt Hotel, the newlyweds took in a movie, *The Swan*, which Van Horne recalled forty-eight years later as "dreadful." They went on to dinner with the Phillipses, who also hosted a party for the couple later that evening. "Many people," wrote Van Horne, "dancing, flowers, cake, champagne, etc." The Pollocks did not attend, but sent "an enormous box of white flowers." The next morning the newlyweds left for a few days at the Phillipses' country house at Great Meadows, New Jersey.

In the summer of 1956, Greenberg and his bride rented a place near the Pollocks', and conveniently near where Greenberg's therapist, Ralph Klein, was vacationing. By then, Lee Krasner was fed up with Pollock's verbal and sometimes physical assaults and, at Greenberg's urging, had fled to Europe. Desperately lonely, Pollock turned to a young woman, Ruth Kligman, who had approached him during one of his drinking bouts at the Cedar Tavern. She was flattered by his tipsy attentions and thought, perhaps, that her affection would sober him up. As Greenberg later told the art critic Cleve Gray, "People should have known that he was a radical alcoholic, the most radical I've ever known." But

Greenberg himself overlooked Pollock's inebriation that summer, as he invited Pollock and Kligman to a dinner party with some of his wife's Bennington classmates. The guests wore jeans and snubbed her, Kligman later told Pollock's biographers, for her elegant white linen dress and gold sandals. "Greenberg turned an abstract discussion of friendship into a pointed inquiry," she said, by asking Pollock what he intended to do about Lee. Pollock said nothing and later told Kligman, "It's very complicated."

On July 27, Greenberg was in Pollock's studio critiquing his recent paintings. What the artist absorbed is difficult to assess; he was consuming a case of beer every day. After spending three weeks with Kligman, he was abusing her, much as he had mistreated Krasner; she fled back to New York. But on August 11 she returned, bringing a friend, Edith Metzger, perhaps as a shield if Pollock again turned aggressive. Kligman was concerned about Pollock's mood when he greeted her at the station in soiled clothes, and again when she attempted to introduce Metzger, at which he merely grunted and walked away. Pollock insisted on stopping off at a bar for "an eye-opener" before taking the two women home. When Kligman prepared lunch, he declined to eat and instead drank from a bottle of gin.

That evening, the two women were excited that they, together with Pollock, were invited to a benefit concert at an upscale venue, The Creeks. Pollock called Greenberg to complain about the price of admission, $3 per person, and to ask if he was going. "He never talked about money before," Greenberg later recalled, suggesting that Pollock was searching for excuses not to go. Finally, the threesome headed for the concert, but Pollock insisted on stopping for more drinks, whereupon Metzger refused to get back into the car. For a while, Pollock passed out. When he awoke and began to drive, Pollock ordered Kligman to calm Metzger, who by then was screaming. Minutes later, Edith lay dead under Pollock's wrecked car in the forest alongside Fireplace Road, a short distance from the Pollock–Krasner home. Pollock and Kligman were catapulted out of the front seat into the woods; he died immediately and Kligman sustained multiple injuries. It was Greenberg who telephoned the news to Lee Krasner at a friend's Paris apartment the following morning.

When Lee asked him to give the eulogy at the funeral service on August 15, Greenberg insisted he would have to mention Edith Metzger, "the girl Jackson killed." Lee refused, and instead asked a local pastor who scarcely knew of the artist to officiate. Among the pallbearers was Ben Heller, a wealthy textile manufacturer who had developed a passion for Pollocks; just six months earlier, he had bargained hard with Lee to acquire a painting originally titled *Number 31, 1950*. Greenberg wanted to call the painting *Lowering Weather*, but Pollock (or more likely Krasner) called it *One*.

Outside the small set of mourners, Pollock's death embellished a tragic myth spawned only seven years earlier in the pages of *Life* magazine. In the wide public's mind, his personality resembled Marlon Brando's 1953 role as a reckless motorcycle biker in *The Wild One*, and his end echoed that of another icon, James Dean, killed at age twenty-four when his Porsche crashed on a lonely California desert highway a year earlier.

Pollock's own broken body had scarcely been buried before the MoMA contacted Krasner to arrange for a one-man retrospective to be held just three months later. The works shown were already valued at considerable advances in price; some were hiked to $12,000, several were now appraised at $9,600, and only two drawings were less than $1,000. While the exhibition attracted a respectable number of visitors, many critics were unimpressed. In an essay titled "The Jackson Pollock Myth," Hilton Kramer discerned a brief "plateau" in Pollock's work, when "the anarchic was . . . domesticated by the decorative," followed by "an abyss . . . which dominates the last four years of his life." Though harsher, this judgment accords with Greenberg's views of the post-1950 Pollock oeuvre.

Looking back many years later, Greenberg observed that Pollock's self-esteem rested solely on his paintings; in everything else he saw himself as "a complete washout. He felt worthless." He had no theory underlying his work, telling Greenberg, "My paintings come from nowhere. I just go into the studio and paint." Pollock would do a streak of perhaps twenty pictures, "then he'd sit around the house for weeks." Greenberg's diagnosis was that Pollock suffered from "low metabolism. He would sleep late in the morning. He told me he always got up tired."

Certainly, Greenberg would have sympathized with such a routine; he himself seldom arose before noon. He would also understand Pollock's fundamental sadness. "I never saw Jackson happy," he told Cleve Gray. "His own inchoateness made him miserable." While Greenberg expressed himself forcefully on paper, his blunt assaults on fellow critics were often counterproductive; as time passed, those he attacked were, at best, alienated and, at worst, became lifelong foes. Like Pollock, Greenberg had trouble expressing himself orally, tending toward the ponderous and, perhaps inadvertently, intimidating his listener. He had begged off from participating in a panel discussion in Provincetown in 1949: "Speaking takes too much out of me in terms of fright and tension." His writings and, often, his conversations conjured an unseen enemy lurking somewhere in the shadows, perhaps a figure from his childhood, most likely his father, unremittingly prodding him forward, demanding that he justify himself and still finding him inadequate.

*   *   *

The art market responded to Jackson Pollock's death not only by adding dramatic new value to his work, but by lifting the prices for many of the other Abstract Expressionists as well. While their works had been selling for $2,000 to $3,000 in 1955, the sale two years later of Pollock's *Autumn Rhythm* to the Met validated his peers: a large de Kooning that had sold for less than $2,500 in 1953 cost as much as $8,500 three years later and doubled again in the following two years. During that time, Baziotes's prices rose to $3,500, Rothko's went to $5,000, and Hofmann's reached $7,500. At those sums, they were reaching levels achieved by earlier American modernists like Stuart Davis.

For serious art investors, however, French Impressionists and Postimpressionists were still "among the world's best," according to the *New York Times* on the first day of 1958. Gauguin, Renoir, Monet, Van Gogh, and company had appreciated 90 to 120 percent, in a year when industrial stocks fell by 11 percent, railroads by 36 percent, and even diamonds fell by 5 to 7 percent. Rise as they might, the prices for Abstract Expressionist works were still far below what a good Matisse was fetching. It was this price gap—in addition to Greenberg's seal of approval—that persuaded new collectors to buy out many Abstract Expressionist exhibitions during the late 1950s.

Internationally, Pollock was leading the upward price spiral for the most recent American art. Particularly after a Pollock retrospective tour throughout Europe in 1957 (funded by the U.S. government as a Cold War propaganda effort), values of his works leaped. By 1959, one painting was appraised at $70,000 and several others at $35,000; and a 1960 article in the *New York Times* singled out works by Pollock as having doubled in value the previous year. By this time, Krasner was living at 147 East Seventy-second Street, a considerably more luxurious location than the isolated clapboard house, reeking of painful memories, on Fireplace Road in The Springs.

The fate of Pollock on the international art market attracted a bright spotlight onto the man who had first championed him, and reflected as well on the other artists he had endorsed. Now established as something of an oracle, Greenberg spent much of 1956 reviewing other people's books, often in testy, quirky tones. He gave a two-volume French account of Impressionism a single, grudging paragraph, the caboose to a lengthy exposition of his own highly theoretical take on that style. He chided Leonardo da Vinci for straying off his subject in the *Treatise on Painting*, and faulted the renowned Italian critic Lionello Venturi for starting his discussion of the road to modernism with Giorgione. And he launched another volley at Sir Herbert Read in a review of his mildly titled *The Art of Sculpture*. "The man's notions that the sense of touch plays a strong role in appreciating sculpture are more than fallacious . . . [they're] downright absurd." Greenberg was particularly enraged over Read's assertion that the welded iron sculpture then becoming prominent "technically would be classified in any museum not as sculpture but as wrought ironwork."

This was a clear reference to the sculptures of David Smith, an artist Greenberg had been nursing for most of his critical career. He had first singled out Smith in 1946 as "perhaps the best young sculptor in the country" and mentioned him frequently. By the time his tirade against Read was published, Greenberg had already completed a multipage appreciation of Smith.

This was one of his most incisive articles after the mid-1950s, for it presented, in fewer than two thousand words, a vivid capsule critique of modernist sculpture. Greenberg began by dashing expectations from previous decades that "sculpture might shortly become the dominant vehicle of figurative art." Then he neatly sorted modernism's icons into national and stylistic groupings, tracing influences and offering judgments. He curtly dismissed areas "where hopes have turned into illusion [and] inflated reputations," in particular those of Moore, Marini, and the postwar

Giacometti. He diagnosed "modernist sculpture's common affliction" as "artiness," a reaction to Constructivism, a "terrorizing agent" bearing "machinery and machine-made look." For readers of *Art in America*, many of them newly interested in viewing art or collecting it, he offered a road map to the marketplace for sculpture, redlining potholes and devoting most of the essay to scenic overlooks dominated by David Smith, "whom I do not hesitate to call the best sculptor of his generation."

Greenberg had a long-standing personal relationship with Smith, making a point of visiting the artist's home at Bolton Landing, a small village in upper New York State, whenever he was in the area. As he had done with Pollock and others, Greenberg also critiqued the artist's work, publicly (and perhaps embarrassingly) in his reviews and privately in lengthy, sometimes alcoholic studio sessions. Smith was three years older than Greenberg and had learned welding while working summers at a Studebaker car assembly line. Arriving in New York in 1926, he studied painting at the Art Students League, and tried to synthesize painting and sculpture into a dynamic art form. Despite Greenberg's support, he met little success until the early 1950s, when a Guggenheim Fellowship allowed him to explore larger, more abstract forms.

Like the other artists Greenberg admired, David Smith gratefully gave the critic pieces of his work. The foundations for Greenberg's growing personal collection had been laid in 1950 with a gift drawing from Jean Dubuffet, whose letter took it for granted, as was the custom in France, that an artist present a work to a friendly critic. The artist had been prompted by dealer Pierre Matisse's dispatch of Greenberg reviews. "I am very happy with your flattering appreciations of my work," wrote Dubuffet. They "testify to your deep comprehension of my aims." In a news release later that year, Betty Parsons, whose gallery Greenberg often praised, included his name among a list of others owning Jackson Pollock works. Robert Motherwell contributed in 1957, asking Greenberg to check "the picture I wanted to give you," then hanging in a show at the Stable Gallery: "Take a look and see if you want it." In 1961, Richard Diebenkorn gave Greenberg an etching and promised to give him a drawing on his next visit to Diebenkorn's studio. While many of the alumni of *Partisan Review* believed that the very essence of being an intellectual was to provide guidance to the wider public on various cultural phenomena, such as literature, music, and art, only art gave its critics a bonus—not just prestige, but also valuable goods.

The chronicler of the Abstract Expressionists, Irving Sandler, told an interviewer that all critics of that time were entangled in conflicts of interest. "None of us could support ourselves on criticism," he said. The typical fee for a review was $3. An article that would take weeks or even months to research and write typically brought in $75. Since not many critics could survive on that kind of income, he said, "we all did shows for museums and galleries, we taught, we consulted, but the one thing you didn't do . . . you weren't a gun for hire. You didn't write for any gallery that paid you."

Maybe Sandler didn't because he taught, but his apartment certainly displays a fine array of valuable paintings, many of them gifts from the artists whose work he reviewed. For Greenberg, who was sixteen years older and now a married man, finding a livelihood in the world of art criticism was more problematic. His job as an editor at *Commentary* was his only regular income. When Norman Podhoretz arrived at the magazine's offices one summer day in 1952, a fierce sun was beating through a skylight upon editors laboring behind crude partitions. "In one of those cubicles," wrote Podhoretz, "his bald head sweating profusely, sat the senior member of the staff, Clement Greenberg, the most influential art critic in America." The youthful newcomer was overjoyed, he wrote, when he told Greenberg of his struggles to acquire an authoritative voice as a writer and the intimidating critic replied that he was "a natural."

In 1957, Greenberg's job at *Commentary* began to crumble. He was an exceedingly skilled editor, but his late arrivals, gruff manner, and strong opinions alienated coworkers and, eventually, the American Jewish Committee, the magazine's publishers. At that time, *Commentary* was overtaking *Partisan Review* as the most prominent of New York intellectuals' publications. Along with Greenberg, the editorial staff included his brother, Martin, the sociologist Nathan Glazer, the young film and cultural critic Robert Warshow, and the political analyst Irving Kristol. Among the contributors were Mary McCarthy, Harold Rosenberg, Paul Goodman, Alfred Kazin, Sidney Hook, Irving Howe, Hannah Arendt, Daniel Bell, and Diana Trilling. At the helm was Elliott Cohen, a brilliant intellectual holdover from the *Contemporary Jewish Record*, who was battling recurrent mental breakdowns. As earlier with the similar array of willful minds at *Partisan Review*, the intellectual discussions among staff and contributors were passionate. Kristol recalled the atmosphere as being "very stimulating." Podhoretz remembered an intellectual free-for-all. "You needed to be brilliant," he said. "And brilliant meant quick . . . able to win arguments with other very smart people, and everyone was brilliant in that way."

In the way of such assemblages of brilliant minds, stresses built up and arguments turned bitter. As his reputation as an art critic blossomed, Greenberg's interest in *Commentary* diminished. He indulged his penchant for late nights and sleeping through the morning, often ambling into the office when the rest of the staff was looking forward to quitting time. As he later wrote to the editor of his papers, "I did not see the job as full-time . . . But I did come in every day . . . and then I did apply myself without break till after 5:30."

When Podhoretz became a junior editor in the mid-50s, Greenberg was "extremely sour" about articles his younger colleague commissioned from writers like Robert Graves and Edmund Wilson. He teased Podhoretz, calling him head of "the department of big names." Upon first arriving at *Commentary*, Podhoretz had been "startled out of my wits" when Greenberg contemptuously described the magazine as middlebrow. But the younger man was dazzled by Warshow and Greenberg's "tales of the patriarchal past: how Mary [McCarthy] had left Philip [Rahv] to marry Edmund Wilson, how Dwight [Macdonald] had once organized nude swimming parties on the Cape . . . Oh to be granted the right to say 'William' [Phillips] and 'Philip,' and 'Dwight,' as I could already say 'Bob' and 'Clem.'" Greenberg's personal demeanor struck Podhoretz as "simultaneously helpful and kind, but also cool," and his relationship with editor Cohen was "strained," to say the least; Podhoretz saw his late arrivals at the office as efforts to spite Cohen.

To his brother, Martin, Greenberg was "an eminence not so *grise*," said Podhoretz. Martin had "a fine literary sensibility, but was not a good editor. He was totally indecisive." Nevertheless, in January of 1957, Martin was made managing editor of *Commentary*, Clement was demoted to associate editor, and Podhoretz was one of three assistant editors. In February, Clement was still associate editor and Podhoretz was one of two assistant editors. By April, Martin, Clement, and Podhoretz were all associate editors. In May, Theodore Frankel became a fourth associate editor and in June, Clement's name disappeared from the magazine's masthead altogether. So did his byline; he would never write for *Commentary* again.

Greenberg had never thought much about money, but now he

was facing lean times, so lean that many years later he could still recall the precise details of his financial shortfall. He was glad to take $50 from *Arts* magazine for the detailed update on "Sculpture in Our Time," and $100 for a lecture at the Utica Museum. He was already living virtually rent-free in an apartment building owned by his father at 90 Bank Street, and now he also got a loan from the old man and even managed to borrow $10 from his therapist. Faced with penury, Greenberg sold a Franz Wols gouache in May to Harold and Hester Diamond for $350. The next day, they returned to buy a Baziotes for $775. Greenberg used some of the proceeds to redeem a bracelet given Janice by her grandmother that she had pawned for $250.

Greenberg's financial nadir contrasted sharply with his rise as an authority. In April 1958, his growing stature was confirmed by an invitation to present six lectures at Princeton University the following fall and winter. The prestigious Gauss Seminars, delivered by prominent critics in the humanities, had been started in 1949 to honor Christian Gauss, the venerable chair of the Department of Modern Languages and dean of the college. While Greenberg worked hard on writing out and obsessively revising his weekly lectures, he started late, less than two weeks before the first session. He was still dealing with his anxiety over public speaking and, perhaps to bolster his courage, Janice—whom he now called Jenny— had bought him a finely tailored blazer at Saks Fifth Avenue to wear at the first lecture, on December 4. The crowd hearing Greenberg's presentation in the Firestone Library that evening included some of his warmest fans, Frank Stella, Darby Bannard, Frank Greene, and Michael Fried. "He was the only critic we admired," said Fried much later. At Princeton, he found Greenberg "at his most apodictic. Naturally, he didn't show slides . . . he despised art history lectures and the apparatus that went with them." Fried was so enchanted that he could not remember what Greenberg had actually said, and guessed that it was about "modernism and self-criticism."

Three days before the next seminar on December 11, Greenberg began writing his text and was still revising it on the train to Princeton. This was the pattern for all the remaining lectures, a late start and frantic last-minute revisions. His method was to prepare a handwritten version, then expand it into a typed text, and finally, as H-hour neared, to pummel and chop it ruthlessly with insertions and deletions. While spending Christmas Eve with Jenny on Cape Cod, he began work on the fourth seminar. He spent most of January 4, still on Cape Cod, furiously revising, and continued two days later in New York; that night he took two tuinals and one Beta to sleep, a habit that persisted, with variations, to the end of his life. After giving the fourth lecture on January 8, he stayed over and returned the following day, noting in his datebook: "read and drank." On January 22, his ordeal was finally over, his sponsors celebrating with a festive late-night party.

Greenberg must have been thrilled to appear as an honored lecturer at Princeton University, a school founded as a Presbyterian seminary in 1752, which had virtually barred Jewish students or professors from its campus until after the Second World War. But while the Gauss Seminars inflated his reputation in the New York art world, they did little to augment his precarious income.

❋   ❋   ❋

Many years later, Greenberg vividly recalled the day, September 20, 1958, when what appeared to be his financial salvation rolled to a stop in front of 90 Bank Street in a black chauffeured limousine. Inside were three men: the public relations wizard Ben Sonnenberg; Robert Dowling, a financier famous for having swum around Manhattan Island; and a man identified only as Mr.

Knight. All three were art collectors, and they told Greenberg they'd persuaded a prominent antiques dealer, French & Company, to start a gallery for contemporary American painting. The company had already leased a space above the Parke-Bernet auction house on Madison Avenue and the sculptor/architect Tony Smith had been retained to design the interior. The only thing lacking was a connoisseur to select the art to be shown there, they said, and Greenberg was an obvious choice. He later described the celebration that followed: all-night merriment at three different parties, and stops at the artists' hangouts, the Five Spot and the Cedar Tavern.

Greenberg spent many months negotiating his position with Spencer Samuels, French's director, haranguing him on the dearth of new takes on Abstract Expressionism and his own discovery of a fresh set of abstract artists outside New York. At any number of bibulous lunches and dinners with Samuels, Greenberg insisted on quality installations, color catalogues, and total control over which artists' work would be shown. Samuels appeared awed by Greenberg's expertise and willingly agreed to his demands as they decided to open the new gallery early in March 1959.

But there was much that Samuels did not tell Greenberg. French & Company had been founded in 1908, specializing in decorating the apartments of wealthy New Yorkers with antique French furniture and bibelots. Throughout the 1920s, French had prospered, with gross sales in 1929 of more than $5 million. But the Depression hit the company hard: the failure of the Harriman bank cost it the $256,000 on deposit there, customers were unable to pay for what they had bought, and repossessed merchandise could not be resold. Bank credit dried up and French, unable to repay high-interest loans, filed for bankruptcy in 1938. After French reemerged in 1943, its managers looked forward to a boom when the Second World War ended. Moneyed people surely would again snap up the thousands of status-defining items crammed into French's huge warehouse on East Fifty-seventh Street. But at war's end they found that the public's taste had radically changed. Gilded wall sconces, antique-looking paintings of questionable attribution, and curvaceous bronze-slathered chests and secretaries were no longer in demand. Household help was scarce and expensive, and many well-off New Yorkers favored sleek, low-maintenance Scandinavian modern furniture, or its American equivalent designed by Charles Eames.

Early in 1958, French sent a massive collection worth $1.25 million, so the news release said, to be sold in Puerto Rico, Havana, and Venezuela; the company's "painting expert" said it included "a rare and early 'Enthroned Madonna and Child' dated about 1285 A.D. which is possibly Florentine." Later that year, a few weeks after Greenberg had begun discussions with Samuels, French announced an exhibition to celebrate its fiftieth anniversary, "The Taste of Connoisseurs." In gold lettering on velvety royal blue cardboard, the invitation described items from private collections and museums, a vast array of Louis XIV, XV, and XVI furniture, *objets d'art*, paintings attributed to Delacroix, Degas, and Vigée LeBrun, Chinese screens, and Oriental rugs; all sales would benefit the upscale Spence-Chapin Adoption Service.

Despite these strenuous efforts, sales for the last six months of 1958 were only $556,000, half of the same period in the previous year, and gross profit had slumped alarmingly, from $528,000 in 1957 to just $199,000 in 1958. Paintings bought for more than $47,000 were sold for less than half that amount, while the gross profit in the Decoration and Services Department declined from 40 to 16 percent. Some jobs for customers and company officers went unbilled. However, Spencer Samuels's salary had leaped from $38,726 to $47,031; in addition, the payroll included Mitchell Samuels at $24,500 per year, Spencer Samuels, Jr., at $19,300,

Robert Samuels at $20,180, and Robert Samuels, Jr., at $10,820. By contrast, Greenberg and one other employee in the contemporary art gallery would receive only $5,200 each.

No one breathed a word of this background to Greenberg. Robert Dowling did not reveal that his City Investing Company had sunk more than $1.5 million into French & Co. stock and cash advances secured by notes. At no time during a lavish meal did Samuels reveal to Greenberg that he was desperately hunting for new investors. Nor did he mention, as they shared drinks in some plush Midtown *boîte*, that auditors, in early 1959, had noted that no one was guarding the gallery doors against theft, that shipments in and out were improperly recorded, that three hundred items shipped to another gallery went untracked, and, most alarming, that the IRS was examining French's tax returns and had already complained of "dilatory tactics" to delay its audit.

Unaware of standing atop a sinking ship, Greenberg presided over the opening of the contemporary art gallery on March 10, 1959. More than forty-five years later, the art dealer André Emmerich described it as "the largest and most spectacular gallery in New York," a skylit penthouse at East Seventy-sixth Street and Madison Avenue. With considerable fanfare and not too much effort, Greenberg chose to reprise a one-person exhibition of Barnett Newman he had curated almost a year earlier at Bennington College. In that catalog, he had challenged viewers: "If you are color-deaf, you will focus on the stripes," which, indeed, were the only motifs visible in those super-size canvases. He insisted that further viewing would reveal "shaped emanations of color and light," and that, despite their rectilinear simplicity, Newman's works had little to do with Mondrian, and "far more to do with Impressionism." At Bennington and now in New York, Greenberg bet his reputation on this artist, whose work left him "exhilarated."

Neither critics nor customers were exhilarated by Newman's

stripes, which he called "zips," or by his grandiose titles, such as "Onement," "Day One," and "Vir Heroicus Sublimis." However, selective hindsight has credited Greenberg with the "storm of renown" that established Newman firmly as a pioneer in what the critic called Color-field Painting or Post-Painterly Abstraction.

For his next exhibition, Greenberg chose an even more difficult figure, Morris Louis, then an obscure creator of large, color-drenched canvases living in Washington, D.C. The critic had been following Louis's career since 1953, after being introduced to him by another Washington artist, Kenneth Noland. Back then, Greenberg had taken them to Helen Frankenthaler's studio to view her poured stain paintings. The following year, Greenberg included three large Louis paintings in the "Emerging Talent" exhibition at Kootz Gallery, and publicized him through an *Art Digest* article. In 1957, he promoted Louis for a one-man show at the Martha Jackson Gallery. On frequent trips to Washington, Greenberg had groomed and channeled Louis's work into confor-mance with his own notions of quality. In April 1955, his severe criticism had prompted Louis to destroy about a hundred paint-ings; in the next two years, he destroyed roughly another two hun-dred works.

Since 1949, when he had quit reviewing art on a regular basis, Greenberg had steadily moved from simply viewing and analyzing the art shown at various galleries and museums, to himself ranking the works in the artist's studio, to mounting exhibitions, and inevitably amassing a valuable personal art collection, all gifts from grateful—or hopeful—artists. He had also developed more than friendly relationships with art dealers, beginning with Pierre Matisse, the painter's son, in 1948. At the time, Greenberg had written a slim biography of Joan Miró, an artist represented by Matisse, that was substantially illustrated by pictures supplied by the dealer. The forty-four-page text was cobbled together from secondary sources and lacked anything Miró himself had to say. While the book received warm reviews from Greenberg's colleagues at the *Nation* and *Partisan Review*, Thomas B. Hess, as noted earlier, published a highly damning one. Despite this, Greenberg continued his role as Pierre Matisse's pen with a text for a pocket-size pamphlet on Henri Matisse, part of a series on modern artists published by Harry N. Abrams. Perhaps because of the relationship between patron and subject; Greenberg's usually sharp commentary was absent, buried in a sea of platitudinous admiration.

At French & Co., Greenberg refined his skills as an impresario for new art. Before his stint there ended, in 1960, he was able to show many of the artists he had "discovered," such as Kenneth Noland, Jules Olitski, and Adolph Gottlieb. In the summer of 1959, Greenberg was in Paris scouting for artists to show at French the following season. To Spencer Samuels, he wrote tepid recommendations for two sculptors whose Paris gallery would share the costs of shipping their work to the United States, while also assuring him that French & Co. was viewed as "the most advanced gallery in New York." He nonetheless complained that "we could have sold Louis and Olitski better than we did."

More to the point, he seems to have been completely unaware of his employer's financial problems. As his letter arrived in New York, Samuels was digesting a dire report on operations in the first half of 1959. Sales were down by one-third from the previous year; the slim profit of $141,000 in 1958 had dissolved to a $411,000 loss. Some $150,000 had been spent on equipping the contemporary art gallery, plus another $70,000 for the first three exhibitions, which had attracted only five thousand visitors. Although the gross profit to June 30 was $62,500, other expenses of $86,800 spelled a net loss of almost $25,000. Nevertheless, an ambitious round of exhibitions was planned for the 1959–60 art season: David Smith and Adolph

Gottlieb, and repeat shows for Newman, Louis, Noland, and Olitski. Greenberg also wanted to show Jackson Pollock, but Lee Krasner insisted that he also give her a show. Greenberg agreed, but his evident reluctance so angered her that she canceled both her and Pollock's shows.

Still, French & Co. executives expected that contemporary art sales would get a boost from an upcoming Greenberg article about modern art, to be published in the mass-circulation *Saturday Evening Post* in July. This lengthy essay was part of the popular magazine's effort to reach a more serious readership via an educational series called "Adventures of the Mind." In its solid blocks of earnest text, Greenberg made "The Case for Abstract Art." He urged the reader to enrich his life with regular doses of art, to "take time out to stand and gaze, or sit and listen, or touch, or smell, or brood . . ." But Greenberg also rendered judgment on what was patently unfamiliar to him, as he indulged his penchant for seldom-used words: "Think of how encrusted and convoluted Arabic poetry is by contrast with our most euphuistic lyrical verse." The thoughtful reader might have consulted a dictionary to learn that "euphuistic" meant "affected elegance of language," but the word probably convinced more readers that they were not up to such highfalutin' diction.

Unlike the vivid response to *Life* magazine's article about modern art ten years earlier, not a single response pro or con was published in the *Saturday Evening Post* in the following weeks. Despite this strong article, and despite Greenberg's plea to Peggy Guggenheim for a loan show of her "war babies," French & Co.'s downhill slide continued. In the last six months of 1959, cash reserves dwindled from $113,000 to $44,000; losses were more than $82,000, of which $28,000 was attributable to contemporary art, swelling the accumulated deficit to some $470,000. Despite these ominous numbers, Spencer Samuels traveled in Europe in grand style during the fall, staying at the posh Royal Danieli Hotel in Venice and buying costly antiques, including a Louis XV commode. The European representative he hired to buy and sell items was paid $100 per week, plus commissions, more than the renowned art critic stocking the contemporary art store.

Greenberg's foray into gallery management ended abruptly when French & Co. was forced to close the contemporary gallery in 1960. Nevertheless, the public for new art was growing quickly and was clamoring insistently for guidance to the Next Big Thing. Despite his continuing financial straits, Greenberg's star was in the ascendant.

57/60
60/61 (2v)

Chapter VII

THE NEXT BIG THING

WHEN *ART AND CULTURE*, Clement Greenberg's first book of essays, was published in 1961, it was hardly a blip in the universe of American readers. That June, they were engrossed in such best sellers as Irving Stone's fictionalized biography of Michelangelo, *The Agony and the Ecstasy,* and William Shirer's *Rise and Fall of the Third Reich*; President John F. Kennedy's *Profiles in Courage* had inhabited the best-seller list for more than two years.

Yet within the growing discipline of art history, among professors and graduate students at Ivy League schools no less than at state colleges, *Art and Culture* was a bombshell. The editor of *Arts Magazine*, Hilton Kramer, hailed the book's author as having applied "the finest mind" to "art criticism in our time." Barbara Rose, then a graduate student at Columbia University, looked back on *Art and Culture* as "the point of departure" for her own generation of art critics. Greenberg's voice, she wrote, "was a unique and welcome call to clarity, logic, and meaning."

Before delivering the manuscript to Beacon Press in Boston, Greenberg had spent months poring over his published writings, selecting what to include in a book of fewer than three hundred pages, and revising—sometimes drastically—what was finally published. On February 1, the page proofs for *Art and Culture* arrived, and he devoted days to correcting them. He was rising as early as 9:30 A.M. and spent frequent mornings in therapy with Ralph Klein; often he took prescription sleep medication and dosed himself with martinis in the afternoon.

Pursuing his review of the past, Greenberg took advantage of a May 1961 *Newsweek* interview to fire yet another salvo at Harold Rosenberg for the essay he had written nine years earlier, in which he'd argued that the Abstract Expressionists were creating their identities through the act of painting. Calling them "Action Painters," Greenberg said, "smacks of the label for a new kind of dance." Elsewhere in the brief article, he played a handful of familiar cards: excitement "in watching art in your own time"; regret that he "didn't have the scholarship" to write about the Old Masters; triumph that enthusiasm for the artists he favored had become widespread; and satisfaction that "nobody ever called me on the people I've overlooked." The interviewer added the accolade: "His insights have always been profound, and his pronouncements steady and clear."

Despite such praise, Greenberg seemed restlessly to court the kinds of slings and arrows that he so liberally launched at others. When the *New York Times Magazine* paid him $300 for his triumphant article about Jackson Pollock's acceptance by museums as well as the marketplace, he quibbled, not about his piddling fee, but about the editors' title for the piece: "The Jackson Pollock Market Soars." When two readers ventured mild disagreement on Pollock's achievement, he pulverized them with a demeaning reply: the Pollock drawing illustrating the article was not "grossly inaccurate," and Pollock did not repeat himself; the letter-writer was at fault, unable "to discern the difference within a class of things," like the Europeans who thought all Chinese looked alike.

Even Thomas B. Hess's benevolent *New York Times* review of *Art and Culture* elicited a nit-picking letter from Greenberg. He was embarrassed by how Hess "exaggerates my role as a champion of advanced American art." It was all "too highly colored to be true"; furthermore, he had never "been anything like a 'baron' among New York abstract artists. Ask them." Nor had he rejected the art of Willem de Kooning, Greenberg wrote; rather, he had praised the artist's first show in 1948 and had written a catalog note for his retrospective in Washington. No mean wit, Hess lightly mocked "Mr. Greenberg's sudden modesty," recalling his speaking "loudly and clearly on all occasions about vanguard American art and artists." Hess would "defer to his renunciation of a barony; the aristocracy is a slippery class; 'brigadier general' might have been a more appropriate rank."

In *Partisan Review*, Robert Goldwater expressed deep admiration for *Art and Culture*. He noted that Greenberg was unique in mastering the "combination of personal and critical involvement and . . . [the] conviction and insight to make himself the champion of one significant painter [Pollock] of his generation." In *Art News*, the magazine edited by Hess, a reviewer called the book "tonic" and its author meeting "again and again, and with almost no letup in polemical force, the most diverse challenges," dealing "almost in literal succession, with a forgotten American painter, an overpraised modern European master, a brand-new and original French artist, a misunderstood and rambunctious American who would become the mythical painter of his generation."

Among *Art and Culture*'s most fervent fans was James McC. Truitt, identified in the *Washington Post* only as "a staff reviewer." In fact, Truitt and his wife, Ann, were close friends of Greenberg; he had often stayed with them overnight in Washington, and had given intensive studio advice to Ann, one of the few women artists he supported. In his review, James Truitt wrote that Greenberg was "a rightfully opinioned critic," whose "eye and taste . . . have usually proved right in time." He quoted an essay in which Greenberg named Washington "the painting capital of the United States," principally because his protégés Morris Louis and Kenneth Noland lived there.

Some pieces in the book differed considerably from those originally published, and often in capricious ways. Wisely, Greenberg had not changed a word of the book's lead essay, "Avant-Garde and Kitsch." Despite its many outdated references and its strong Marxist undertone, this article had already been reprinted in *The Partisan Reader* and, in abridged form, in a widely read collection of essays on mass culture. Later, it would reappear in three more anthologies, and it continues to be a standard reading in many college courses on art, sociology, history, and communications.

In the late 1950s, a newly discovered art movement succinctly labeled "Pop" had reinfused this essay with a powerful urgency. It was an art dealer, not a critic, who recognized the new trend's importance—if not aesthetically, then commercially. After trying to survive in the sweater business, Leo Castelli and his wife, Ilana, opened a gallery in their own home in 1957. They had fled Italy on the eve of the Second World War; in New York, their enthusiasm for new American art had blossomed in the wake of Abstract Expressionism. In 1958, Alfred Barr bought three pictures from their Jasper Johns exhibition for the MoMA, including a mocking depiction of the American flag priced at $900. When the museum's acquisition committee balked, Philip Johnson donated the picture in honor of Barr. The acquisition "was like a gunshot," Hilton Kramer told an interviewer years later. "It commanded everybody's attention."

The museum's purchase of American canvases with the paint barely dry marked the arrival of the MoMA as a new player in New York's taste-making game. Since its founding, the museum had been slow to recognize emerging artists, particularly Americans, concentrating instead on established Europeans. But when Barr's annual European trips yielded scant discoveries, he began to look beyond the Abstract Expressionists among the Americans. In 1954, he had already bought a large canvas that conveyed the same sort of mockery of traditional values as Johns's flag painting: Larry

Rivers's spoof titled *Washington Crossing the Delaware*. At a discussion that year on the future of abstract art Barr had confidently predicted that history painting, like the Rivers opus, would replace abstraction. That evening, Greenberg joined Hilton Kramer in supporting abstraction, what he characterized as "the 'master current' of the modernist era."

Greenberg saw the artists he had shown at French & Co. as the vanguard of this master current and continued to do all he could to establish "Post-painterly Abstraction" as the heir to Abstract Expressionism. Reprinted in *Art and Culture* was an article, "New York Painting Only Yesterday," published just four years earlier in *Art News*. Greenberg not only changed the title to "The Late Thirties in New York," but substantially changed the text. To his observation that in the 1930s "Social Realism was as dead as the American Scene," he added, in brackets, "Though that is not all, by far, that there was to politics in art in those years; some day it will have to be told how 'anti-Stalinism,' which started out more or less as 'Trotskyism,' turned into art for art's sake, and thereby cleared the way, heroically, for what was to come."

Greenberg's original essay claimed that the MoMA was unfriendly to abstract American artists and faulted the aesthetic judgment of Alfred Barr in "betting on a return to nature." In the revision, Greenberg twisted the stiletto by describing Barr parenthetically as "that inveterate champion of minor art." The museum's chief curator of painting, William Rubin, later told an interviewer that when he questioned Greenberg about that remark, he replied cryptically: "Well, I hate to say it, I even hate him, but I have to admit that Barr is a great man." Greenberg was never able to tell this to Barr directly, as the museum director sedulously avoided seeing him socially. However, Barr did mail Greenberg a review of *Art and Culture* published in a Soviet magazine. As expected, a translation of the article revealed deep criticism, especially of Greenberg's assertion in "Avant-Garde and Kitsch" that the typical Russian art viewer was "a rude, uneducated boor."

Greenberg was by no means alone in decrying the new art's turn toward mockery and return to subject matter. Perhaps he blamed the failure of his own foray into dealership at French & Co. on the arrival of this upstart movement, clearly based, as he saw it, on the "kitsch" he had so artfully hammered twenty years earlier. Pop Art had begun appearing in storefront galleries on Tenth Street in the late 1950s. But scarcely six months after *Art and Culture* was published, Claes Oldenburg's dripping plaster cheeseburgers and other excrescences of daily life filled a one-man show. Six months after that, Pop Art invaded the uptown art scene via Sidney Janis's expansive exhibition of "The New Realists." As the artists migrated to the uptown mainstream, it seemed that the adventurous Tenth Street galleries were played out, or so wrote *New York Times* art critic John Canaday after a Saturday visit in the spring of 1963. Only three people were touring the galleries, he said, like "lost lambs on a darkling heath . . . How piteous their bleats . . . how touching the tremble of little legs that once capered."

Greenberg's nemesis Harold Rosenberg was so shaken by the art that had emerged from Tenth Street that in 1964 he published a bitter "geography" of the visual experience to be found there. While studiously avoiding the word "kitsch," he nevertheless drubbed Pop Art for abandoning the American artist's traditional nonconformity and instead turning to "a kind of metaphysical retirement, a dissident self-insulation from as many areas of social contact as possible." Cynically, the new artists had withdrawn, a parallel with the "interior immigration" of intellectuals behind the Iron Curtain. Rosenberg was no less shocked than Greenberg by the persistence of Pop Art, its impudence that seduced the righteous Alfred Barr as well as a fast-stepping crowd of new collectors.

In 1963, he angrily called it "slapstick art." A year later, when Pop had dipped even lower into popular culture, he took a more measured tone, dismissing it as merely "elevated commercial art."

Yet the youthful Pop artists clashed vigorously with the aging Abstract Expressionists. Andy Warhol, who was considered the worst offender, was once heard to say in his deadpan voice, "I love the New York School, but I never did any Abstract Expressionism . . . don't know why, it's so easy." Years later, Warhol approached Willem de Kooning at a Hamptons party, holding out his hand. The elderly De Kooning screamed at him: "You're a killer of art. You're a killer of beauty and you're even a killer of laughter! I can't bear your work!" Hilton Kramer recalled an East Side collector's party where someone asked whether a Claes Oldenburg soft telephone actually worked; Adolph Gottlieb snorted, "Yeah. Pick it up and a voice says, 'Hello schmuck.'"

The publication of *Art and Culture* confirmed Clement Greenberg's transformation from a tetchy champion of underdog artists to a respected elder guide to the mainstream of modernism. Greenberg's personal life was also changing. His young wife, Jenny, was pregnant and insisting that they find better housing than the cramped apartment in what she called "the tenement" at 90 Bank Street. The sale of a "large-ish" Pollock painting financed their move to 275 Central Park West, into a seventeenth-floor corner apartment, rent-controlled at $600.

Greenberg himself described it two years later in a letter published in an architectural magazine. For three pages, he carried on about all the handsome vistas seen from this apartment, in the magazine's featured series "My Favorite American Scenic View." The view from most windows was to the north, facing a Stanford White apartment house built in the late nineteenth century. On clear days, he could catch a glimpse of the Hudson River and the Palisades in New Jersey. But the most rewarding view, in real estate value no less than aesthetically, was of "a good piece of Central Park," including the reservoir directly below. To the east was a black bridle path, spanned by a metal bridge—"one of the best pieces of Art Nouveau design I have ever seen." Unlike most New York apartments, the Greenbergs' was spacious and included a living room with ample wall space for hanging his growing art collection. At that time, the walls featured paintings by Kenneth Noland and Jules Olitski, both artists to whom he had given one-man shows at French & Co., and who would enjoy his unwavering support to the end of his life.

*   *   *

At the age of fifty-two, Greenberg should have been enjoying robust health; certainly his busy schedule of gallery visits and writing indicated he was brimming with vitality. But he also ate and drank to excess and was hardly ever seen without a glowing cigarette clamped between his index finger and thumb. For him, even a sniffle seemed to turn into a lengthy siege. In mid-May 1963, for example, he took Coricidin for a cold, was overcome by his aspirin allergy, and had to rush to a physician for a shot of adrenalin. He was still suffering upper respiratory symptoms late in June. Greenberg was also using pills to fall asleep and experimenting with drugs cadged from friends: chloral hydrate, phanodorm, and phenergan, to the point where he had started taking daytime naps. And he was drinking a great deal: in July, after a day of drinking and swimming in the pool at art dealer Samuel Kootz's Westchester mansion, he met an acquaintance on the train back to the city and went barhopping with him until 3:15 in the morning.

While he was wary of the feisty younger, and better-educated, art critics, Greenberg enjoyed entertaining his admirers at home. As a nineteen-year-old junior at Princeton, Michael Fried had written to Greenberg in 1958 after attending the Gauss Lectures.

He soon received a typical Greenberg postcard: "Call me and by all means come." Perhaps busy or shy, Fried delayed, until he received another postcard: "Letters I've sent out seem to have gone astray; perhaps that's happened with you." Greenberg repeated the invitation and this time Fried paid him a visit, the first of many. As he was revising the essays for *Art and Culture*, Greenberg told Fried that art criticism was "a low enterprise . . . most art critics were hopeless." For years afterward, as he advanced toward a Ph.D. at Harvard and into post-doctoral studies, Fried often dropped in and remained "completely on the Greenberg wavelength."

Henry Geldzahler was another young art historian who paid his respects to Greenberg beginning in 1961. In 1963, still in his twenties, the pudgy son of a wealthy Belgian diamond dealer was already associate curator of American painting and sculpture at the Metropolitan Museum of Art. He wrote to French & Co., requesting catalogs of Greenberg's exhibitions there. "The brief life" of the contemporary art gallery, he wrote, "was of major historical importance." Greenberg received a carbon copy of that letter. Even though Geldzahler became an enthusiastic patron of Pop Art, he respected Greenberg. In 1965, when Geldzahler curated the Met's comprehensive survey, "American Painting in the Twentieth Century," the young man singled out Greenberg as author of "a body of essays that stands as the most important achievement in the history of American art criticism."

*   *   *

On December 20, 1961, at 11:40 A.M., Jenny went into labor and Greenberg took her to Doctor's Hospital. In the waiting room, he opened Henry James's *Spoils of Poynton*, one of many James novels he was reading that year. At 8 P.M., he had a sandwich, "waiting," he wrote in his datebook. At 9:30 P.M., red underlining emphasized shattering news: "Girl baby born dead." He spent the evening with Jenny and left just before midnight; outlined in red at the foot of that day's page, he wrote: "Little girl gone (anencephalic)." Greenberg spent most of the next four days with Jenny at the hospital, buying her Christmas presents at Saks Fifth Avenue, and arranging for the baby's cremation at Universal Funeral Chapel. Kenneth Noland came by once to have coffee and drinks with Greenberg, but no one from either family appeared. On December 24, Greenberg brought Jenny home for a cheerless Christmas Eve. The next day, they opened presents and then, Greenberg noted in his datebook, "drank; lunch in." On New Year's Eve, they dined alone and watched television.

Greenberg's laconic entries in the datebook over the following weeks covered over his anxiety and grief, much as his attentiveness to Jenny contrasted with his behavior toward the birth of his first-born, Danny. In the inner dialogue he conducted with his personal inquisitor, he asserted how thoughtful and responsible he had become. Still, overall his actions show little difference from his previous life, and his datebooks mainly detail a succession of books read (Hegel, Wölfflin, Mann), visits to or from a few friends and acquaintances, perusal of his own youthful letters to Harold Lazarus (at age fifty-three, was he reflecting on how quickly life passes?), and an increased intake of alcohol and pills, especially sleeping pills.

By mid-February the mood had lifted a bit, and the Greenbergs hosted a large cocktail "party chez nous," including artists and dealers. And in the spring, they drove south for Greenberg's appearance at the University of North Carolina, before vacationing in St. Armand's key in Florida—a leisurely round of driving, sunning, swimming, and, at least for Greenberg, drinking. Back in New York, he raced around Manhattan, popping into most galleries for a quick look-see before drinks and dinner at a different restaurant with a different group almost every night. Early in April, the Greenbergs drove to Bolton Landing for a visit with David Smith. At a party on April 7, marijuana was passed around along with the whiskey. While there, Greenberg noted in his datebook, he and Smith, "walked, talked, looked, and drank." A month later, Greenberg relaxed with marijuana after a long day of socializing with artists in Washington, D.C. But at bedtime, he continued to use various combinations of sleep medicines.

Although the datebooks at this point make no further mention of the stillborn child, Greenberg's manic activity and intake of drugs and drink suggest a lingering depression. Perhaps to deal with it—and certainly to put food on the table—he embarked on a multitude of writing projects. Most viable was a biography of Jackson Pollock, for which he did an enormous amount of work, collecting voluminous notes about the extended Pollock family, its origins, professions, travels, and lore. He also amassed an array of other people's clichés describing Pollock's personality and work: "demonic fury," "epic sweep," "heir of Whitman, Faulkner, and Melville," "enormous cosmic thrust of his whiplash lines," "dynamic action of the creative process," and "unique art without boundaries." Clearly, he was preparing to savage anyone who claimed Pollock as his own. Perhaps in order to generate interest in the book, Greenberg also wrote a long essay about the painter's impact on postwar art critics; but despite his heavy editing and re-editing, this essay languished in his files, along with a folder stuffed with clippings about Pollock.

The idea of a Pollock biography had been simmering since the artist's death in 1956. By 1960, Greenberg was shopping around a book proposal in both the United States and Britain. He had carefully saved Pollock exhibition catalogues and compiled extensive lists of paintings, with their completion dates and their current locations. It is possible that Greenberg dedicated *Art and Culture* to Margaret Marshall, his mentor at the *Nation*, because she was then working as an editor at Harcourt, Brace and World publishers.

In June and early July 1962, the Greenbergs house-sat Samuel Kootz's spacious home in Yorktown Heights while the art dealer and his wife were traveling. Greenberg was still working on the Pollock book, but took many days off, swimming naked in the pool and reading an array of volumes, principally about Spanish history and culture. As though justifying his vacation to the inner taskmaster, he noted in his datebook the days he did "no Pollock." Back in the humid city on July 25, he learned from Marshall that, despite his standing in the art world, Harcourt had turned down his book proposal. The fact is, Greenberg's writing was best suited to a short form, a magazine or newspaper article honed by his overactive pencil through multiple revisions. The few books he published were either collections of these short works or transcripts of lectures printed posthumously by his widow. The drafts of his proposal for the Pollock biography, on the other hand, reveal his confusion in structuring something as sustained as a book, and in the end, Greenberg abandoned the project altogether.

Greenberg's lingering depression was reflected in his few published writings over the next two years. He worked almost throughout 1962 on "After Abstract Expressionism," writing, rewriting, polishing and reediting, and even mailing follow-up corrections until it was published in October. This essay was a return visit to the offspring of Cubism, trying to fit the second generation Abstract Expressionists into the orderly progression he had earlier set forth in appointing the likes of Pollock, Gottlieb, and Newman the true heirs of Cubism. He rapidly sorted through new abstract painting in Europe and America, while studiously avoiding that other new American painting that caused him and other critics so much heartburn—Pop—until the final paragraph. He dismissed that work as "Neo-Dada" and claimed that it was hardly avant-garde, since the artists had not broken with "safe taste." In the discussion of successors to Abstract Expressionism, Pop represented only "novelty, as distinct from originality," and it "has no staying power."

The doctrinaire and impatient tone evoked an equally doctrinaire and impatient retort from a newly minted art historian, Max Kozloff. He was art critic of the *Nation* and also publishing his rabbinically honed disputes on art in the pages of *Artforum*, a new magazine published on the West Coast. In Greenberg's theory, Kozloff discerned "a bastion of aesthetic necessities, any one of which, if granted, instantly locks arms with another, until a very formidable chain is constructed." Greenberg's ideas attain power, he wrote, "from their very directness and capacity to over-simplify complex phenomena." While many others had previously attacked Greenberg's choice of artists as purely personal preferences, or his theories as overly complex, this was the first to attack him for over-simplifying. In tiny type stretched over five double-column pages, Kozloff argued that Greenberg's Color-field painters were "isolated abstractionists" in a dominant art culture that had turned figural in the form of neo-Dada, Pop, and assemblage.

Kozloff's anger may well have been simmering since Greenberg failed to help him obtain a grant a year earlier, a refusal to which he'd reacted with a three-page, closely-spaced letter, replete with invective. Beyond personal spleen, however, Kozloff's response to Greenberg's article, a lengthy letter to the editor of *Art International*, heralded the arrival of a new cohort of art historians, the products of rigorous training mostly instituted by refugee German art historians during the late 1940s and 1950s. It was they who had introduced American students to the aesthetic theories of German philosophers, including Greenberg's favorite source, Immanuel Kant. Just thirty years old, Max Kozloff had received an M.A. from such a program at the University of Chicago in 1958 and was finishing Ph.D. studies at New York University's Institute of Fine Arts when his attack on Greenberg was published.

Even the title of Greenberg's last essay of 1962, "How Art Writing Earns Its Bad Name," promised a vicious outburst—and the text amply fulfilled it. As so often in his longer essays, Greenberg started this one with a brief, self-justifying dip into history. He recalled how no one twenty years earlier dreamed that American painters could soon "challenge the leadership of Paris"; how a Pollock show there in 1952, though commercially unsuccessful, led to his being "taken more seriously in certain quarters of the Paris art world than anywhere else, including New York." Greenberg seemed to have forgotten *Life* magazine's multi-pagee splash back in 1949, when it had asked whether Pollock was "America's Greatest Artist." After savaging Rosenberg's "Action Painters" article for four long paragraphs, Greenberg blamed an English critic, Lawrence Alloway, for rescuing Rosenberg's essay from the disregard it deserved. At the peak of a tirade, Greenberg often turned to obscure words, and this time, he hurled "amphigoric" at the "piece of art interpretation" by Rosenberg that Alloway had so readily accepted.

Greenberg then spewed disdain at other English art critics for seizing upon Rosenberg and Alloway as a means of downgrading Americans to minor status, and blamed them for exporting their views to the Continent. He complained that the French critic Michel Tapié, after giving Pollock his first Paris show, then joined with Alloway in falling for "false dawns" hawked by "comedians like Mr. Rosenberg." And he assailed Robert Goldwater, the husband of the sculptor Louise Bourgeois. Despite this critic's friendly review of *Art and Culture*, Greenberg dismissed him as a "campfollower," whose catalog essay for a current Rothko exhibition then touring Europe was "typical of contemporary art writing," in implying that the artist "has come out of nowhere and owes practically nothing to anything before him. It's as though art began all over again every single day."

Finally, Greenberg indicted all current art criticism as "the only place where the absurd has made a new lodgment in the area of art." He flung "absurdity" upon "its rhetoric . . . its language . . . its solecisms of logic . . . its repetitiousness." He then presented examples of the kind of prose he was trashing: de Kooning's colors that "erupt through the ceiling, coherent in their poetry and ambiguity," a Pollock described as a "scornful technical masterpiece, like the 'Olympia' of Manet," and another Pollock cited as "an abyss of glamour encroached upon by a flood of innocence." The perpetrators went unnamed, but anyone up on art writing could identify Thomas B. Hess on de Kooning and Frank O'Hara on Pollock.

Greenberg's peroration heaped ridicule upon "the widening of the gap between art and discourse," which led to "perversions and abortions," so that "art itself has been made to look silly." This rant was over the top, even from a writer whose style featured strong rhetoric. As Pop Art cavorted into the spotlight, Greenberg was stunned by the silence or approval of other art critics in the face of what he considered rampant kitsch. He had also suffered a grievous loss, a child stillborn, and its parents abandoned to solitary grief by both families. For Greenberg, the dead baby had represented a second chance at parenthood, while Danny was still a source of private anguish and reproach. Finally, there was the yapping brood of young art historians, frisky puppies intent on forging a career at his expense.

Retribution arrived quickly. Herbert Read, the English critic whom Greenberg had repeatedly attacked, staunchly defended Harold Rosenberg and called attention to "the wit and intelligence" of a collection of his essays, *The Tradition of the New*, published in 1959, which included "Action Painting," the essay Greenberg had savaged. Read attributed British interest in Pollock, not to the latecomer Lawrence Alloway but to Peggy Guggenheim, who had written to Read in 1943 about her "new discovery." As for the art pioneered by Pollock, Rosenberg's articles were the "most illuminating." Read cited several unclear passages in Greenberg's essay and then pointed out the new role for contemporary critics: "the unprecedented task . . . to try to convey to a public, generally outraged and ignorant, the sincere, but obscure motives" that impel artists to produce "provocative images." Greenberg devoted an entire week to obsessively composing, editing, rewriting, retyping, touching up, further revising, and re-retyping the reply to these donnish quibbles, and issuing further quixotic challenges while landing a few more jabs at Rosenberg.

What motivated Greenberg to cast Rosenberg as Beelzebub remains murky—perhaps both men's heritage of Talmudic disputation, or perhaps simple territorial jealousy. But there is no question that Rosenberg mustered his considerable resources to reply in kind. He was just three years older than Greenberg, and since their days together in the orbit of *Partisan Review*, he had forged a vivid persona as a sparkling, witty, all-purpose intellectual into a profitable career. As early as 1947, while still holding down a remunerative but vague job with the Advertising Council, he had published an essay about actors, onstage and off, in *Les Temps modernes*, edited by his friend Jean-Paul Sartre. The following years yielded a series of articles on Marxism and political history in various prestigious journals. His papers show that in 1962 alone, his rapier wit and verbal fireworks were sought for appearances at Columbia University, the Baltimore Museum of Art, MoMA, Brandeis, Oberlin, Cornell, and the California College of Arts and Crafts. His usual fee was $1,000, plus transportation, housing, and meals. He was also invited to present the Gauss Lectures at Princeton in March 1963. Norman Podhoretz eagerly sought his book reviews for *Commentary*, while the editor of *Artforum* begged him for his take on West Coast art, and Collier Books gave him a contract for a book on Herman Melville.

In May 1963, *Encounter* published Rosenberg's riposte to Greenberg's thrusts at his theory of Action Painting. He insisted that Abstract Expressionism grew out of 1930s activism as "painting became the means of confronting . . . the problematic nature of modern individuality." His former protégé De Kooning had generously said that Pollock "broke the ice," but "behind Pollock," Rosenberg wrote, "came a veritable flotilla of icebreakers." He then ripped "those who have an interest in 'normalizing' vanguard art so that they may enjoy its fruits in comfort . . . dealers, collectors, educators, directors of government cultural programs, art historians, museum officials, critics, artists . . . 'the art world.'" Finally, Rosenberg focused on Greenberg's efforts to connect Abstract Expressionism with previous art movements. In this "burlesque of art history," he wrote, "artists vanish and paintings spring from one another with no more need for substance than the critic's theories." Greenberg, he charged, had "elected himself as First Cause."

Hindsight and distance indicate that Rosenberg and Greenberg would have benefited handsomely from cooperating instead of perpetually bickering. As the 1960s dawned, both men were seen as patriarchs by the younger art historians emerging from graduate schools. "If you stepped into art criticism," wrote one, "you stepped one way or the other into their gravitational field."

By 1964, it was quite clear that Pop Art, which both critics ceaselessly belabored, was no longer an upstart but was disporting itself stridently in the center ring of the New York art world. And the following year, they were both soundly trounced by Max Kozloff. Reviewing how enthusiastically they had reacted to Abstract Expressionists, he faulted Greenberg for failing to understand how those artists had been influenced by the automatism of Surrealism, an art movement that Greenberg regularly dismissed, and Rosenberg for perceiving "risk" as the artists' response to a vague "crisis" dreamed up by both critics. Kozloff argued that they had transferred "their earlier left-wing dialectics to an embattled aesthetic minority." For both Rosenberg and Greenberg, the villain was "a philistine, implacably middle-of-the-road society without any historical or cultural consciousness." But both men were taken aback by that same villainous group, which avidly embraced a new art that also seemed to lack historical or cultural consciousness.

By the time this analysis appeared, both Rosenberg and Greenberg had retreated from their duel. After several stints as a visiting professor, Rosenberg found a permanent academic perch in 1967 at the University of Chicago, as professor of art and member of the Committee on Social Thought. His duties there were so light that he could also carry on as art critic for the *New Yorker*, where his starting pay was a generous $600 per article. Although his predecessor. Robert Coates, suggested he was "a demon for punishment" in taking the job, Rosenberg managed to write his extensive column for more than ten years based on a quick once-a-month foray around New York galleries. Simultaneously, he tossed off numerous articles for *Vogue*, and recycled his papers and speeches as articles, before collecting them into lucrative books.

Greenberg, by contrast, fled from the New York scene in 1963, writing nothing of substance there, while plowing new terrain, both personal and professional. He organized yet another exhibition of works by the Color Field painters Louis, Noland, and Olitski. In his introduction for that show, he seemed tickled that this exhibition was flying under the New York art scene's radar: it opened in January at the Mackenzie Art Gallery in Regina, Canada, the capital of Saskatchewan, a vast grain-producing province with fewer than one million inhabitants. The works shown did not arrive "with ribbons tied around them," wrote Greenberg, but "the prevailing tide in New York abstract art" had turned: Noland had become a "name"; the reputation of Louis, who had died in 1962, "grows from day to day"; and Olitski had taken a second prize for painting at the Carnegie International in Pittsburgh. He noted that the New York art world's indifference to those artists "may have changed to nervousness . . . in the face of a threat to established tastes."

It was not the first time that Greenberg had strayed outside New York to "discover" both new artists and new audiences. He had found David Smith in rural Bolton Landing, New York; Louis and Noland in Washington, D.C.; Olitski near Bennington, Vermont; and Jack Bush in Toronto. These provincial artists would rely on Greenberg for critical advice in the studio and critical publicity in the art media, not to mention entrée to various galleries. Soon after the Regina show, Jules Olitski's paintings went on display at New York's Poindexter Gallery, with quotations in the catalog taken from Greenberg's introduction to the Canadian show: "some of the most unconventional [work] to be seen anywhere in American painting."

The notion that a far-flung agricultural community would some-how throw open its doors to avant-garde art captivated Greenberg. It might have been the romance of wide-open spaces that drew him to Canada, or perhaps memories of his own peripatetic youth. At that time, Greenberg had been lonely and frightened, forced out into an uncaring world at his father's demand. Now, Greenberg clearly basked in adulation from "the enlightened art public of western Canada," a fancy description indeed for what were largely wheat farmers and ranchers living in towns like Moose Jaw or Swift Current, battling bitter winds and sub-zero temperatures in prairie villages in a land of thousands of lakes. He would make many return trips to Regina and summertime visits to the Emma Lake Artists' Workshops, 230 miles due north; already, he had met with twenty-four of the Regina artists the previous summer.

Greenberg was so taken with the Canadian abstract work he termed "prairie art"—and perhaps also impressed with his unquestioned influence there—that he wrote a lengthy survey of it for *Canadian Art,* published in April 1963. In it, he saw Canada reflecting the American situation, with Toronto and Montreal analogous to New York, and Vancouver to San Francisco. The city folks could only imagine that the provincials looked to them for culture just as they themselves looked toward Europe. But, "unlike Podunk or San Francisco," he wrote, Saskatchewan "does not waste its mental energy in conjuring up illusions of itself as a rival to New York or London . . . This may explain why I found both Regina and Saskatoon far less provincial . . . than I had expected." Of course, the very fact that Canada had to bring in an American authority to describe the work of its own painters indicated a certain provincialism.

But alongside his delight in new discoveries, Greenberg's shift of interest from American to Canadian artists, and his long absence from New York, resembled his flight from becoming a literary critic in the early 1940s. Back then, he had been intimidated by the somewhat older, more experienced literary folk around *Partisan Review*. This time, he may have been influenced by pangs of anxiety over issues at home—Jenny was in the early stages of a new pregnancy—as well as feeling besieged by rivals such as Rosenberg, along with the younger, better-educated art historians emerging from prestigious colleges and challenging his stature more severely by the day.

＊　　＊　　＊

Greenberg's return to New York early in 1963 did not automatically mean a return to writing. Part of this was caused by depression: "dark night of soul; fitful sleep," on March 29, followed by sleep medication the next night. But the main reason for Greenberg's silence in 1963 arrived on Thursday, April 16. That day, he returned home after a round of gallery visits with Kenneth Noland to find that Jenny had gone into labor. Noland drove them to Doctors' Hospital, where, at 8:17 P.M., according to Greenberg's datebook, Jenny was taken into the delivery room. Greenberg started reading Nathaniel Hawthorne's *Scarlet Letter.* Their baby girl was born two and one-half hours later. Greenberg was home by 12:15 A.M. and retired with but one tuinal sleeping pill. He spent the next morning washing the baby's crib and bassinette before returning to the hospital for a long look at his offspring, and to sit with the new mother. Over the next few days, he "cleaned and readied things for Dora," as he had decided to call the infant. Following Jewish tradition, he wanted to name her after his mother; still, he went along when Jenny insisted on naming the baby Sarah. The next day, he brought the two of them home from the hospital. "Champagne with all till 1:30 [A.M.]," he noted; William Rubin, then a professor of art history at Sarah Lawrence College, was among the few visitors.

The baby's birth was greeted by jubilant letters from artists in Saskatchewan, London, Paris, and of course New York. But, at least according to Greenberg's date books, neither his nor Jenny's family sent so much as a card to welcome her. When the infant was just ten days old, Greenberg seemed to be returning to his busy round — but there was a difference: on April 25, he boarded a train to Wilmington, Delaware, juried a show at the art center there, and then, uncharacteristically, rushed home that same evening and "dandled and fed" Sarah. Jenny was now seeing a therapist who had the same unorthodox views as Greenberg's: the conviction that close personal relationships were unhealthy. Greenberg, on the other hand, could not resist forging an intense relationship with the infant, and by July was immersed not in Kant or Hegel but in that parental bible, Benjamin Spock's *Baby and Child Care.*

The details of infant care seeped into the rest of Greenberg's life. On a typical evening, for example, he fed the baby and was in bed by the remarkably (for him) early hour of 11:30 P.M. The contrast between his attitude toward Sarah and that toward his first-born could not be more acute: on Friday, July 26, Danny arrived after Greenberg had read his unpublished, unperformed play, *Tomorrow*, which Danny seems to have sent him earlier. Apparently Greenberg did not think very highly of the the young man's dramatic efforts, as his datebook records: "Brawl with Danny; he left then back; left finally at 9:45." So intense was the irritation the twenty-seven-year-old could evoke in his father that Greenberg lost his meticulous control over grammar. He spent the weekend at home feeding the baby, watching television, nursing a headache, and feeling slightly nauseated.

At the end of the summer, Greenberg submitted an application for a $10,000 grant from the Ford Foundation program for reporters, editors, and critics in the visual and performing arts. He was planning a book of essays on the Old Masters, he wrote, with "the least possible injection of scholarship or literary research," an effort facilitated by his "lack of academic grounding in art history." He would spend six months in all major European art museums, doing much of the writing "on the spot," followed by "two or three months of work at home, since I have the unfortunate habit of revising endlessly." To this self-deprecating proposal he added a list of twelve references, all respectable art world figures, but none from any major New York museum or any Ivy League art history department. The Ford's sharp humanities grant director, W. McNeill Lowry, must have wondered who would read a book about Old Masters by a critic who guaranteed minimal scholarship or research; he politely declined two weeks before Christmas.

Between the dandling, the diapering, and the feeding, Greenberg actually managed to get a few things written. Published early in 1964 was a dense discussion of "The 'Crisis' of Abstract

Art" for a symposium in the French magazine *Preuves*. Surely more enjoyable, since he agreed to do it less than twenty-four hours after he was asked, was his text describing his own art collection for *Vogue*. Illustrated with photos by Hans Namuth, who had gained fame by photographing Jackson Pollock at work, the article contradicted much of his elaborate theory of why new art had to be abstract; after years of insisting that subject matter in art was passé, he enumerated the representational artists he admired, among them Edward Hopper, Richard Diebenkorn, and—that antithesis of abstraction—Andrew Wyeth. Greenberg also wrestled with new territory in a long review of four books of photography. His datebooks reveal him attacking his text day after day, editing and rewriting and editing once again. The prose that appeared to flow so effortlessly in his reviews for the *Nation* now seemed clotted—partly, to be sure, by the disarray normally surrounding a new baby, but also by his realization that these words, too, would someday be collected in book form, an oeuvre that future critics could dismember at will.

Already, there had been a few pinpricks of opposition. In a review of an Adolph Gottlieb exhibition in Paris in 1959, a young critic, Annette Michelson, had noted that Greenberg's introduction seemed dredged up from previous writings and appeared "vague and tentative," stressing "past performance" and suggesting "a malaise about the present." In *Artforum*, she would join Max Kozloff in questioning "the academy of Clem." Another young art historian, Lucy R. Lippard, held that Greenberg had not written "anything important after 1962." She recalled questioning Greenberg after a lecture on what he meant by "quality." If he had to tell her "what quality is," he retorted, "I have to tell you the difference between green and red." Much to the audience's amusement, Lippard shot back, "You mean like Greenberg and Rosenberg?" Afterward, she introduced herself to Greenberg and he said, "Oh, you're Lucy Lippard. I thought you were a school-teacher from the Bronx." She tried to continue the discussion later at a party at Lawrence Rubin's house, but Greenberg grudgingly said, "Well, I must say you have guts." For Lippard, it was a defining moment: "I just realized that I was wasting time worrying about Greenberg. I could have my own trajectory."

But for the moment, these were just ripples of dissent, hardly disturbing to a critic warmly welcomed at the many galleries he visited during the art season, and bombarded with pleas from artists to visit their studios. Each year, he received scores of invitations to lecture at museums or to spend time in campus art departments. In 1961, he had even agreed to be the sole juror for the Oklahoma State Fair's exhibition of Southwest art. The local newspaper was agog over this "first-rate chamber of commerce job," which associated the Oklahoma Art Center "with a cultural effort of major importance." The demand for his presence was so strong that Greenberg could exact $1,000 for a lecture, plus first-class air transportation and luxury overnight lodging, if needed. He gradually devoted a great deal of effort to denouncing Pop Art as more about fashion than taste; at the Guggenheim Museum in 1962, he insisted that he was not upset that Abstract Expressionism had been displaced after a twenty-year run. This, he erroneously claimed, had befallen classical painting in Florence and Rome "in about the same amount of time."

In January 1964, Greenberg embarked on a strenuous three-week tour of his artistic fiefdoms outside New York. In frigid Toronto, he spent two days with Jack Bush, the artist he had been currying on frequent trips north since 1957. As with many before him, Greenberg's relations with the younger artist were equal parts mentor and taskmaster. Following his typical path, he found an ambitious unknown, browbeat him into compliance, helped market his work, and in return received more paintings for his collection. Bush's large canvases became under Greenberg's tutelage "calm beautiful formal statements, emphasizing color and flattening the illusion of spatial depth." But the relationship took its toll on the painter's self-confidence as well. The following January, he confided that "the whole group of small paintings that I did has proved disastrous, with the possible exception of the one you chose for yourself [the previous year]." In May, he reported that he had "cut up and destroyed the two canvases you didn't like, have painted two new large ones which look good." And by 1965, he was complaining that Greenberg's "harping on my 'clumsiness' and 'awkwardness' is making me self-conscious."

Nor was the critic's promotion of Bush's work uniformly beneficial. An exhibition he obtained through Greenberg at the Elkon Gallery in the fall of 1964 netted him only a tiny, lukewarm paragraph in the *New York Times*. When a group of his paintings were shown at London's Waddington Gallery the following spring, the *Observer* snidely noted, "Another trans-Atlantic painter makes his first appearance. He has sailed in on a Greenberg ticket and tied up at the Waddington Gallery." A newspaper in Bush's hometown disclosed that the artist "hates that connotation, but respects Greenberg as a man and as a person of outstanding art perception, and refuses to deny Greenberg's influence."

Still, despite his resentment of the implication, there is no question that Bush and other artists who in the previous decade had submitted to Greenberg's massage of their work were profiting from his connections. And the benefit was mutual. While Morris Louis was alive, Greenberg's coaching persuaded him to destroy several hundred paintings. This, plus the critic's promoting of his reputation, caused prices for Louis's paintings—including some owned by Greenberg—to skyrocket after his death. Works of a type and size that a Paris gallery owner had bought for $700 each in late 1961 were selling for as much as $4,000 only a year later.

In early 1963, Greenberg convinced the Morris Louis estate, Kenneth Noland, and Jules Olitski to supply pictures for an exhibition he was organizing at the Los Angeles County Museum of Art. Among the other artists Greenberg chose for this exhibition was Gene Davis, a painter he had coached during repeated visits to his New York studio in 1962 and 1963. "Some of your comments really shook me up," Davis had written after Greenberg's first visit. And he promised to paint ten pictures "along the lines of the red one you seemed to like." After another Greenberg critique, Davis wrote, "You were right beyond all my expectations." And following another visit a few months later, Davis again followed all his recommendations and found the effect "startling . . . You have the sharpest eye I have ever encountered." After he was included in the LACMA show, Davis was "honored" to offer Greenberg one of his paintings as a gift.

The Los Angeles show, which later traveled to the Walker Art Center in Minneapolis and the Art Gallery of Toronto, ran from April 23 to June 7, 1964. It included thirty-one painters, among them Jack Bush, Frankenthaler, Ellsworth Kelly, Friedel Dzubas, and Paul Feeley. Overall, the attempt was a disaster. For selecting all the paintings, obtaining photographs and writing most of the catalog, Greenberg received minimal payment: only $2,250, including expenses and travel. Nor were the reviews particularly favorable. John Coplans, who would become the editor of *Artforum* and curator at various important museums, found Greenberg's choice of artists seriously flawed, especially if its purpose was—as Greenberg insisted—to show the work of the legitimate heirs to Abstract Expressionism, what he called "Post-Painterly Abstraction." Coplans accused Greenberg of failing to recognize that new art was moving in many different directions, and instead was trying to establish one style as correct; his worst blunder was avoiding Pop Art altogether, even Robert Rauschenberg. "It is obvious," wrote Coplans, "that Greenberg has thought up some kind of category, made little effort to define it, and then tried to find artists to fit it . . . A clumsy attempt full of holes." Even the artists themselves had begun to voice dissent: Robert Irwin, a California artist Greenberg had hoped to include, withdrew from the show before the opening, saying, "There are differences of opinion that demand I stay out of your classification." Behind the barricade he called Post-Painterly Abstraction, Greenberg was erecting a narrow platform for what he considered worthy new art and vigorously pursued those he deemed acceptable—whether they wanted to be pursued or not.

*　　*　　*

In retrospect, Greenberg's trip across Canada at the beginning of 1964 seems dreary, an aimless ramble through a barren frozen landscape, less a journey than a flight from intolerable challenges in New York. After Winnipeg and Calgary, he stopped in Vancouver and Seattle, then continued on to San Francisco, where he most likely visited artists or galleries. He started drinking at midmorning and continued wherever he was taken, to Palo Alto in the south, to San Rafael in the north, to have nightcaps with the Diebenkorns. When he reached the Los Angeles area, the drinks, dinners, and "nightcaps" continued into the early morning. With Paul Feeley, he traversed the Southwest, stopping in Dallas to view the melancholy site where John F. Kennedy had been shot barely three months earlier. He was home by January 24, but five days later he was off again to give a lecture in Philadelphia.

As though he had no wife and young daughter at home, Greenberg continued to travel widely, lecturing and feeding off the adulation of his sponsors. In October 1964 he was in Montevideo, Uruguay, for a talk at the General Electric Institute. In the spring of 1965, he made his first visit to Greece, breezing through the Acropolis and on to the usual tourist sites—Delphi, Cape Sounion, and Corinth—before flying on to Israel. There, he was feted at a museum opening and a press dinner, plus a lunch with Jerusalem's legendary mayor Teddy Kollek. After spending more than two weeks in Rome, Greenberg moved on to Portugal for several days before returning home on June 12. Two days later, he was watching *Love's Labor's Lost* with Jenny at an outdoor theater in Central Park. The play's title, though not its humorous plot, could describe the fraying relationship between this couple, little more than two years after their daughter was born.

This was the year when Greenberg's datebooks drastically changed. Instead of a full page for each day, crammed with notations of activities, people seen, drinks and meals consumed, and medications taken, he switched to datebooks with an entire week on two facing pages. Many days had no entries at all, leaving the impression that a great deal of activity had seeped out of his life. Still, each of the datebooks recording the forty-three most active years of Greenberg's life includes an ample section for addresses; each year, Greenberg laboriously entered the names and addresses of people with whom he wanted to stay in touch. While some names appear repeatedly, most of them changed over time, a fast-moving panorama of people met long enough to get an address and then discarded in favor of the next group.

After publishing only two book reviews for the rest of 1964, Greenberg's 1965 publications were also sparse. Faced by challenges from a growing cadre of critics, he seemed to shrink from debate and retired into a round of travels outside New York. In July, he was again seeing Ralph Klein, sometimes for two-hour sessions. Once again, he was seeking justification for his problems in maintaining intimate relationships. Years later, he would tell an interviewer that "Ralph Klein turned my life around." Greenberg said that before Klein's treatment, "I could never take my feelings seriously; my impulses. I was always looking to the world to get my bearings."

Certainly, he tried to take his family relationships seriously. In August, he vacationed on Cape Cod with Jenny and Sarah, before heading once again to Saskatchewan for ten days of critiquing artists and partying. In September, a visit to the theater was notable enough to be recorded in his now-truncated datebook. On October 9, he left for England and Paris, where he spent more than six weeks, socializing with contacts, shopping for Jenny's favorite perfume, Fracas, and attending the opening of an exhibition for Anthony Caro, a sculptor whom he warmly admired in an essay published at the end of the year.

This essay was part of a relationship with the British art scene that Greenberg had energetically cultivated. He often entertained English visitors to New York and would maintain his relationship with dealers like Leslie Waddington until the end of his life. In May 1963, a group of British sculptors in Anthony Caro's circle had chipped in to buy Greenberg a round-trip air ticket to London to critique their work. His colleagues, Caro wrote, would benefit from "the confidence gained from your belief in the work as well as your criticism." The head of the sculpture department at St. Martin's School, where Caro taught, begged Greenberg to lecture at the school while in London. He suggested that charging admission would enable the school to pay Greenberg's hefty speaking fee. In November 1965, Greenberg returned to England to chair a three-member jury for the John Moores art exhibition in Liverpool.

While Greenberg's publications were dwindling, a great many drafts of unpublished, and unpublishable, essays were accumulating in his files. This record shows a trail of attempts to cover large, complex subjects within the confines of a magazine article. He had been working since 1956, for example, on draft after draft of an essay called "Why the Old Masters Have so Little to Say Directly to the Practice of Ambitious Contemporary Painting." According to the editor of his papers, John O'Brian, Greenberg had inserted some portions of it into "The Case for Abstract Art" (1959), "Modernist Painting" (1960), and "How Art Writing Earns Its Bad Name" (1962). Aside from the awkward title, Greenberg added to his byline "the old man." It was not his age, however (Greenberg was only in his late fifties), but the contradictory content that doomed this piece. For he seemed to be criticizing contemporary painters for ignoring the Old Masters, something he himself had often urged upon avant-garde artists. And when one of those sassy Pop artists, Larry Rivers, painted a mocking series, "Dutch Masters and Cigars," in 1963, things had obviously gone beyond taking any essay like this seriously.

Greenberg's drafts for what may have been intended for essays or lectures show a stark contrast with his earlier writings. His crisp prose often dissolves into scribbled ramblings. One folder at the Getty contains twenty-four typewritten pages titled "Painting in a One-City Culture," drafted for delivery in Washington, and thirty-two pages of preliminary drafts for "Art Outside Metropolises," plus a twenty-page revision that began with deletion of the first fifteen pages of the preliminary draft. Unlike the sharp editor who would have caught such awkward phrasings as "factual truths," or tendentious assertions, such as that the audience for contemporary painting gives "a kind of interest and emotion [that it gives] to none of the other serious or highbrow arts," the current Greenberg floundered in a morass of verbiage. His goal in the latter essay was to demonstrate that throughout Western history, new art had emerged in urban areas outside large cities (perhaps like Regina, Saskatchewan?)—which found him asserting that medieval courts and monasteries were urban, since they produced art, and that Gothic churches were built only in small towns (which made it difficult to account for Paris and Cologne). The more Greenberg busily tried to scribble over hopeless oversimplifications, distortions, and errors, the more he seemed like an over-inflated balloon whose air was seeping slowly out.

Chapter VIII

THINGS FALL APART

A_S GREENBERG_ STRUGGLED to bring coherence to his writing, his enemies were on the watch for any sign of his flagging talents. The publication of *Art and Culture* had by now become a double-edged sword: his early pieces were readily exposed to criticism, and the sharply edited versions of some of them signaled that he himself had changed his mind. The book energized what had been underground murmurings and suspicions regarding Greenberg's central theory, codified as Formalism. On the one hand, it set forth some kind of Marxian historical necessity controlling the evolution of art, but on the other Greenberg freely summoned Kant to support the verdict of his now-famous "eye." Looking back to the Cubists of the early twentieth century, Greenberg's formalism traced a route that seemed to drive artists into increasing abstraction, while also emphasizing the flatness of the canvas. Such an emphasis on form drained the painting of all subject matter except itself. For some years, this appeared to be the only "scientific" way of looking at art; it offered a decent philosophical cloak for what had always been naked sensibility: I like it, I don't like it. However, by the mid-1960s, the covert connection between the "eye" and commerce surfaced in an unending wave of commercial speculation. Ivan Karp, the dealer who had sold Pop Art for Leo Castelli and discovered Andy Warhol, told a reporter that "the eye" was "a great mystique" that "doesn't require great intelligence or learning." He had identified "ten or twelve buyers who have the eye and manage to hit one in five buys."

Greenberg did not consider his own forays into selling artists he liked as being in the same class as the crass commercialism of someone else dealing in art he despised. When he liked an artist's work, Greenberg's efforts on his—and it almost always was *his*—behalf knew no limits. One of these artists was David Smith, whose sculpture Greenberg had lauded as far back as 1943. Over the years, he had visited Smith innumerable times at his home in Bolton Landing and had written any number of articles praising his work. The show of his sculptures that Greenberg organized at French & Co. in 1960 was the most successful of any Smith exhibition to date. When a collector at a subsequent show refused to pay more than $10,000, an artist standing nearby, Piero Dorazio, suggested Smith give it to Greenberg. Such was Smith's gratitude that he handed it over to Greenberg on the spot. Smith's violent death by alcohol and driving on May 23, 1965, presented a macabre echo of Jackson Pollock's death nine years earlier. This time, Greenberg was out of the country when Janice phoned with the news. He was staying in Rome with Dorazio and his wife, Virginia, and he paced anxiously for hours until another call gave him some details.

Upon returning to New York, Greenberg learned that he was one of three executors named in Smith's will; the others were Robert Motherwell and Ira Lowe, a Washington attorney. The State of New York, under its art-loving governor Nelson Rockefeller, was already eager to buy a Smith sculpture for a reflecting pool in front of one of fifteen buildings planned for a government office complex in Albany. The Smith estate included hundreds of sculptures of variable size and condition, as well as (a sign of his recent success) more than two thousand premium cigars, bought by the sculptor in Tampa, Florida, and stored in a climate-controlled vault at Dunhill's in New York.

Within six months of becoming an executor, Greenberg prepared a lengthy article ardently describing some of the works Smith left behind and stating that "the pace of his art . . . was developing faster than ever before." He was also active in setting policy and prices for the estate. In the two years before Smith's death, only five works had been sold, at prices ranging from $6,000 to $40,000. But such is the phenomenal escalation that often follows an artist's death that sales in the first year amounted to more than $500,000, and in the second year jumped to $2 million. Such rampant inflation caught the attention of the IRS, which in 1969 accused the executors of drastically undervaluing the Smith estate. They had estimated its worth at only $700,000, rather than the $5.25 million the IRS claimed. After a costly five-year journey through various courts, the estate was finally assessed at only an additional $71,433.

Meanwhile, the executors faced a dilemma common to most artists' legatees: should they flood the market and risk price declines, or dole works out slowly to maintain demand? Greenberg insisted on the slow option. By 1968, fewer than half of Smith's remaining works had been sold, and Greenberg had devoted several months to estate business, traveling numerous times to Bolton Landing to choose works for sale and meet with photographers, museum officials, critics, and prospective buyers. As compensation from the estate, he requested—and received—$150 per day, a total of less than $10,000 so far, for work that he estimated an outside expert would have charged at least $60,000. Finally, in 1970, the remaining Smith sculptures were turned over to the Marlborough Gallery to be sold at prices averaging in excess of $38,000.

Greenberg was still industriously writing, but by then he was publishing little. While a few interviews and musings were published later, the collected writings sanctioned by Greenberg dwindled to an end in 1969, when he was exactly sixty years old. The complete body of his writing was not published until twenty-four years later, just a year before he died. At this point, the only book setting forth his ideas remained *Art and Culture*. Sidney Tillim, an artist and critic who admired Greenberg, noted that his reputation "was created by his enemies because he did not write enough any more and consequently they keep alluding to articles way back when."

In the intervening years, the public's perceptions about art had changed drastically. Greenberg's early writings had been addressing an audience largely ignorant about art and eager for guidance into this uncharted realm; his goal was to educate the reader's taste in preparation for travel on the high road of upward mobility. But as the 1960s waned, most art writing was addressed either to professionals (dealers, collectors, museums) or to academics burnishing a career. People anticipating the Next Big Thing were confronted by an assortment of Big Things, and instead of two or three critics guiding the public's taste in new art, there was an array of museum curators, art historians, and other experts. But at the center of it all was a vacuum, a void in which all value judgments, including Greenberg's, crumbled. For better or worse, art criticism veered from the judgmental to the didactic; the critic would not endorse or disdain a particular artist, but instead would explain what the artist was trying to do; would not exercise personal taste or apply standards, but rather view art strictly as a creative product worthy of interest.

Several profound changes in American culture encouraged this new, more permissive attitude. The general loosening of societal norms seeped into all cultural expressions. In music, for example, the rock beat, the sensual swiveling of Elvis Presley, and the liberated tunes and lyrics of the Beatles had enchanted American youth and a good many of their elders, and now that public was ready for even more extreme music in the form of acid rock and the Rolling

Stones. Nudity and sexuality thrilled New York theatergoers, and readers were lapping up *The Joy of Sex*. In the face of such a thrill-seeking audience, critics shrank from judgments about new art. For most of them, it was difficult enough to make a living writing about art; rushing to promote artists, as Greenberg had done, could backfire when those artists failed to find success. The publication of Harold Rosenberg's dire analysis of "The American Art Establishment" in the middlebrow men's magazine *Esquire* was itself a new departure. He was astounded that people were paying $100,000 for a Pollock, $70,000 for a de Kooning, and $30,000 for a Jasper Johns. He was stunned by the establishment of countless new museums and the continual expansion of existing institutions. In the previous five years, a new museum had opened every three or four days in North America and established museums organized crowd-pleasing blockbuster exhibitions. Rosenberg described "earlier collectors . . . ridden down by people rushing to anticipate the market." He noticed that this new art universe's primary characteristic was constant flux: "One never knows who or what is going to put an artist across."

Lecturing in Australia three years later, Greenberg sounded a similar alarm over the American art world's "state of confusion." He saw that "innovations follow closer and closer on one another and, because they don't make their exits as rapidly as their entrances, they pile up in a welter of eccentric styles, trends, tendencies, schools." He worried that "boundaries between art and everything that is not art are being obliterated," while "high art is becoming popular and vice versa."

But while Rosenberg and Greenberg urged a return to standards, the exertion of taste, and defense of the traditional artistic order, younger, better-educated scholars viewed art increasingly in historical terms—"how any art related to, expanded, or deflected an established stream," wrote Amy Newman, an editor at *Art News* who chronicled the development of a new art periodical, *Artforum*. From its first issue in June 1962, *Artforum* deviated widely from its peers among art trade publications. It was published in San Francisco, not New York, and was the first American art publication devoted entirely to contemporary art. Its format was an awkward 10 1/2 x 10 1/2 inch square; any advertising prepared for the typical 9 x 11 inch magazine page would have to be resized. Years later, a French contributor suggested that *Artforum*'s style was a reaction to "the moody prose published by *Art News*," a style that hewed to "the French belletristic tradition of the poet-critic." Yet, *Artforum*'s early issues revealed a less ethereal struggle to find its voice and an economic niche. A year after its rocky start in San Francisco, the fifty-eight-page July issue included only five pages of advertising; as though in mourning for lack of support, the inside front and back covers were solid black. Long paragraphs of dense text about West Coast art filled most pages, broken only by small black-and-white illustrations.

Five years later, *Artforum* was an entirely different entity, in testimony to the overheated market for contemporary art. Now published in New York, its summer 1967 issue was nearly twice as long. While some articles by Minimalist artists like Robert Smithson, Donald Judd, and Sol LeWitt were distinctly unfriendly to Greenberg, most of the published art historians—Michael Fried, Barbara Rose, Robert Pincus-Witten, and Sidney Tillim—were devoted to Greenberg's formalism. Under the guidance of its editor, Phil Leider, *Artforum*'s circulation had doubled to nearly eleven thousand, and it had acquired a wealthy new publisher in the person of Charles Cowles, a scion of the Iowa newspaper and magazine clan.

Greenberg's partisans at *Artforum* most admired the theory he had expressed in "Modernist Painting," a Voice of America broadcast published in 1960 and widely reprinted thereafter. In it, he re-emphasized that Modernism was not "anything like a break with the past"; rather, the abstract art of the mid-twentieth century simply continued the Western canon. He credited Modernism with triggering the improved reputations of Uccello, Piero della Francesca, El Greco, Georges de la Tour, and even Vermeer. Modernism also enhanced Giotto's reputation while maintaining "the standing of Leonardo, Raphael, Titian, Rubens, Rembrandt, or Watteau." Such assertions were potent reassurance for young art historians, mainly graduate students schooled on the Old Masters and now trying to make sense of contemporary art. Barbara Rose observed that in the mid-1960s, *Artforum* was "dedicated to the propagation of Clement Greenberg's ideas."

But only a few years later, those who had espoused Greenberg's formalism in the pages of *Artforum* began to question his disdain for Frank Stella (who was then married to Barbara Rose), as well as the Pop artists and other innovators of the 1960s. As Rosalind Krauss put it, the younger critics "wanted to see the determinist 'choo choo train,' move forward a few stations." And as the 1960s ended, the congeniality between *Artforum* and Greenberg clashed increasingly with the magazine's bread and butter: the September 1970 issue contained thirty-two pages of advertising, half of them for art Greenberg scorned. Nor were the reviews of exhibitions in New York, Los Angeles, San Francisco, Chicago, Boston, and Texas based on the Greenberg gospel.

The following month, *Artforum* published "An Ad Reinhardt Monologue," the text of a newly discovered tape recorded before the artist's death in 1967. In it, the artist famous for producing a long string of large all-black paintings rambled on angrily about the art world, including a phrase accusing Greenberg of being an art dealer and a paid consultant to Andre Emmerich. Greenberg telephoned the magazine and curtly ordered Phil Leider to retract the offending phrase. "I could not retract a dead man's words,"

Leider argued, and suggested that Greenberg write the magazine a letter. When Greenberg insisted on a retraction, Leider said he was "stuck. And the next thing I knew there was a letter from a lawyer." Nothing legal materialized from that contretemps, but Greenberg assaulted Leider personally in a slashing letter: "When I first met you years ago I had the impression that you were some not quite identifiable kind of rodent. I then allowed us to have certain sorts of friendly relations. But this latest exchange teaches me once again how important it is to trust first impressions."

Greenberg's relationship with *Artforum* was ruined, but Phil Leider's tenure as editor also was shaky. Despite its advertising surge, the magazine was losing money. Charles Cowles's name was on the masthead as publisher, but the actual owner was his father, Gardner Cowles, who was pouring in $5,000 every month. Charles accepted art works from galleries as payment for advertising and romped through a lavish expense account. Near the end of 1970, Phil Leider was dismissed. When his replacement, John Coplans, discovered that there was no money to pay writers or the printer, he momentarily collapsed from the strain. Then he slashed expenses, persuaded Charles Cowles to stop flying first-class on the magazine's dime, and lent it $9,000 in exchange for one-third of the profits. Within four years, *Artforum* was earning $100,000 a year. For Greenberg, this change boded ill, as Coplans was skeptical of formalism and favorable to the waves of new art — Assemblage, Pop, Minimalism — cresting on the New York scene.

Greenberg's confrontation with *Artforum* could not have been more self-destructive. In October 1967, the magazine had been willing to accommodate his dim view of contemporary art writing by publishing his "Complaints of an Art Critic." In it, he had urgently backed away from his own theory that new art evolves according to certain history-driven rules. Instead, he now proclaimed that "aesthetic judgments are given and contained in the immediate experience of art" and "are involuntary: you can no more choose whether or not to like a work of art than you can choose to have sugar taste sweet or lemons sour." After decades of insisting that "history" decreed that successors to Cubism were Pollock and the Abstract Expressionists, followed by the Color Field painters, he now resented "imputations . . . that his aesthetic judgments go according to a position, a 'line.'" Greenberg's bitter foe Max Kozloff pounced upon this shift with a sarcastic letter, accusing Greenberg of shrinking from "the most interesting, because in part debatable, issues in our relation to art. How queasy of Mr. Greenberg, how fearful!" The conclusion of Greenberg's brief reply was equally personal: "Last and least, the sarcasm in Mr. Kozloff's letter is on a level with its matter."

Within the small world of New York art publications, news of Greenberg's bluster traveled quickly, and with a horde of newly minted art historians eager to acquire a portfolio of publications, not many editors wanted to tangle with an irascible art critic, a man whose views were now alienating many advertisers. At all four established art magazines circulation had risen swiftly. *Art in America*, which had been an anemic quarterly in 1930 and counted only an estimated ten thousand subscribers as recently as 1960, swelled in the following decade to a circulation of more than forty-one thousand. The September 1970 issue sold for $2.75; its glossy cover introduced 148 colorful pages, forty-nine of them advertising. Its editorial consultants included Alfred H. Barr, *New York Times* art critic John Canaday, Whitney Museum director Lloyd Goodrich, and Guggenheim Museum director Thomas S. Messer. *Art News* had also blossomed from an estimated sixteen thousand readers in 1950 to thirty-eight thousand in 1970, with one-third of its eighty-two pages given over to advertising. By April 1978, after Milton Esterow's purchase of the magazine, *Art News* was able to fill more than half the 158 pages in its April issue with ads.

Greenberg's relationship with *Art in America* had faltered back in 1963, when he had been commissioned to write an article on "Perspectives on the New York School." Instead, he had submitted something entirely different. The editor, Jean Lipman, wrote back that she was sadly unable to publish "this very generalized essay." The magazine did publish two more of Greenberg's pieces, in 1965 and 1966, but none thereafter. Unpublished articles, mostly the kind of "generalized essay" Lipman had rejected in 1963, piled up in Greenberg's files. Among these papers were twenty-four pages on "The Agony of Painting," with which Greenberg had intermittently struggled since shortly after Paul Klee's death in 1940. "The Newness of Color" was possibly prepared for Greenberg's Gauss Lecture series in 1958–59; unused then, its many pages show obsessive editing and retyping without a final manuscript. As his publications waned, Greenberg's concepts for essays or articles ballooned into hopelessly cloudy formulations. While the American art magazines of the 1970s sought out sharp writing and were not averse to theoretical pieces with footnotes, there was no market for Greenberg's views on, say, "The Decline of Art" or "Art Criticism and American Art." Nor was there interest in his five-page proposal for a television series titled "Why Modernist Painting Looks the Way It Does."

From a distance of almost half a century, Greenberg's displacement by younger art historians looks like the disrobing of an emperor—in part the normal evolution of generations, but couched in particularly venomous terms. Still, the stripping had little impact on the emperor's everyday activities. He was welcomed at galleries, dined and drank with his many contacts, and read prodigiously; artists by the dozen begged him for a studio visit, and invitations to speak poured into his mailbox. Institutions all over the world pampered Greenberg with first-class air travel, deluxe accommodations, and fancy fees simply for being there.

In 1966, the U.S. State Department sent him on a lavish six-week tour to Japan, where he accompanied a MoMA-sponsored exhibition, "Two Decades of American Painting" and met with students, artists, and professors "to explain . . . the meaning and significance of modern American art through interviews, lectures, and discussions." Armed with background data on all the people he would meet and accompanied by a State Department minder and a Japanese translator, Greenberg visited provincial art schools, museums, and libraries, participated in roundtable discussions, and was interviewed for local newspapers. At a roundtable with the Japan Art Critics' Society he received a fervent compliment from a retired professor of art history at Tokyo University: "I have been anti-American," he said. "You are the first American I met who has a real cultural-exchange personality amply representing America as she really is." No wonder that Greenberg kept every scrap of paper from this trip: assorted maps, an envelope with Japanese lettering from the Takamatsu Japan-America Cultural Society, and a banner reading, "Welcome Mr. Greenberg."

He quickly arranged for a similar trip to India the following year, accompanying the same exhibition for which he had toured Japan. It was the largest collection of American paintings ever seen in India, ninety-seven works by thirty-five artists. While the number of daily visitors never exceeded five hundred, many left provocative comments in the guest book: "inexplicable," "decadent and boring," "extremely exciting," "mystifying in a nice way," "delicious," and "tragic." At a roundtable, the director of India's National Gallery of Modern Art observed that "the principles underlying your art are diametrically opposed to the principles underlying traditional Indian art." To which Greenberg retorted: "Traditional Indian pictorial art died 100 years ago . . . You can say that I have no business coming here as an outsider and saying that. But you say it yourselves—those of you who are closest to art."

Barbara Rose believed that Greenberg was traveling as a CIA agent: "He had a kind of apostolic, evangelistic style," she said. "It was, 'You'll believe in me, my revealed truth, or you're not a true believer.'" In fact, Greenberg was simply a foot soldier in the decades-long American "cultural offensive" against the Soviet Union. A key feature of this campaign was to demonstrate the contrast between Soviet persecution of artists and artistic freedom in the West. The high hopes for Soviet liberalization of the arts, raised in 1956 by Nikita Khrushchev's denunciation of Josef Stalin's misdeeds, were dashed in succeeding years as the dead souls of party hacks retained their hold on Soviet arts. During a July Fourth visit to the American embassy in Moscow, the Soviet leader loudly criticized the art he saw on the walls there; he "did not agree that something good might come of experimentation in the arts." With Benny Goodman on hand, Khrushchev "commands jazz to go away . . . but it won't." So wrote the *New York Times*'s Moscow correspondent. It was the opening shot in an extended campaign by that powerful newspaper on behalf of artistic freedom in the Soviet Empire.

The quantity, the prominent positioning, and the disapproving tone of these articles persuaded a preponderance of American opinion makers that criticizing new art gave comfort to the Communist enemy. The subtext implied that anything calling itself art was good and that supporting abstract art was a blow for artistic freedom. Hammered as philistines, the critics of abstract art had melted away. This sea change in the serious public's view of new art lent strong support to Greenberg's argument on behalf of his chosen artists. While younger art critics might be nipping at his heels, his strong early support for the likes of Jackson Pollock, Barnett Newman, and David Smith lent conviction to his more recent selections of Color Field painters. Moreover, contrary to the quasi-Marxist underpinning of his early writings, such as

"Avant-Garde and Kitsch," his unswerving brief for abstract art had become a mantra for artistic freedom.

＊   ＊   ＊

After his public squabble in *Artforum* over "Complaints of an Art Critic," Greenberg left the unfriendly New York art scene in a huff. As that article was published, he was again receiving weekly therapy from Ralph Klein. Jenny was also seeing a therapist who held views similar to Klein's. Sarah had started school and her parents had quietly drifted into separate lives. For most of 1968, Greenberg saw Klein every week that he was in New York. However, he was also traveling a great deal, trying to stay away from the now hostile city. Like an aggrieved ten-year-old, Greenberg simply picked up his (very considerable) marbles and continued to play the game before friendly audiences somewhere else.

In May 1968, he was in Australia, giving the first of the series of locally prestigious John Power Lectures in Contemporary Art at the University of Sidney. With the hindsight of many aging people, he recalled a golden era in the late 1940s and 1950s when the Abstract Expressionists held center stage. In this talk titled "Avant-Garde Attitudes," he described the current scene as fraught with "nervousness of art opinion . . . One knows what is 'in' at any given moment," he said, "but one is uneasy about what is 'out.'" The uncertainty, he said, could "explain why critics have lately begun to pay so much more attention to one another than they used to." Then, the man who years ago had so lovingly described an avant-garde ceaselessly innovating while surviving on the margins of society lamented that "today, everybody innovates. Deliberately, methodically. And the innovations are deliberately and methodically made startling." With some reason, he blamed Marcel Duchamp, along with "the art journalism of the 60s," for the acceptance of Pop Art, but he confidently predicted that such art would be brought down by those who still applied "qualitative comparisons."

By then, Greenberg had realized that verbal expression offers an author more leeway than the printed word: speech travels lightly, impressing the audience without leaving vulnerable tracks, while an enemy can scrutinize writings at leisure, picking out inconsistencies or contradictions. An interview served a defensive strategy—getting his views before the public without the risk of being challenged. Even in interviews, Greenberg always insisted on reading the final text and reserved the right to edit it. A model for the many interviews to come was his conversation with the art critic Edward Lucie-Smith, published in *Studio International* in January 1968. For that British publication, Greenberg poured out his verdicts on various English artists. He was not a fan of Francis Bacon or Henry Moore, finding that they "share the capacity to impose oneself." He discerned in some Bacons "the cheapest, coarsest, least felt application of paint matter . . . along with the most transparent up-to-date devices." He still deemed the best American painters "the best in the world," but deplored the current, self-styled avant-garde as occupying "the *foreground* of the art scene," the same position, he said, as the much-maligned academic painters of the late nineteenth century, Bouguereau, Gerôme, and Alma-Tadema.

In a long and respectful interview for broadcast and distribution by the State Department's propaganda arm, the United States Information Service, Greenberg was never identified as a youthful left-wing radical or author of fiery articles opposing America's entry into the Second World War. Instead, the interviewer hung on his every word about the superiority of American art, New York's rise as the center for new art, and the impending collapse of Pop Art, followed by the failure of minimalism. As though reflecting on his own increasingly marginalized position in the New York art world, Greenberg concluded with an assertion that art should not be overrated: "The quality of art in a society does not necessarily . . . reflect the degree of wellbeing enjoyed by most of its members . . . The weal and woe of human beings come first," he concluded. "I deplore the tendency to overvalue art."

Greenberg was referring to the moral or aesthetic value of art. But he had worked hard on both sides of the Atlantic Ocean to raise the monetary value of works by the Color Field painters and the welded steel sculptors he favored. In 1965, he arranged for a successful London exhibition of Kenneth Noland's paintings; Noland's wife, Stephanie, gushed to Greenberg that even artists were "surprised, pleased, awed, or just plain worried" about the show's strong impression. Acting on behalf of the Morris Louis estate, Greenberg also arranged for Louis exhibitions at the London gallery of Leslie Waddington. Early in 1966, the gallery donated a Morris Louis to the Tate Gallery, a gesture dealers often make to lend prestige and to lift the prices of a particular artist's work.

Greenberg endured a prominent but mixed reputation within the British art world. His encouragement of Anthony Caro in the early 1960s had emboldened that sculptor to teach his students at St. Martin's College how to create welded metal sculptures that, according to one critic, "changed the look of British sculpture forever." At around the same time, by contrast, Greenberg had sent a postcard to John Latham, a part-time teacher at the same school, calling his sculpture "patly Cubist." Jurying a Liverpool exhibition, Greenberg had kept out a work by Latham. The artist retaliated by organizing a "Still and Chew" event in August 1966. He invited artists and students to his home to chew up one-third of the school library's copy of *Art and Culture*, and spit the wet mash into a flask. Latham then performed a quasi-occult ceremony distilling the book's essence into a small glass vial. When he received a "very urgent" overdue notice from the library almost a year later,

Latham instead returned the vial to the library. The deed cost him his job, but he later gathered all the documents and objects connected with "Still and Chew" into a black leather case. In 1991, it was "respectfully displayed" at the Oxford Museum of Contemporary Art as a key example of Conceptual Art.

And *Studio International*, while hosting Greenberg's own comments, was also a frequent forum for his detractors. In its pages, the critic Patrick Heron argued that while Greenberg's earlier writing presented a persuasive case for formalism, "he is now so overconfident that he merely massacres his victims." An American foe, the sculptor Donald Judd, accused Greenberg of trying "to impose a universal style." He found "despicable" the critic's assertion in a *Vogue* article that Judd's Minimalist brand of art did not sell well. Yet another writer labored academically over Greenberg's early writings, discerning a "Hegelian search for absolutes" that he found wanting in the current "chaotic, fragmented society" and totally "incompatible with Marxism."

Perhaps Greenberg's most engaging moments in Britain were the informal gatherings he hosted whenever he was in London, in the bar of the Dorchester Hotel. For those young English art enthusiasts who were willing to brave his prickly remarks—"I'm a highbrow. What are you?" was typical—he offered the insights gained from decades of savoring art. Steadily smoking and sipping straight vodka, he set forth his values. They did not include the Pop, Minimalist, and Conceptual art that was then popular; this he called "novelty art" and deemed it more threatening to art than the middlebrow culture he had deplored in the past. One of his young listeners, Tim Hilton, then a postgraduate scholar at the Courtauld Institute, revered Greenberg as "a tutor of ferocious kindness, or dismissiveness." Decades later, he recalled a man "thin as a refugee," a head with "an immense bald dome," possibly representing "the original 'egghead.'" In his "curiously English clothes," perhaps a jacket with oval leather patches, Greenberg exuded "an aura of wealth" as he preached to disciples in the bar of that elegant hotel. He would appear when the bar opened at 11 A.M., demanding "a triple vodka on the rocks! Not too many rocks! And the same for this Limey pansy!" Then he would hold forth for hours. A critic at bay, he was called "a reactionary, a tyrant, a would-be manipulator of the art market . . . and probably an agent of the CIA, for had he not contributed to *Encounter* [later revealed as covertly funded by the CIA] and broadcast on the Voice of America?" But to Hilton, he was unforgettable.

At home, Greenberg was also beset, not only by those who disagreed with his views on art, but by the steady unraveling of his marital ties. Jenny was often out with friends, and Greenberg spent many evenings with one or both of the Rubin brothers: William, who in 1968 had become chief curator of painting and sculpture at MoMA, and Lawrence, who exhibited many of Greenberg's favorite artists at Knoedler Contemporary Art in New York and at his Paris gallery. On other evenings, he dined with various women friends, identified in his datebooks only as Meg, Jill, Martha, Lia, Ceria, Tanya. Near the end of 1968, he was again seeing Ralph Klein at least weekly. That year he spent Christmas Day alone.

While Greenberg and Jenny had trouble living as a traditional couple, their therapy had prepared them for an open marriage and they came to terms with leading separate lives. Jenny started taking acting lessons and in 1970 moved out of the Central Park West apartment, with Sarah. But Greenberg "hated to deal with money," his daughter recalled, so Jenny continued to take care of the couple's finances, controlling the checkbook and paying bills. She also pressed Greenberg to demand more payment for appearances and lectures. Sarah received a "very progressive" education at the private Manhattan Country School and believed that "money was never an issue."

Although Sarah sometimes lived apart from him, her father gave her "unconditional love," took her on many trips, and willingly paid for her Vassar education as an art history major, even though, as she recalled, "a part of him was aghast." "Why not study French or Latin?" he asked her. Despite her obvious affection for her father, Sarah had few illusions about him. She realized that his over-consumption of alcohol was chronic and concluded that he had for many years been an alcoholic: "He just maintained a certain level of alcohol in his system," she said. He could be bombastic, she said, as he was portrayed in the 2000 film *Pollock*, and even overbearing, but he was never ostentatious. "People would give him boxes of Cuban cigars," she said, "but he made no show of smoking them."

Sarah fondly recalls her first trip with her father, in 1974, when she was barely twelve. They went to Paris "in style," she recalled. "It was a constant party." The following summer, Greenberg took Sarah and a school friend to South Africa, where he had been invited by the Art Institute to participate in roundtables and symposia, jury an art show, and give lectures. With the two girls, he also visited Kruger National Park, a game lodge, and Victoria Falls. The total experience was so memorable that he kept every scrap of paper he encountered there, including all the hotel and restaurant bills. When Sarah was sixteen, her father took her on a trip to Moscow and Leningrad. Soviet authorities had barred them from visiting artists' studios, but at the Hermitage they were invited to the storage rooms where the curators brought out their hoard of early modern paintings—Picassos and Matisses that were still locked away from public view. Greenberg was "tireless" in seeking out art, his daughter recalled; wearing sneakers, he was always ready for the next work. For Sarah, "It was a turning point. I decided I liked art." After graduation, Greenberg questioned her determination to open an art gallery, but made only muted protest when she financed it by selling a sculpture David Smith had given her when she was born. Although she felt confident of her taste in art, Sarah, like her father, hated dealing with the financial side and the salesmanship involved, and the gallery did not last long.

Dark-haired and pretty, slender, bright, and a confident New Yorker, Sarah found her calling as a photo editor at a national magazine and as a wife and the mother of two daughters. The oldest, Clementine, talks of her grandfather, even though she was born three years after he died. The younger daughter was born in 2001 and has learned to pat the head of an Anthony Caro bust of Greenberg in her home.

*   *   *

In 1972, Jenny located an unusual house in Norwich, a small town in upper New York State some 150 miles north of the city. She and Greenberg bought it, probably as a vacation retreat. The house is based on plans drawn by Frank Lloyd Wright in 1940 for a moderately priced 1,250-square-foot dwelling that could be mass-produced. Playing on the initials "USA," Wright called it a "Usonian House" and expected his carefully thought-out design to drive out the "stupid makeshifts," the "stuffy and stifling little colonial hot boxes" commonly built in America. The house is set on a concrete pad, hidden from the rural road down a steep driveway. The entry opens into a living room dominated on the right by a massive fireplace wall of native stone extending from the floor to the apex of the cathedral ceiling. Straight ahead, a wall of windows opens on a forest view. To the right, off a corridor lined with storage areas, are two bedrooms, a small powder room, and a spacious full bath. Natural materials dominate the house, a slate floor in the entry and hallway, and natural wood beams and window framing. A boiler, recently replaced, provides hot water to kitchen and baths, as well as to copper heating pipes in the floor.

This version of the Usonian house was built in 1954. The design had failed to catch on for mass production, and is probably the only such dwelling in the northeast. The Greenbergs purchased it from the original owners. The current owner, Bonnie Gale, who bought it from the Greenbergs in 1990, is still impressed with 'how it relates to the site." The building was so carefully positioned that on sunny days, the pump sending hot water to the radiant heating ducts embedded in the floor turns itself off. Greenberg's daughter recalled the house as dark, enveloped by trees, and her father tossing coffee grounds onto the lawn, saying he was feeding the grass. When Bonnie Gale moved in, she scraped away the starved lawn down to bedrock and trimmed some of the trees, revealing a sylvan landscape fading to blue toward the horizon.

In a town drenched in its colonial past, this distinctly modern house modestly offers a breath of fresh air, but is so well hidden that hardly a neighbor is aware of its existence. Despite its relationship to a distinguished American architect, it is omitted from any lists of local historic landmarks. Beginning in 1974, Greenberg spent most of his time here, commuting from New York City to Binghamton and covering the remaining forty-five miles to Norwich in a rented car. It was a long day's trek, and treacherous in winter storms, but something about the charm and long history of Norwich spoke to him. Perhaps it was the village's leafy streets lined with fine examples of every northeast style of architecture: Puritan white clapboards, white stone Greek Revivals, and colorful gingerbread Victorians. The front porch survives here still, its roof often supported by ornamental pillars and posts; by contrast, windows are small, to help husband warmth during fierce winter weather. In that town, there was a hint of the Ocean Parkway house in which Greenberg grew up, but without those contentious Jews. Perhaps he was attracted to the unvarnished serenity of the place, contrasting so starkly with the frantic Manhattan life and the confrontations that beset him there.

It may be that Norwich's mainstream mentality provided a setting more accepting and less argumentative than the podium Greenberg was increasingly defending. His daughter recalled an intense relationship he developed in the town with a man named Al. Her father spent many happy hours arguing with Al, who was a Catholic, over passages in the Bible; when Al died, Greenberg wept bitterly. On the other hand, Greenberg's sojourn here of more than fifteen years left hardly a trace in Norwich. Less than a decade after his death, a diligent search turned up not a single person who remembered him or had even heard of him.

In 1973, Jenny moved into the house full time. She sent a reluctant Sarah to the local public school, helped to revive a historic opera house in the nearby village of New Berlin, and taught drama in the local high school. Mother and daughter lasted only a year in Norwich. Then Greenberg made the house his primary residence, triumphantly reminding his many correspondents that he was now to be found at Chenango Lake Road. It was there that Greenberg ripened into a notable curmudgeon, in a house designed by one of the twentieth century's most gifted curmudgeons. There, stretched out before a roaring fire, he can be pictured reading many of the works he faithfully recorded in his datebooks during those years: Wittgenstein's *Philosophical Investigations* and Richard M. Huber's *The American Idea of Success*; Gerda Taranow's *Sarah Bernhardt* and Terence McLaughlin's *Music and Communication*; and, still on a lifelong track, Michael Podro's *The Manifold of Perception: Aesthetic Theories from Kant to Hildebrand*, Erich Fromm's *The Crisis of Psychoanalysis*, Lars Gustafson's *Selected Poems*, Charles Rosen's *Classical Style*, Robert Bridges's *The Spirit of Man*, Lionel Trilling's *Sincerity and Authenticity*, and Allan Staley's *The Pre-Raphaelite Landscape*. He was even interested in the pioneer of the Dadaists, reading Noël Arnaud's *Alfred Jarry d'Ubu Roi au*

Docteur Faustroll. So went Greenberg's enduring quest for what the towering nineteenth-century intellectual, poet, and literary critic Matthew Arnold defined as criticism: "a disinterested endeavor to learn and propagate the best that is known and thought in the world."

In 1974, Greenberg's relatively serene semiretirement as a scholar was shattered by a woman who for years had sat at his feet. In the early 1960s, Greenberg had often met with Rosalind Krauss, then a graduate student at Harvard University. Greenberg was "courtly . . . affable," she said. Like other graduate students, she would come to New York to visit art exhibitions and then, near the end of the day, stop by at his apartment for a drink. "It was sort of a ritual," she recalled. She had expected to write a doctoral thesis in modern French art, but in 1965, when she heard that David Smith had died, "a light went on in my head," and she began work on a catalogue raisonnée of the Smith oeuvre. In 1966, Greenberg recommended that she be given access to all the David Smith Papers that the estate had deposited at the Archives of American Art. He considered her catalogue raisonnée an important contribution, so he also suggested that she contribute to a catalogue for an exhibition of Smith's sculptures being prepared by the MoMA.

On a lecture tour through the Midwest, Krauss was surprised to find that many private and public art collections were "look-alikes," most including something by Noland, Olitski, Poons, Warhol, and Lichtenstein, "a sort of explosion of art collectors and art centers" built around "essentially the same collection," with four of every six paintings by "Greenberg-approved artists." Greenberg "saw himself as Mr. Clean," Krauss told an interviewer much later, "the disinterested observer whose motivation was beyond question. He freely involved himself wherever art he championed was concerned and he was rarely circumspect."

Toward the end of the 1960s, Krauss's relationship with Greenberg became "tortured," she recalled. She disagreed with his hawk-ish views about the Vietnam War and resented his vehement dis-missal of the sculptor Richard Serra as "a fake." While teaching at Harvard in the summer of 1970, Krauss had an epiphany. With the slide of an early Picasso landscape as a backdrop, it suddenly occurred to her that her lecture was merely a regurgitation of Greenberg's views—"the general rap about the paintings getting flatter and flatter and blah-blah-blah"; when she turned around to look at the slide, however, she saw "this huge amount of space in the painting." She told her students, "Everything I said to you in the last twenty minutes is a total lie." After that point, she recalled, "I began to see that this gang had become totally doctrinaire." And when she wrote about a Cubist exhibition a year later, Greenberg deemed her "apostate" and began to be "very, very rude to me." It was not long after this that Krauss left behind "ten years of my experience and a kind of juvenile relation to authority figures."

In 1974, Krauss consummated the break by publishing a graph-ically illustrated article, in which she revealed that Greenberg was responsible for stripping paint from Smith's sculptures and leaving them outdoors to rust in wintry northern New York. She added that some had been coated with "another substance" resembling "shiny opaque brown paint . . . This gravy-like slipcoat transforms the crisp, assertive, light-reflecting white or yellow-painted shapes and surfaces into dark, light-absorbing forms." Others were rusted practically beyond repair. She contrasted "the whole chocolaty contingent of 'new' Smiths," with pristine examples in a Newport, Rhode Island, exhibition, asking, "Is a Smith of another color still a Smith?" The text of the article wound around photographs of Smith's original painted sculptures and what Krauss described as "an aggressive act against the sprawling, contradictory vitality" of Smith's oeuvre. She found it "particularly disturbing" that Greenberg and Motherwell were executors of Smith's will. Also mentioned was a letter Smith himself wrote about unauthorized painting of one of his works.

In strictly legal terms, however, there appeared to be no impediment to altering works of art, although moral rights for the integrity of a work of art were frequently cited. Nor was the matter as straightforward as Krauss claimed even in moral terms, for Greenberg had at least two contradictory letters from Smith in his files. In one, the sculptor wrote that he had been "obsessed with the sculpturally painted concept for years." The other, written a year before his death, asserted that "paint is something I'm never finished with . . . solid color is too easy and not my challenge." In a letter responding to an account of the scandal in *Newsweek*, one longtime owner of a Smith recalled the sculptor telling him: "Paint it. Repaint it, let it rust, do anything you want with it." Interviewed by Hilton Kramer in the *New York Times*, Greenberg took full responsibility for ordering the removal of white paint—which he considered only primer—from a number of Smith sculptures. The sculptor had never intended it to be the final coat, he said; the paint "misrepresented Smith's intentions." A follow-up the next day reported that many experts found the painted sculptures less impressive than the bare ones. However, even Kramer, who subscribed to Greenberg's formalism, deemed his actions questionable. Kenneth Noland wrote to Kramer asserting that he had had many discussions with Smith about color and was certain that Smith would have condoned Greenberg's changes. The art chair at a college near Bolton Landing also defended Greenberg on the basis of interviews with Smith's assistant Leon Pratt. Greenberg himself drafted a testy letter to the *Christian Science Monitor* about its own critical article on the Smith sculptures. None of his critics "happens to have a self that I respect," he wrote. "When someone with a character I have a regard for does the exclaiming, I'll be given pause, if only privately."

The immediate fallout from the article was intense. Robert Motherwell abruptly resigned as executor of the Smith estate. Soon, a high-powered panel was discussing the issue at New York's Cooper Union art school. It included Krauss, the art critic Dore Ashton, College Art Association president Albert Elsen, and the association's attorney Franklin Feldman. Kenneth Noland told a reporter covering the event that he would gladly make Greenberg the executor of his own estate. Greenberg did not deny removing the paint, but grumbled that so far, no protests had come from anyone "whose character and competence I respect." And he continued to defend his paint-stripping: as late as 1991, he was sure he had done the right thing: "They looked better with the naked metal," he told an interviewer.

Still, the damage was done and the controversy shadowed the rest of Greenberg's life. Barbara Rose noted that with publication of that article, "his entire cover was blown . . . a man who would alter the work of an artist posthumously really is not credible." Some thirty years after the event, and three years after Greenberg died, Robert Hughes considered the incident worth including in his epic history of American art. It was "an extraordinary violation of an artist's posthumous rights in the name of a critic's opinion," he wrote in the late 1990s. Irving Sandler, who chronicled the New York School of the 1950s and 60s, was sure more than forty years after the event that Smith would have been furious at having paint stripped from any of his sculptures. Sandler recalled Smith showing him a piece painted white and saying it had at least ten coats of paint, as he was trying to get the color just right.

The scandal further marred Greenberg's reputation. Having exiled himself from New York, he seemed to be unable to write anything publishable. His relationship with Jenny was practically finished. In 1970, they had agreed on a friendly separation: they nonetheless wrote separate wills in favor of each other, filed a joint tax return, and bought a car together. Jenny and Sarah moved to a loft on West Twenty-first Street. They communicated often and Sarah frequently stayed with her father. As she later described the arrangement, "They lived apart much of the time I was growing up. They had an 'open marriage,' and each had affairs with others."

The Smith scandal had barely subsided before another anti-Greenberg barrage arrived from a totally unexpected direction. In April 1975, *Harper's* published a lengthy article by Tom Wolfe, a well-known journalist brandishing a mordant wit and a Yale Ph.D. in American Studies. "The Painted Word" targeted several art critics who had promoted the Abstract Expressionists, but at the bull's-eye stood Clement Greenberg, the seer whose prose "would veer from the most skull-crushing Göttingen Scholar tautologies, 'essences' and 'purities' and 'opticalities' and 'formal factors' and 'logics of readjustment' . . . to cries of despair & outrage as would have embarrassed Shelley." For thirty-five pages in this prestigious magazine, Wolfe railed against the pernicious art theories spouted by postwar critics, most egregiously "Greenberg, Rosenberg and Flat." The goal of flatness, Wolfe went on, "inspired such subtle distinctions, such exquisitely miniaturized hypotheses, such stereotactic microelectrode needle-implant hostilities, such brilliant, if ever–decreasing tighter-turning spirals of logic, that it compares admirably with the most famous of all questions that remain from the debates of the Scholastics: 'How many angels can dance on the head of a pin?'"

A rakish full-length portrait of the author occupied the entire back dust-jacket of the slim book that soon emerged. He was posing in an immaculate white three-piece suit and white shoes—his jaunty hip-shot pose backed by a Chippendale doorway with gleaming brass fittings. Spread over just 121 pages, it was liberally illustrated by the Wolfe's own drawings. The text also was riddled with factual errors, but Wolfe's baroque prose—impeccable clauses hitched together with colorful, if reproachful, adjectives—was amusing, even habit forming.

Wolfe's screed galvanized the various factions of the New York art world. William Phillips of *Partisan Review* offered Greenberg as much space as he needed, "and, of course, a decent fee," to write a reply. "All kinds of culturally well-intentioned people who make up the world of semi-educated opinion are affected by Wolfe's kind of thinking," he wrote. Always feisty, Greenberg replied that Wolfe did not deserve an answer as a "keen enough graduate student" could point out Wolfe's errors of fact. "And since when," he asked Phillips, "has *Partisan Review* addressed itself to semi-educated opinion?" Elsewhere, *The Painted Word* was widely reviewed, including a three-page, self-flagellating *New York Review of Books* article in which Barbara Rose blamed herself and some colleagues for such publications. "We were so enthusiastic about the art that moved us," she wrote, "that we oversold it to an uninformed audience unwilling to make the effort to understand difficult works . . . a public that could only . . . resent . . . the art and the criticism they were bound to find unintelligible."

Beyond the outrage of art insiders, Tom Wolfe's lampoon amused many readers but his message found few converts. Greenberg continued to be in strong demand as an art juror and speaker. And the more he spoke, the less he prepared. For a talk about Matisse and the Fauves at the National Gallery in April 1973, he had only a brief text, holding forth on the basis of a few pieces of paper covered with scribbled abbreviations and addenda. As time went on, his daughter Sarah noticed that his formal talks grew "shorter and shorter," and eventually "they got down to ten minutes." But then he would go on for a long time answering questions, "which is what he really relished."

✳   ✳   ✳

Greenberg was in Norwich when his father died at the age of nine-ty-six, on July 15, 1977, and there is no record that he attended the funeral. Although the old man lived at 360 Central Park West, only eight blocks away from the Greenberg apartment, Sarah recalls seeing her grandfather only twice and barely meeting her cousins. Greenberg had long ago broken with Joseph, and had spent most of his life fighting the vicious and demanding specter that he had internalized as representing him. Although the unspoken messages that pass between a father and a son are often incomprehensible, even to the participants, Greenberg appeared never to have come to terms with the demons that his father represented.

The estrangement was embodied in Joseph Greenberg's will: his second wife, Fan, received the mandatory one-third of the estate; of the remaining amount, Greenberg's brothers, Martin and Sol, were given more than 30 percent each, while Greenberg received only 2.5 percent. Six months before he died, Joseph had also given $10,000 in real estate holdings to every child, except Clement. The reason for such allocations, Joseph noted in the will, "was not that I have less or more affection for any one of them as opposed to any other, but [it] simply represents my own judgment concerning their respective financial needs and resources." Even by the typically low appraisals of estates for tax purposes, Joseph's properties were substantial, well in excess of $500,000. Greenberg's estrangement from his father was costly, not only for himself but also for his daughter, whose trust was roughly half of what her cousins received.

At around this time, perhaps bolstered by this inheritance and some $300,000 Jenny had inherited from her mother, the long-separated couple decided to legalize their division, and in 1979 they divorced. Near the end of the year and in faraway Australia, Greenberg discussed his own failures with surprising frankness. The interviewer from *Weekend Australian Magazine* found him not only agreeable, but perfectly candid as he ticked off his mistakes: his first marriage, his embrace of socialism, his overconfident rhetoric, which, he admitted "covered up a lot of insecurities." A "really good writer," he now asserted "lets his insecurities hang out—that would have been a lot more fun." He now realized that he had "provoked a lot of needless anger just by my manner . . . The way I presented myself in my prose was a symptom of . . . insecurity." When he was asked in a survey how he would like to be in another life, he replied that he "would like to be born with different parents" and "with innate gentleness." At the age of seventy, on the threshold of old age, Greenberg had acquired some capacity for self-knowledge and some tolerance, even of his own foibles. He appeared comfortable with his interviewer's description of him as "a much-mellowed man."

Chapter IX

IN THE POSTMODERN WILDERNESS

By the end of 1978, Greenberg could well have relaxed the severe self-criticism that underlay so much of his harsh disparagement of others. His two most vocal opponents, Thomas B. Hess and Harold Rosenberg, had passed away earlier that year, a mere twenty-four hours apart. While their feud with Greenberg had entertained the art crowd for decades, their fundamental approach to writing about art in many ways mirrored his own. All three had made do with only scant formal training, and instead practiced what was now seen as an old-fashioned, moralistic brand of criticism. Their role was essentially liturgical, to guide the reader away from the tawdry or superficial toward what they deemed the best, an approach that the younger cohort of art historians considered not only unnecessary but deplorably elitist.

Greenberg's longtime bête noire, Harold Rosenberg, had died of a heart attack on July 12 at the age of seventy-two. Along with Greenberg, he had taken a dim view of the new art, but never once, in all the millions of words he had spoken and written, had he acknowledged a common cause with Greenberg. The very next day, and one day before his fifty-eighth birthday, Thomas B. Hess also succumbed to a heart attack. He collapsed at his desk at the Metropolitan Museum of Art five months after he had been named consultative chairman of the Department of Twentieth Century Art, succeeding Henry Geldzahler.

Only a year before his death, Hess had curated a widely praised exhibition of the New York School at the New York State Museum in Albany. Among the admirers of that show was Hess himself, who gave it a rave review in *New York* magazine. Perhaps it was his patrician background that muted criticism of such blatant self-dealing, but more likely it was his sparkling personality and wicked wit. The novelist Donald Barthelme, who briefly served as director of the Contemporary Art Museum in Houston, gleefully recalled Hess's description of a 1965 Op Art exhibition at the MoMA as "gadgetry bitten by art, dreaming about science." At a dinner party less than a week before his death, Hess entertained a group that included Helen Frankenthaler with his usual "ferocious, man-eating, illuminating jokes." Others in a long tribute to Hess in *Art in America* noted that during his brief tenure at the Met, he had already reinstalled three galleries of twentieth-century art, that he was "the funniest man" that the London *Times* art critic John Russell had ever met. Several others drew favorable comparisons between Hess and Greenberg. One noted that for Hess, "the work of art was not something to be snared in a web of ideas, rather, the painting would emerge from his comments as if newly cleaned." Another recalled that Hess had once written that Greenberg "had his teeth straightened and capped—thus marring the only honest feature in his face."

With the passing of Greenberg's two main rivals, a poetic style of critical writing all but disappeared. Originating in France, finding some of its most potent formulations in the prose of the nineteenth-century poet Charles Baudelaire and the twentieth-century poet and cultural impresario Guillaume Apollinaire, this form of criticism now struck many as hopelessly outdated. Rosenberg's razorlike wit and mercurial personality were recalled with affection and awe, but of the enormous body of his writings on art, only his 1952 essay presenting the Abstract Expressionists as "Action Painters" had much traction outside the academy. As for Hess, his career as an editor was widely admired—Barbara Rose called him "the most talented . . . who had taken art as a subject since Baudelaire . . . a genuinely literary personality with a breadth of culture unmatched in what was essentially still a provincial New York scene"—but by the 1980s he, too, had become a marginal figure. And the artist they had championed, Willem de Kooning, was seen by many as "a Frankenstein" created by Rosenberg and Hess in their effort to give 'life' to their romantic fantasies about art."

Greenberg was outside the country when Rosenberg and Hess died. In June, he had joined the faculty of the Salzburg Seminar in American Studies, an annual gathering of arts notables sponsored jointly by the Austrian and American governments. As another skirmish in the Cold War cultural offensive against Soviet Russia, the two-week session at Schloss Leopoldskron on "The Creative Arts and Contemporary Society" also attracted the heads of the National Endowment for the Arts, the Ford Foundation, and the National Council on the Arts. Afterward, Greenberg and his daughter Sarah traveled—somewhat ironically—to the Soviet Union.

It was most likely during this trip that Greenberg gave an interview about the future of the avant-garde to a German radio program, with the text later published in a leading German art periodical. Conveniently forgetting the Cubists and Surrealists, among others, he remarked that the Abstract Expressionists were the first avant-garde to achieve recognition in their own time. He did not consider Pop Art a genuine avant-garde, he said, because it was "too easy to grasp." The rule for the past century, he said, was, "The more powerful the art, the more resistance to it . . . Conversely: The faster an artist is successful, the less significant his art."

These modifications in his theory of how art evolves confirmed Greenberg's new situation as a conservative, a defender of modernism, which he now saw eclipsed by that carelessly named new trend, Postmodernism. Like Hess and Rosenberg, Greenberg was temperamentally and chronologically unable to accept the mocking, skeptical, ironic, and often trivial shenanigans at the cutting edge. As early as 1970, Irving Howe, the literary critic Greenberg had fostered so long ago at *Commentary*, had also noticed that the search for the "new" was "often reduced to a trivializing of form and matter," dwindling speedily to "the predictable old." He deplored that "alienation has been transformed from a serious and revolutionary concept into a motif of mass culture, and the content of modernism into the décor of kitsch." A few years later, in *Partisan Review*, Howe explained that the union between radicalism and modernism, as expressed in the early years of that periodical, "was neither a proper marriage nor a secure liaison: it was a meeting between parties hurrying in opposite directions, brief, hectic, and a little messy." William Barrett, another veteran of those late 1930s and 40s radical frays, was also disappointed by the successors to modernism. Instead of being displaced by another worthy avant-garde, as had been expected, "the Zeitgeist was to find its expression in a riotous proliferation of new schools, often tendentious and in conflict with each other." The entire notion of good taste had become suspect and "sounded 'elitist,'" an attitude that postmodernist jargon condemned as "damnable."

With his peers gone and his own status questioned, Greenberg himself weighed in with a rare *Partisan Review* article on "The State of Criticism." It is doubtful that Hess or Rosenberg would have found much to quarrel with as Greenberg bemoaned the new critics' penchant for analyzing art rather than reacting to it. In support, he cited the elitist literary critic E. D. Hirsch, who faulted the self-described New Critics for replacing the value question that had ruled literary theory since Plato—"Is it good?"—with the more neutral "What does it mean?" In that context, wrote Greenberg, "art will get explained, analyzed, interpreted, historically situated, sociologically or politically accounted for, but the response that brings art into experience as art, and not something else— these will be unmentioned."

When the MoMA celebrated Picasso with a blockbuster exhibition in 1980, the quintessential modernist artist was reinterpreted with a postmodernist overlay. His legacy, wrote a reviewer in *Art in America* "was his subversion of accepted attitudes concerning illusion and reality." Hardly represented were Picasso's haunting early Pink Period and Blue Period paintings, his Classical Period of the 1920s, and his vast body of graphic works. Such an attitude signaled the arrival of the arch-jokester Marcel Duchamp at the center of a new anything-goes aesthetic. Ignored by that superficially more inclusive judgment about art was the yawning chasm between those who were enchanted by imitative creations based on Duchamp's uniquely cerebral art, mostly academics and academically trained artists, and the wider art public that strenuously resisted the nihilism and mockery proposed by Duchamp's followers.

In response, staunch opponents of postmodernism around the world rallied to their typewriters. In order to reassure themselves of the continuing value of the kind of art they had for years collected, they would summon the venerable critic for a lecture. The postman on Greenberg's rural route brought frequent letters warmly inviting him to speak on whatever subject he wished.

In October 1979, Greenberg gave the Fourth Annual Sir William Dobell Memorial Lecture at the University of Sydney on "Modern and Postmodern." While his original draft was laden with abbreviations, emendations, and interlinear afterthoughts, the two hundred copies of the printed and bound edition crisply elucidated his quarrel with postmodernism. As reprinted in *Arts Magazine* the following February, he described modernism as "the continuing endeavor to stem the decline of aesthetic standards threatened by the relative democratization of culture under industrialism." He viewed the consumers of postmodernist art as philistines in disguise, and their patronage as a way "to justify oneself in preferring less demanding art without being called reactionary or retarded."

While such views were largely ignored by the self-styled devotees of the "cutting edge" in the academic world, they continued to be in demand at many other institutions—including academe—where modern art lovers gathered. A lecture on "The Decline of Taste Internationally" near the end of 1980 attracted an appreciative audience to the Kalamazoo Art League, and Greenberg was welcomed to repeat his talk the following evening at the University of Western Michigan. He attributed the decline of taste to the increasing centralization of art, in Paris during the nineteenth century and in New York following the Second World War. Such a concentration of art producers and consumers, he argued, led to "provincialization" of the rest of the western world. Although he himself had done much to promote this state of affairs, he now found it troubling that even art that originated elsewhere had to be confirmed in New York.

Following up on his disillusion with the New York art scene, Greenberg traveled to Vancouver, Canada, to offer, at another conference on modernism, a prescription for coping with what he diagnosed as decadence. He reviewed his scheme for the development of modernism as a reaction to the "radical lowering of esthetic standards" in the mid-nineteenth century, and insisted that the modernist spirit was still vital, able to "resist decline."

While resisting the new as adamantly as he had earlier embraced it, Greenberg experienced no dearth of audiences, which allowed him to carefully select his venues and honoraria. When a Guggenheim Museum curator of a forthcoming 1981 exhibition of works by Arshile Gorky asked for his recollections of that artist, Greenberg quietly ignored it. When invited to participate in a one-day seminar on "Questions of Method in 20th Century Studies" at the National Gallery's Center for Advanced Study in the Visual Arts, Greenberg wrote on the invitation, "not ansd"; among the invitees was Meyer Schapiro, who had frequently crossed scholarly lances with Greenberg, while Rosalind Krauss was the seminar's senior fellow. But Greenberg eagerly accepted $1,000 for a half-hour talk plus questions in connection with the exhibition "The Abstract Expressionists and Their Precursors" at the Nassau County Museum of Fine Art. And in the spring of 1981, he was pleased to receive a free trip and three-star lodging in Lausanne to participate in a two-day colloquium at the Cantonal Beaux Arts Museum. The discussion was on a topic often sponsored by various American government propaganda agencies during those Cold War years: "Dialogue between America and Europe."

Like many an intellectual pioneer who spends his later years deploring whatever came next, Greenberg had built up a tidy following as a sort of fire brigade, summoned to stamp out the flames of innovation. But clearly it was a holding action; for better or worse, time was on the side of the younger, better-trained, and more energetic art historians and critics who were filling the art trade press with learned—if sometimes unintelligible—articles. Moreover, these periodicals were prospering from a preponderance of advertisers for the new kinds of art; their editors were unlikely to welcome the views of an art critic who insisted that this same art was decadent and essentially worthless.

Still, in the late 1970s Donald Kuspit, an art historian with serious credentials and numerous publications, prepared a monograph on Greenberg's criticism. In 1979, his scholarly study, *Clement Greenberg: Art Critic*, was published. "The importance of the artists Greenberg singled out for attention is no longer in question," Kuspit wrote, even though "the principles of his art criticism . . . remain controversial." By recognizing and publicizing the American art he considered superior to the Europeans', Kuspit wrote, Greenberg "had done as much for the development of American abstract art as any artist." Kuspit also suggested that Greenberg used his formalist theory to counter "a romantic component to aesthetic experience. For it is a reminder of the way life slips out of control of art . . . It is a reminder of the raw emotion that artistic exhilaration means to sublimate."

Kuspit's book was intended for a scholarly audience and its reviews provide evidence of how postmodernist scholars were thinking. *Art News* remarked that it couldn't imagine its readers being interested in a book written "with the intelligence of a scholasticist theologian" in "glutinous prose . . . [with] very little affection for the sensual, the tragic, or the richly disorderly." The *Journal of Aesthetics and Art Criticism* called Greenberg's views "limited" and questioned Kuspit's effort to cast him as a "philosopher critic." In the posh periodical *Leonardo*, the reviewer expressed the postmodernist critique most clearly, finding "insufferable snobbishness" in Greenberg's embrace of "the objects of ordinary people when they take the form of naïve folk crafts associated with the pastoral scene" while he "despises whatever is produced for their appeal in urban circumstances." Furthermore, Kuspit failed to mention how Greenberg's principles "expressed the ideology of the marketplace."

Already branded an elitist art marketer, Greenberg was next pilloried in New York's *Village Voice* by two women offering "A Double Take." Purporting to review Kuspit's "clumsy, difficult take," Kay Larson called for "a real biography" examining "his leverage on the art market, his commanding tone toward artists, his repainting of David Smith sculptures . . . [and] his peculiar dominance over three generations of critics." Larson then rolled out her most damning critique: "'Feminine was a pejorative for Greenberg." Her colleague, Carry Rickey, attacked Kuspit for writing "an epic shell game: you shell a ton of pods and yield a dozen peas." Furthermore, Kuspit's book was "so densely written that it must be the most potent soporific ever devised." Greenberg did not exactly defend Kuspit, but he did reply with some sober corrections: He had never organized traveling exhibitions of American art, he wrote, but only lectured about exhibitions organized by the MoMA; he had not painted Smith sculptures but only removed primer from seven of them. As for the "leverage on the art market" cited by Larson, "Could she do me the favor of documenting that? Would that it was, or had been a fact." Rickey's riposte appeared along with Greenberg's letter. She took issue with Greenberg's taste, suggesting that taste was an elusive quality and the "chase for taste" resembled "a supermarket sweep—a rush through the aesthetic grocery store for reassurance that all art modes are created equal." To which Greenberg apparently felt compelled to reply once again. He quibbled with Rickey's assertion that many of his "acolytes" were professors. She should "put up or shut up," he wrote, "'acolytes' is an invidious word." Then he quoted Plautus on how "ad hominem critics invite facetiousness" and Goethe's *Mephistopheles*'s warning about trading jokes with women. To which Larson replied: "Didn't I say that if you scratched 'the father of criticism,' you'd discover a paternalistic woman baiter?"

*   *   *

In early June 1982, Greenberg received a letter that would be the key to reviving his reputation and securing him a prominent place in the history of American art. John O'Brian had begun reading Greenberg's critical writings after hearing him speak in Toronto. Born in Britain, he was raised in Canada after his parents emigrated following the Second World War. He had majored in political economy at the University of Toronto, then embarked on what he described as a "tolerably successful" ten-year career as an investment banker. Along the way, he had married and fathered three children, while cultivating friendships with artists and writers; he had also published poetry. Now in his early thirties, O'Brian had taken a B.A. in art history at York University, then an M.A. at Harvard. His faculty advisor was the art historian T. J. Clark, who analyzed nineteenth-century art through a Marxist lens, but whose approach to American art had often placed him in open conflict with Greenberg. O'Brian had published a few articles in small Canadian art magazines when he contacted Greenberg.

The critic swiftly responded, inviting the Canadian to Norwich, a six-hour drive from Montreal, and suggesting he plan to stay two or three days. After a phone conversation, O'Brian agreed to meet Greenberg on August 7, "so that we could see the whites of the other's eyes." At that first meeting, O'Brian recalled, "we talked, we walked, we had dinner." After that visit, O'Brian frequently telephoned Greenberg and finally suggested "a project"—that he edit Greenberg's writings for publication. "You convinced me of that a long time ago," Greenberg replied. Elated, O'Brian followed up with dozens of visits, every five weeks or so, to Norwich or New York; often Greenberg would drive to Boston to meet his new editor. Though Greenberg drank steadily whenever they met, he "always made sense," said O'Brian. "He always spoke in fully formed sentences, and he always smoked Camels."

By November 1, O'Brian had drafted a proposal to submit to publishers. He envisioned a single book of about one thousand to fifteen hundred pages, including all of Greenberg's writings for the previous forty-three years. He noted that "increasingly, serious scholars hold the view that Greenberg's writings are the most rigorous and significant produced by an art critic during the past forty years." It was, he said, "a commonplace among artists, critics, art historians, and the informed public that Greenberg [is] the most influential art critic of our time." When he sent the draft proposal to Greenberg, O'Brian had already set up a meeting with an editor at Beacon Press, the Boston publisher of *Art and Culture*. Greenberg had mixed feelings about O'Brian's project. On the one hand, he wondered why O'Brian was putting so much time and effort into this work, but he also reminded the would-be editor that, more than twenty years after publication, *Art and Culture* was still earning him $500 annually. After considering the proposal for more than five months, a senior editor at Beacon wrote to O'Brian that "we could not work out the economics so that it would be a viable project for us." The rejection letter was written by a woman, prompting one of Greenberg's outbursts: "Women in positions of authority remain an affliction," he wrote to O'Brian. "I'm not a male chauvinist, but I bow to experience."

O'Brian had meanwhile submitted the proposal to academic presses at Yale, Princeton, MIT, Cornell, Harvard, and Chicago, of whom only Chicago was willing to go forward. O'Brian then tried to persuade Greenberg to write an introduction for the book, "an assessment of your career as critic and essayist." Greenberg refused, as he also refused to write an updated introduction for a new edition of *Art and Culture*, which Beacon was bringing out in 1984. With a contract from Chicago likely, Greenberg and O'Brian engaged in several months of polite fencing over allocating the royalties. They discussed sharing the profits equally until Greenberg urged O'Brian to take more than 50 percent, "given my ex-wife's immersion in the bond and money market." He proposed that O'Brian, who was undertaking most of the work, receive two-thirds plus reimbursement of expenses. Later, O'Brian confessed that the project was so appealing that he would have settled for a fifty-fifty split. As the sparring ended, Greenberg suggested, "It's time you called me Clem." He questioned O'Brian's dedication to assembling all of his writings, confessing that he, himself "wdnt go to anything like the same trouble for messages from the true Messiah."

Such apparently sincere self-deprecation, balanced against Greenberg's lapses into overweening arrogance, demonstrate his lifelong uncertainty over his self-image. Was he really the eminent art critic who had made the reputation of many an artist? Or was he just a wayward boy, a twice- failed husband, father of a troubled son, and exile from the New York art bustle? The ambiguity may well have spawned the drawn-out depression that drove him to seek relief from a bottle. He was plagued by "senility and booze," he wrote to O'Brian, adding parenthetically, "I enjoy the latter much more than the former."

As they worked together, Greenberg revealed his private troubles and quirks to O'Brian. He described the extensive dental work performed on his teeth from childhood. He grumbled about the weather, saying that "spring doesn't come the way it used to forty years ago in Flatbush, like a hot breath from heaven. Nor does the fall, which once came like a whiff of cocaine." When O'Brian sent him the draft of his introduction to the first volume, Greenberg found it too complimentary. O'Brian complied by removing "all suggestion of congratulation . . . I simply take for granted that you are a great critic." Greenberg confessed that writing now came hard, that the unnamed book he planned was "not cóming at all," which he blamed on "laziness."

As O'Brian committed himself, at the behest of the publisher, to dividing Greenberg's oeuvre into four volumes, Greenberg decided to rewrite some of his earlier pieces. "Reading my old stuff makes me squirm," he wrote to O'Brian. He felt "revulsion against my past prose." The two men discussed the issue many times, and O'Brian finally prevailed, even to including the original versions of the essays Greenberg had revised for *Art and Culture*. A few times,

Greenberg angrily resisted O'Brian's questions. Once, they were driving to Syracuse, where Greenberg was judging an exhibition, and O'Brian asked for specific dates and details about the critic's past. "You're writing a biography!" Greenberg exclaimed in irritation. O'Brian assured him that he was "just trying to pin down the facts for the chronology he appended to each volume.

As O'Brian tracked down every last scrap of Greenberg's published writing, the critic concentrated on lecturing. At a second visit within three years to Western Michigan University he tried to describe "true taste" in art (as opposed to more inclusive contemporary taste) in a lecture for which he wrote a fresh beginning, then added material from other talks. At a conference on modernism, he roved through literature, music, and art, pointing out that shock, "at first to cultivated 'elite' taste, not just to that of philistines," was a salient characteristic of modernism. However, he contended that during the previous twenty years art professionals and the educated public had stifled all shocking art in a smothering embrace before the new art had a chance to develop. He revised the transcript of his talk into an article, published in *Arts* magazine in April 1986.

"I'm allergic to lectures, including my own," he wrote to O'Brian a year later. Nevertheless, he continued crisscrossing the United States and Canada to speak, with a few European side trips for good measure. Over time, his written remarks dwindled to as little as a page, as his formal talk became briefer and more extemporaneous. Now a seasoned speaker, the nervousness he suffered in his earlier appearances was replaced with a sometimes combative certainty; he relished the challenge of post-lecture questions from the audience. He usually deplored the current New York art scene, and on at least one occasion urged his listeners to savor "the pleasure, the joy, the exhilaration to be gotten from art . . . in any medium, and from nature, too."

Greenberg's fees kept up with inflation, and then some. For a half-hour talk plus questions at Skidmore College, he received $1,000, plus free lodging and meals; writing something for the college magazine, *Salmagundi*, earned him another $500. Vassar, where his daughter was a student, received a special discount: $200 for a five-minute talk and a half-hour of questions, plus mileage from Norwich ($58). Western Michigan University, where he had spoken twice before, gave him an honorary doctorate in fine arts in March 1984, for which he received $1,200 plus airfare and accommodations for his family. When Rhode Island School of Design awarded him another honorary degree, he also gave the commencement address for which he was paid $500 plus all expenses. The program included a dinner party the night before, a "robing" breakfast before his talk, and a luncheon afterward.

Greenberg was not exactly an endearing guest. He waited almost a month before accepting an invitation from Carnegie-Mellon University to be the President's Distinguished Speaker on April 19, 1984. He negotiated double the original honorarium to $3,000, plus a round-trip air ticket in first class and lodging in a first-class hotel, all for a talk along lines he had previously pursued elsewhere: "The Current State of Art."

For a lecture to begin at 4:30 P.M., he had cut the air trip so closely that he arrived a few minutes late, as some five hundred people waited in a ballroom. His guide, the art history professor Elaine King, noticed that his speech was slurred and he appeared drunk. She quickly sent a student for a mug of strong coffee, which he willingly drank. He then spoke for some twenty minutes, but was eager to address questions, staying at the podium about ninety minutes. After the lecture, he attended a reception and an elegant dinner at a leading restaurant, where alcoholic beverages freely flowed.

The following day, King picked him up at his hotel with a car and driver for a tour of the Carnegie Museum collection. He was sober and, because he had probably learned from experience that vodka is the least likely intoxicant to cause a hangover, appeared perfectly chipper. As King was clambering into the back seat of the two-door coupe, she heard Greenberg muttering *sotto voce* to the driver: "There are too many God-damned women in the art world." She shot back: "Yes, there are too many God-damned women getting people like you to speak on art." In recalling the exchange twenty years later, she was still miffed but nevertheless found Greenberg's lecture "a tour de force," and the critic himself "an innovative radical . . . now stuck in his own theory . . . a period piece, but an important one."

The "period piece," now seventy-five years old, blithely pursued a series of appearances that might have exhausted a younger, less alcohol-soaked and chain-smoking figure. In May 1984, he was again in Saskatoon, a happy reunion with a provincial group that offered unconditional affection. In September, he was at New York's Whitney Museum, sharing his recollections of finding new art in the late 1930s and the sad fate of many of those artists who were unsuccessful. A few days later, he was at the Oklahoma Museum of Art, speaking on "The David Smith Tradition" at a symposium.

Even with his travels and commutes to New York, Greenberg could not resist a call for a contribution to *Partisan Review*'s fiftieth anniversary issue, an immense *omnium gatherum* of American writers and intellectuals who had cut their teeth in that now marginalized publication's heyday. While its circulation, never robust, had dwindled to just under six thousand, the periodical's pages encompassed the American intellectual elite; contributors to that issue included John Ashbery, Harold Brodkey, James Dickey, John Hollander, Bernard Malamud, Philip Roth, Vladimir Nabokov, Joyce Carol Oates, Norman Mailer, Isaac Bashevis Singer,

Stephen Spender, and Robert Penn Warren, along with the brightest essayists of the postwar years: Jacques Barzun, Daniel Bell, Sidney Hook, Alfred Kazin, Milan Kundera, Mary McCarthy, Robert Motherwell, Cynthia Ozick, and Muriel Spark, plus generous excerpts from the journals of Lionel Trilling, who had died in 1975.

Greenberg's contribution to this grand reunion was a feisty restatement of his well-known views about art: Modernism was a response to decadence, painting is the central avant-garde art, a creeping crisis was undermining a "culture in decline, Spenglerian decline." But he had drastically changed his political outlook since the early days of *Partisan Review*; he no longer believed in socialism and had become "a political agnostic," revolted by leftist cant yet unable to vote Republican.

While his writing was sparse, Greenberg still relished preparing a sharp, if not furious, letter to the editor whenever a magazine article diverged from his revealed gospel. In 1986, he fired off a nitpicking letter to the *New Criterion* responding to its assertion that New York was still at the center of contemporary world art. He argued that while the city was central to shaping taste in contemporary art, it had lost out to "the hinterland" as "a center of production." Artists need no longer live in the city, even though their work is validated there. "And now, New York spreads bad taste, incubates it . . . Trends may not be born in New York," he wrote, "but New York is where they get certified."

*　　*　　*

When the first two volumes of Greenberg's writings were published in 1987, at least two generations of art historians and critics became aware of just how broad the spectrum of his early work had been. *Perceptions and Judgments* was the subtitle of volume one, covering 1939 to 1944. For the first time in decades, readers had access to the workaday art reviews published in the *Nation*, the ill-advised essay against American entry into the Second World War, the many book reviews, the thoughtful literary discussions, and Greenberg's sympathetic report about the camp for German prisoners of war near Tishomingo, Oklahoma. On the cover, as it would be repeated on all four volumes, were two versions of a single photograph — Greenberg's bald dome, his eyes judgmentally squinting, and two fingers pressing the ever-present cigarette to his lips. The photo was by Hans Namuth, a photographer whose career was capped by the photos he took of Jackson Pollock at work.

The second volume, *Arrogant Purpose*, covered only four more years, to 1949, but it defined the certainty of judgment in Greenberg's style as it reached maturity. Near the end is one of his last pieces for the *Nation*, displaying Greenberg's self-assured, moralizing tone. Summarizing the lackluster 1948–49 art season, he writes that, despite new galleries opening in New York, "It remains as difficult as ever for a young American painter or scholar working in an advanced mode to win real attention in New York." He castigates the city's leading galleries for promoting only European art: "There are galleries and dealers that create values and there are others that exploit values already created." He steps out of his role as a critic of art to urge the city's leading dealers to promote "more of an overlapping between the two kinds on 57th Street." Then follow his summary marching orders for "the more powerful organs of American public opinion" to realize that "our new painting and sculpture constitute the most original and vigorous art in the world today." Finally, he invokes shame: "It would be very embarrassing . . . if the Luce magazines . . . boarded the train before the powers on 57th Street did." That is precisely what had happened less than two months afterward, when *Life* profiled Jackson Pollock.

As might be expected, the reviews of the first two volumes

dwelled almost exclusively on Greenberg: his moralistic tone, his harsh verdicts for some and never-ending praise for others, his flawed theory of modernism, his dicta for artists, and his imperiousness, picked up in the second volume's title. There was little discussion of John O'Brian's patient pursuit of every Greenbergian scrap, the chronologies and bibliographies that would aid generations of scholars, and his evident diplomacy to appease a notable curmudgeon. In the introduction to the first volume, O'Brian hints at his project's challenge: "to record faithfully his activity as a critic," not to illustrate the "haste and waste" of Greenberg's "self-education," which he described as the impetus for publishing *Art and Culture*. Despite Greenberg's horror of a biography, O'Brian's introductions and chronologies provide many relevant glimpses into the critic's development. From O'Brian's introduction to volume one, for example, many readers became aware for the first time that Greenberg had written widely on literature, that his youthful radicalism was part of a dynamic left wing among New York intellectuals of the 1930s, and that Greenberg interested himself in all sorts of visual endeavors, even cartoons, photographs, and Currier & Ives prints.

Reviewers of the first two volumes in all corners of the intellectual world found confirmation of whatever they had previously believed. Robert Storr, then a MoMA curator who had known Greenberg only from *Art and Culture*, found him "at once overbearing and absent," showing "astonishing brilliance and equally astonishing dogmatism." He was horrified that Greenberg "issued edicts and sanctioned movements from behind the screen of his own taste." He compared Greenberg unfavorably with Harold Rosenberg, and was particularly infuriated by Greenberg's assertion in a recent issue of *Art News* that Andrew Wyeth's art was superior to Robert Rauschenberg's. Sidney Tillim in *Art in America* was considerably kinder, stressing Greenberg's emphasis on values, arguing that the mission of modernism was to preserve high culture from destruction by the tasteless: "Quality became for him something of a moral imperative."

Greenberg's writings were also reviewed in scholarly publications in which art criticism was seldom given space. In *Salmagundi*, Elizabeth Frank, who would later win the Pulitzer Prize for her biography of Louise Bogan, characterized Greenberg as "an aesthetic generalissimo" who issued "verdicts with bloodless arbitrariness" and who "has to be the most hated man in the New York art world." Still, she said, while his manner was perhaps "arrogant," it was "the arrogance of a large, hungry talent visibly fulfilling itself . . . He was after Athene"—the virginal Greek goddess of combat and victory, wisdom and patron of the arts— but "neither she nor Greenberg gets around much any more." And Sanford Schwartz in *American Scholar* acutely analyzed Greenberg's personality as he dissected his writing, highlighting "a fearfulness and an uncertainty" behind his judgments. Like Greenberg's own assessment of Franz Kafka, Schwartz noted that he "weighs, ponders, and questions everything from many sides in the effort to establish certainties that will survive chance and history."

The review that Greenberg saved among his files, however, was not a scholarly analysis published in a serious journal but a brief notice in an obscure publication, *Jewish Exponent*. There, a little-known writer highlighted Greenberg's assertion from 1944 that, although he was totally secular, "a quality of Jewishness is present in every word I write." The reviewer admired his "prescience in commending artists who are today recognized as the century's best" and concluded that his influence benefited the art world.

The publication of Greenberg's early writings fanned renewed interest in the Abstract Expressionists and revived debate over the avant-garde: was it still vital or was it a cadaver awaiting an autopsy? When the Albright-Knox Gallery in Buffalo organized a massive exhibition of Abstract Expressionists, one critic noted that Greenberg "looms like a gray eminence" over the show; he was "insistently cited" in the catalog, but omitted from the acknowledgments. None of the pictures in his collection were in the show. Harold Rosenberg was also mentioned, "but no one is still arguing with him."

Greenberg himself seemed less argumentative. In 1991, he visited the Pollock house at The Springs on Long Island for the first time in more than thirty years. He had joined a small gathering of graduate students and faculty at the New York State University at Stony Brook, which had taken over the property as a museum and study center. Still chain-smoking, he defended Jackson Pollock: "I've known plenty of drunks, including myself, and his character change was the most radical I've ever seen. When sober, he was one of the nicest human beings I've ever met." Then, "talking about the painter as though he were a pitcher," wrote the *New York Times* art critic Roberta Smith, "Greenberg said that Pollock lost his stuff." At age eighty-two, Greenberg struck Smith as "candid and evasive, gossipy and perceptive . . . not without the confidence that is essential to any critic." Asked to comment about current art, he replied that it would take "a whole monologue and I'm not being paid enough." And he passed along his latest—and most condensed—art theory: "Let nothing come between you and art, nothing: no ideas, nothing . . . When something really works, you're helpless . . . when you don't like something, the words come more readily."

Greenberg had not been back to that house since 1959, when he'd had a falling-out with Pollock's widow, Lee Krasner. He did not like her work, he told Roberta Smith. "I couldn't help myself. You don't choose what you like . . . your likes and dislikes are given to you." Such a remark was a far cry from Greenberg's earlier formalist theory, which had given reviewers of the first two volumes of Greenberg's papers an opportunity to cast a few more stones at a critic who had not published much in twenty years.

*   *   *

In 1989, Greenberg and Jenny reconciled and remarried, and the following year they sold the Norwich house and he moved back into the apartment overlooking Central Park. The move made him more accessible to interviewers, and Greenberg basked in their attentions. On the fiftieth anniversary of the publication of "Avant-Garde and Kitsch," he acknowledged that he had not thought enough about the essay's suggestion of a moral avant-garde. "It was brash and rash and blunt," he acknowledged. "I spoke too soon." He also regretted asserting that mass culture appropriates high culture and waters it down. As for kitsch, he had come to like some of it: "I loved and still love popular music," he said. "I loved to dance."

Greenberg also circulated again to gallery openings, sometimes nudging artists to do what he thought would improve their work. One of the dealers he befriended was Jacquie Littlejohn, who had trained as an artist at Rhode Island School of Design before opening her Soho gallery in 1985. She was impressed with his "extraordinary presence" and "powerful intelligence" and managed to get past his obsessive "editing [of] other people's works." After visiting another show at her gallery, he invited her to his apartment, where he promptly made a pass at her. "Clem loved ladies," she recalled. "He was so funny . . . but he was also respectful." Perhaps Greenberg appreciated Littlejohn because he suffered "jitters" when his daughter Sarah opened a Soho gallery in 1989. The critic and Littlejohn often met for dinner; she understood that Greenberg enjoyed being provocative, but also appreciated his "sweet side." In 1992, he attended the grand opening of her gallery in the Fuller Building on Madison Avenue, and sat in her office's executive chair "like a king on a throne." She was showing the work of an artist with tendencies toward Surrealism, a style Greenberg disliked, but he restrained himself, said Littlefield, saying he was "impressed by her ability to paint."

The following year, the last two volumes of Greenberg's collected writings were published, eliciting a good deal of appreciation for his clarity and even for his sharply defended opinions. Possibly a few more observers of the contemporary art scene had been repelled by the sea of kitsch threatening to overrun any aesthetic standard. Others may have been put off by the incomprehensible hash of deconstructionist cant masquerading, in many cases, as art writing. To many, it was probably a relief to delve into texts that offered a judgment, no matter how bold or misguided, after the lukewarm bath of influence and history that had become the art critical norm. Some may have been disturbed that the anything-goes ethos of postmodernism had brought forth basketballs floating in tubs of water, canned excrement, and an artist crucified on a Volkswagen Beetle. Perhaps a few were perturbed by the government funding of photographic shows of sexual sadism and performances featuring an artist urinating into a toilet or smearing herself with chocolate.

Whatever the reason, the final two volumes, *Affirmations and Refusals, 1950–1956* and *Modernism with a Vengeance, 1957–1969*, formed a bracing contrast to the current fragmentation, and attracted a wide spectrum of reviewers. Donald Kuspit, who had written on Greenberg's theories in 1979, connected readers of the *New York Times Book Review* with Greenberg's Jewish heritage: "The true issue of his development," he wrote, "is not how Stalinism became Trotskyism became art for art's sake, but how unconscious Jewish iconoclasm changed into conscious love of abstract art." Kuspit saw Greenberg as "a great, very discriminating connoisseur and esthete, the last . . . in a tradition that begins in the 18th century." Kuspit was deeply moved by the "air of urgency" in Greenberg's writings, "as though the fate of civilization hung on the fate of high art, and the mission of art criticism was to defend it to the death."

In the *New York Review of Books*, Robert Hughes offered a distinctly astringent view of Greenberg's oeuvre. He had no dispute with Greenberg's status as "the most influential art critic in American history," even though a "ritual denunciation of Greenbergian formalism" in 1980s art magazines "was a way of clearing the throat, establishing credentials." Feminists and multicultural activists had pummeled the critic as a demon of elitism and patriarchy. Hughes noted that Greenberg's onetime disciple Rosalind Krauss had rehearsed his putdown of "smart Jewish girls with their typewriters" four or five times in a recent book. He also deplored Greenberg's relatively meager writings: *Art and Culture*, brief monographs on Miró, Matisse, and Hans Hofmann, plus four slender volumes of criticism. In comparison, Hughes cited John Ruskin's thirty-eight volumes, with an index that alone ran to 689 pages. Nevertheless, Hughes held his fire in this review, waiting until Greenberg was dead to crucify him in a monumental history of American art published in 1997.

Greenberg himself kept appearing at various gatherings, speaking now from brief jottings and in reply to questions. In 1992, he spent a week in Tokyo, lecturing and attending art events. The following year, he appeared in Chapel Hill, North Carolina; New York's Hunter College; Dallas; New York University; and Yale. While offering little new, he continued to criticize contemporary art and complain that there was not enough negative criticism of it. But he was clearly flagging. There had been a warning in the late 1980s when the Canadian artist James Walsh and his wife dropped by the New York apartment for drinks. As they were leaving, Greenberg was fumbling in his back pants pocket for money so they could buy him a pack of Camels to send up with the doorman. He fell backwards, cracking his head against a corner of the wall. Looking at Greenberg's bleeding scalp, Walsh "felt I was looking down into the abyss, watching the thought processes . . . here a thought of Kant, there a thought of Camels," while Greenberg "was shrugging off the whole affair." Walsh called 911 and when two police officers arrived, the critic complimented one of them, a young woman, on her looks. The Canadians accompanied Greenberg to a hospital emergency room where his wound was stitched, and when they returned to Greenberg's building, he invited them back up for a nightcap.

As the O'Brian volumes were garnering their share of criticism and praise, Greenberg developed a sudden hatred for his editor. The cause may have been O'Brian's discussion, in the introduction to volume three, of Greenberg's transformation in the mid-1950s from left-wing radical to militant anti-Soviet cold warrior. They had been close friends and collaborators for eleven years. Then, without ever airing his grievance, he told Peter Plagens of *Newsweek* that O'Brian had made him "retroactively politically correct." Greenberg continued, "I should have known that there was something . . . not quite right about John O'Brian. It's an inappropriate introduction." In the same interview, he noted: "I inadvertently offend people . . . and I don't mean to." In this case, however, he clearly meant to offend O'Brian.

Once again, and for the last time, Greenberg had responded to a close friendship with another man by suddenly cutting it off. After fifteen years of intimate correspondence with his college friend Harold Lazarus, Greenberg abruptly stopped writing him. In May 1978, he had written in his journal, "Cutting off from HL: How long ago was that? What a relief. And yet I still feel a little guilt." And in January 1990, he recalled Harold as "the best thing to happen to me at college, yes. But I didn't like him. Didn't like his nearness."

Time and again throughout his life, Greenberg reacted to "nearness" of men with abrupt flight and, usually, anger. After collaborating with Dwight Macdonald on a strident antiwar essay in 1941, Greenberg soon dropped the relationship and reacted with rage to Macdonald's death in 1982. Greenberg quickly broke with Harold Rosenberg during the early 1940s, and brushed off Jackson Pollock after 1952, ostensibly because the artist had "lost it." For years during the 1960s, Kenneth Noland was like a member of Greenberg's family, and then suddenly he was gone. During the 1970s, William and Lawrence Rubin appeared weekly, sometimes daily, in Greenberg's datebooks—and then it was over. The datebooks show a steady parade of people arriving in Greenberg's life, lingering, and then abruptly disappearing. If it was a rash impulse that drove Greenberg to cut off John O'Brian, the scenario had been rehearsed many times before.

*　*　*

As the final O'Brian volumes were appearing, Greenberg's health and finances deteriorated. In February 1993, a lingering flu sent him to Lenox Hill Hospital for five days. That spring, he learned that his accountant had cheated Jenny and Sarah out of some $750,000. Friends said he was "in dire financial straits," the *New York Observer* reported in August, "but he did have medical insurance." In January 1994, Greenberg was hospitalized with a breathing problem; while there, he fell and broke his hip. He recovered somewhat, as Jenny and Sarah rationed his alcohol and persuaded him to stop smoking. They threw a party for his eighty-fifth birthday. On April 5, an interviewer found him "very energetic. He continues to go to galleries . . . and reads very much, including the writings of the French structuralists whom he undoubtedly does not hold in high regard."

But, after more than half a century of chain-smoking,

Greenberg's breathing problems persisted. On May 2, he was again admitted to Lenox Hill Hospital, where he died on May 7, 1994, at 3:50 P.M. The last person to see him alive was Dr. Vladimir Smirnov, who filled out the death certificate. On May 10, Greenberg was cremated in West Babylon, Long Island. A memorial service was held on May 18 at the exclusive Manhattan Century Club and, in what he called "a message from the grave," John O'Brian was invited.

Chapter X

THE LEGACY

By the time clement greenberg lay dying, many people in the art world had come to view him as a fossil, a remnant of a bygone age called modernism. Having defined the course of modernism and having dared predict what new directions it would take, this outspoken critic had spent the last third of his life vehemently fighting a rearguard action; his enemies as he saw them were the armies of mediocrity undermining aesthetic standards and the followers of fashion polluting time-sanctioned taste. But, despite prattle about sex, drugs, and drunken carousing in the critic's apartment, serious art historians continued to request interviews and to consult his writings; *Art and Culture* and the four volumes edited by John O'Brian remained in print. While he wrote little after 1969 and medicated himself into an alcoholic haze, audiences interested in the fate of fine art all over the world listened raptly to this chain-smoking fellow with a bald dome as though he were some kind of biblical prophet.

Considering Greenberg's background, this image is more apt than it might at first appear. While he pursued a militantly secular life, he could not escape the moral penumbra of the traditional Jewish world built around a faith that strictly sequestered the sanctioned from the forbidden. In that world, every detail central to daily life—food, sex, work, and play—fell into one or the other category. The immigrants like Greenberg's parents who deviated from the old ways sought out other systems that could regulate their lives. Like the youthful Greenberg, they often turned to Marxist visions of paradise on earth. Greenberg imaginatively extended that view of history to art, by expounding his theory of how new art develops. Long after he abandoned Trotskyism, he clung to the shreds of that theory, even when it became obvious that his visceral reaction to what he saw, his "eye," dictated which artists received his backing. To buttress these seemingly capricious choices, Greenberg summoned authorities of the past in much the same way that contemporary rabbis reverently cited bygone Jewish sages.

*   *   *

The outpouring of obituaries and appreciations that followed Greenberg's death testified to the central place he occupied in the art world, an industry critical to New York's status as a cultural hub. Because of an early deadline for its Sunday edition, the *New York Times* obituary ran on page thirty-eight. Still, the four-column spread, illustrated with a three-year-old photo of a wan Greenberg sans cigarette, more or less accurately summarized the high points of his career. "Avant-Garde and Kitsch" was erroneously credited to the *Paris Review* rather than *Partisan Review*, but some of his more pungent remarks appeared, such as: "When you don't like something, the words come more readily."

Two days later, the *Times's* chief art critic, Michael Kimmelman, published a long "Appreciation" of Greenberg. It was illustrated by Greenberg's signature photo, his eyes squinting in the smoke from a cigarette pinched between his thumb and forefinger, and his brow furrowed in concentrated appraisal of—a newly discovered Pollock? another Warhol sacrilege? For Kimmelman, he was "the most important art critic the United States has produced . . . At once the most admired and excoriated writer on art, as much a touchstone of postwar American painting and sculpture as any of the painters and sculptors in whose circle he moved as an oracular presence." In Greenberg's critical practice Kimmelman discerned "an ability to get inside a work as if it were a watch, and he were analyzing its mechanism."

A chorus of appraisals of Greenberg's career swiftly followed. Hilton Kramer deemed him "the greatest art critic of his time" and dismissed allegations that he had manipulated the art market. "The thing about Clem was that you didn't have to agree with him to find him the most interesting writer around." Greenberg's fellow critic Robert Rosenblum found his "psychological power astounding," as he became "the dictatorial father to a whole generation of critics who either followed him slavishly or rebelled against him." William Rubin, estranged from Greenberg after their many years of intense friendship, minimized his career as merely "meat for a couple of Ph.D. students," even as he admitted that the older man "brought something rather special into my own life: his feel for painting, the dialogue one could have with him about German Romantic poetry, about Kant . . . [he] was not just an art critic."

However, Greenberg's ashes were hardly cold before more severe critics pounced. The painter William Feaver found the critic "so ridiculously authoritarian he could be ignored" and his "bizarre certainties and arbitrary scorn" irrelevant. This complaint was typical of the sharp turn art criticism had taken in the postmodernist world. In the new critical milieu, opinions about art were inevitably formed, but not overtly expressed. Instead, critics were busy explaining what the artist was trying to do, justifying the sometimes unspeakable materials used, and meticulously tracing a connection between what the artist had wrought and an established tradition. Much of this discussion was conducted in a self-referential mumble that was unintelligible even to the educated public. Still, allusions to Greenberg, whether hostile or friendly, continued to pepper academic discussions of art. Thus, the author of a clotted disquisition on *The Metaphysics of Beauty* described Greenberg as a "historically restricted substantive formalist." In the face of such a hash, the less educated public simply shrugged and substantially gave up on decoding the new art. Instead, record crowds surged into the large—and ever-growing—encyclopedic museums to seek communion with the truth and beauty that had always inspired people.

This phenomenon prompted quite a few art historians to re-evaluate the tepid nature of current criticism. In 1998, Robert C. Morgan, who would edit a volume of Greenberg's late writings and interviews, described "the post-Warholian nightmare . . . one big mindless bash, where money talks and nobody listens." He found it inconceivable that any commentary on current art could take place "without the subtle intervention of publicity, management, and marketing strategies." All contemporary art, he concluded, "is seen through the shroud of the market."

In his expansive obituary in the *New Criterion*, Hilton Kramer had asserted that Greenberg did more than any other critic to per-suade people newly interested in art during the 1950s and into the 1960s to develop a taste for modernism. Those who accused him of dictatorially imposing his views had exaggerated, Kramer wrote, "for the majority of the new reputations to achieve commercial and institutional success in his time never enjoyed [Greenberg's] critical support." Kramer was convinced that Greenberg's "critical oeuvre . . . will outlive the carping and incomprehension of his adversaries." Another sympathizer suggested that Greenberg had become "the consciousness of the art world . . . someone to be reckoned with, a kind of perennial gadfly."

Despite such brave words, those who had always disapproved of Greenberg's theory and his strong pronouncements continued to heap scorn upon his legacy. In his 1997 book *American Visions*, Robert Hughes noted that Mark Tansey's spoof *Triumph of the New York School*, painted in 1984, portrayed Greenberg, "the General MacArthur of modernist formalism," accepting the surrender of Picasso, Matisse, and other European art stars. Strangely, Hughes blamed the dead critic for "the fiction" that Abstract Expressionism was the first American art to find international acclaim, contradicting all the evidence showing that Jackson Pollock and his colleagues were clearly the first American Modernists to engage European art periodicals and museums. Hughes also deplored the dominance of Greenberg's Color Field painters on the 1960s and '70s museum scene as other new art movements were slighted.

Such criticism failed to dislodge Greenberg from his central perch. Three years after his collected writings were published and two years after his death, a reviewer described these volumes as "a climactic stage in the establishment of Clement Greenberg as a veritable institution"; any discussion of postwar art, wrote David Anfam, would have to confront him. Anfam recalled meeting Greenberg in 1977 and being shocked by the critic's "idiosyncratic style that conflated personal views with apparently impersonal criteria." Furthermore, he found the man "devoid of etiquette, feisty, shrewd, declarative, and irritating," behavior he thought typical of New York manners: "One might well have been jostling a rival in the smoked salmon queue at Zabar's deli a few blocks away." Nevertheless, he asserted that the collected writings "contain enough unfinished business to sustain scholarly commentary well into the next century." Even Robert Hughes had raved over Greenberg's writings in a long review for the *New York Review of Books*, published only three years before *American Visions*. "No American art critic has produced a more imposing body of work," he wrote. It stands as "a permanent rebuke to the jargon and obscurantism that bedeviled art criticism in his time and still does now."

Unlike his complex legacy, Greenberg's will was a straightforward document. Written less than three years before his death, it left all his property to Janice, with his daughter Sarah next in line.

There was no mention of Danny, which led the probate court to appoint a guardian to represent Greenberg's troubled son. She located Danny in a group home for the mentally ill in Lorain, Ohio. Now fifty-nine years old, he was being treated with psychotropic drugs for "long term chronic schizophrenia." According to the attorney who wrote Greenberg's will, the critic had no idea whether Danny was still alive: "It is unfortunate that [Danny] and his father did not have any . . . relationship for thirty years," he wrote, "but it explains the omission of any bequest or legacy." In fact, Greenberg had consulted several specialists in schizophrenia on Danny's behalf just fourteen years earlier, in 1980.

According to the widow's sworn list of assets, nonprobate joint or trust property amounted to less than $15,000; less than a year earlier, the couple's holdings had been stripped by a larcenous accountant of some $750,000. The property solely owned by Greenberg or payable to the estate, which Jenny would inherit, was valued at more than $2.3 million. As is typical in probate proceedings, a final accounting set the estate's value at between $500,000 and $1 million, just enough to avoid paying the confiscatory 50 percent federal estate tax.

A paradox faced the widow: she was living in a luxurious apartment at a low fixed rent, surrounded by a valuable art collection, but extremely short of cash. Although Greenberg over the years had sold some of the art that grateful artists gave him, what remained was still an enviable array of mid-twentieth-century works, more than could be hung in his spacious apartment. At one point late in Greenberg's life, the surplus had to be stored at the deluxe Santini Brothers warehouse; later, it was moved to a less expensive facility. After his death, the collection constituted a precious nest egg for the widow.

In 2001, seven years after Greenberg's death, an exhibition of much of the art collection he had amassed opened with considerable fanfare at the Portland [Oregon] Museum of Art. It had previously been offered, with a price tag of $2 million, to many other museums. In the catalogue's "collector's statement," Greenberg's widow, Janice Van Horne, described caring for the works until they had "become as familiar as old friends, the 'furniture' of my life." She described herself as "a curator of this art. I hung it. I toted it. I dusted it."

In announcing the acquisition at the museum's annual meeting in the fall of 2000, the museum's executive director, John E. Buchanan, Jr., described the purchase as "the entire collection of the distinguished New York art critic Clement Greenberg." The collection's curator and coauthor of the catalogue, Bruce Guenther, wrote in the museum's house publication, *Portland Art Museum*, that "these are the objects he chose to live with and keep." But while the collection did indeed include, as Guenther wrote, "works by some of the most important mid-twentieth-century American artists," it was by no means comprehensive. To take only a few examples, a single, fading ink scrawl represented Jackson Pollock, and an oversize birthday card for Jenny was the only work by the sculptor David Smith, while an oil and gouache on paper was the sole painting by Hans Hofmann.

Nor was there a single work by Morris Louis, an artist who had rewarded Greenberg with numerous paintings, and whose widow relied on Greenberg for advice regarding the estate. By contrast, the collection featured twenty-two works by Kenneth Noland and twenty-one by Jules Olitski. These Color Field artists had enjoyed a swift run-up in their prices as Greenberg coached them in the studio, then publicly praised their work and organized their exhibitions. Although his work was represented in thirty-two museums, prices for an Olitski painting reached a peak on May 7, 1990, with a record sale at Christie's of $352,000. A work of similar size went unsold at Christie's East in 1999, despite a bargain estimate of

$24–32,000. In September 2003, another Olitski went unsold, even though the estimate was only $8–12,000. Kenneth Noland, whose paintings hang in thirty-one museums, followed a similar trajectory: a record sale at $2,035,000 on November 8, 1989, followed by occasional sales in six figures and most in five. Of 247 Nolands offered since the mid-1980s, only 169 were sold. Among the unsold was a 1958 Noland offered at Christie's on November 13, 2002, with an estimate of $650,000 to $850,000. In fact, one reason why the collection sold to Portland included no Morris Louis paintings might be that his prices had held up considerably better than the other Color Field painters.

While alive, Greenberg claimed that he had sold no more than thirty items from his collection. But Greenberg's papers and other materials indicate a considerable number of absences. Striking was the lack of work by Barnett Newman, whom Greenberg had given a show at French & Co. in 1960; nor was there Robert Motherwell's "Je T'aime," which Christie's put on sale in 1984. Also sold before the Portland purchase were works by Howard Mehring, Helen Frankenthaler, and a small Pollock gouache. As late as 1990, photos of Greenberg's apartment showed paintings missing in Portland: Jules Olitski's *Nobel Regard*, Friedel Dzubas's *Untitled*, Kenneth Noland's *Sarah Dora's Luck*, Horacio Torres's 1973 portrait of Sarah, and a wide Morris Louis stripe painting, which also had been hanging in Greenberg's living room in 1964.

Despite the gaps, the collection housed in the Portland Museum provides a much-needed West Coast site for viewing the work of many of the artists Greenberg admired. These works, wrote one critic, "hold up well as a demonstration of confidence in the power of color to hold a canvas as well as the power of a critic to determine success."

The bitter attacks that dogged Greenberg during his last decades gradually faded after his death. A biography was published in 1997, and his widow saw to publication of several books by and about him: *Homemade Esthetics*, transcripts of nine Bennington College seminars given in 1971 and articles based on them, published in 1999; *The Harold Letters*, his youthful, revealing correspondence to Harold Lazarus, published in 2000; and an anthology of late writings and interviews, published in 2003.

Those critics who resented Greenberg as a dictator of taste began to notice that not all the artists he endorsed ended up wealthy art stars. One case was the postal worker Arnold Friedman, whose art Greenberg admired in 1944 for "its honesty, for its renunciation of tricks and stunts." While he was editor of *Commentary*, Greenberg had commissioned a profile of Friedman after the artist's death, and wrote the catalog blurb for a retrospective at the Jewish Museum in 1950. For a memorial exhibition in Springfield, Massachusetts, Greenberg wrote an appreciation of the artist's oeuvre: "Had Friedman been more of a showman, he would have bastardized his idiom a little," but because he stayed true to his vision "most spectators miss the point." Hilton Kramer, as art critic for the *New York Times*, also admired Friedman's work, but succeeded in attracting only one known collector to it.

*   *   *

Clement Greenberg's most influential years spanned a singularly fertile period in the art of the Western world. In the 1940s, a critic writing for obscure publications could envision finding an audience for a modest, part-time artist like Arnold Friedman. In those years, the American art world was like a village, an outpost of creative energy in a philistine land, a place where the French term avant-garde resonated defiantly against the grain of the nation's overwhelming middle-class torpor. The country had but a single museum of modern art, a sparsely attended institution founded with Rockefeller money just as the stock market withered in 1929.

It was still supported by a handful of old-money New Yorkers, the few devotees of a vanguard they located in Europe. At the outset of Greenberg's career as an art critic, the few Americans interested in new art assumed that European artists would again lead the way when the Second World War ended.

These patrons—readers of the stodgy *New York Times* or its competitor, the even stodgier *Herald Tribune*—would hardly have seen Greenberg's first substantial essay, "Avant-Garde and Kitsch," published in the low-circulation radical journal *Partisan Review*. However, this ambitious attempt by a callow unknown to analyze how artistic avant-gardes function is still must-reading for students and scholars in a broad spectrum of fields: sociology, literature and the arts, history, and even economics. Moreover, Greenberg also identified the avant-garde's arch enemy, a voracious beast he called "kitsch."

This single essay, filling fewer than seventeen pages in Greenberg's collected writings, has stuck remarkably to the ribs of our cultural corpus: it continues to be widely quoted, analyzed, reprinted, paraphrased, mustered, or dismissed in the articles and books forming the essential lens through which modern society is viewed.

At the time of its publication, not many Americans grasped the originality of Greenberg's proposition: that a stridently commercial culture and a relatively esoteric avant-garde were engaged in an unequal struggle. That struggle played itself out through Greenberg's lifetime and beyond. In a world where the word "diversity" implies the equality of all cultural manifestations, those devoted to defining high art are tagged as elitists and increasingly marginalized. Media coverage of the arts devotes itself largely to entertainment, while art critics and academics shrink from making distinctions of any kind among "artistic" expressions.

Greenberg came of age as a critic just as a unique window was opening, a time when quite ordinary people were seeking information about art: how to look at it, how to understand it, how to profit from it, how to appropriate the objects themselves (or at least knowledge about them) as status symbols. It was a time when art mattered—for many, art was a religion—before it shattered into a dozen short-lived, competing schools; before artists were driven by a pitiless marketplace that promised wealth and fame to the few who succeeded there. It was also a time when artists had few financial alternatives to making art; they depended heavily on the kind words of critics. It was also a time of visual scarcity; there was no television or Internet, and color was an expensive rarity in the print media.

Along with just one or two colleagues, most notably Harold Rosenberg, Greenberg guided millions of visitors into museums and galleries, especially those venues that were beginning to present modern art. Each of these pioneers brought various theories to back up their discussions of art, an innovation that contrasted sharply with the kind of tepid "art appreciation" then appearing in newspapers and magazines.

Despite his relatively sparse writing and his edgy manners, Greenberg has etched a permanent place in the world of aesthetics. He said and did things that impelled people to challenge him, whether about his views on art and artists or his hateful remarks about women or homosexuals. He behaved as though he wanted to attract the kind of wrath he felt his father had directed at him; he seemed constantly to be testing whether he could withstand such wrath. Whatever his inner motivation, his readers could sense the daring implicit in his outspoken views, a journalistic high-wire act without peer. His writings convey a sense of crisis, of last chances before a blade fell, of almost desperate commitment to a cause, whether, in early days, to that rebel among rebels Leon Trotsky, or, later, to that artistic bad boy Jackson Pollock. While his zest for taking risks later led him to stake too much on questionable aesthetic wagers, his rhetoric remains a benchmark for persuasive prose in the field of aesthetics. There is a reason that, despite the millions of words written about art since Greenberg's virtual retirement in the 1960s, he is still a vital presence. For good or ill, his ghost lingers wherever serious people are perusing the many and varied visual manifestations that today constitute art.

NOTES

PROLOGUE: THE INDISPENSABLE CRITIC

xi   "OPEN IT MYSELF": Interview with John O'Brian, Vancouver, B.C., Oct. 31, 2003; CG to O'Brian, undated, Aug. 1984.

CHAPTER I: WHO AM I?

3   SHOEMAKERS, AND HORSE THIEVES: John O'Brian, ed., *Clement Greenberg: The Collected Essays and Criticism, Volume 1: Perceptions and Judgments, 1939–1944* (Chicago: University of Chicago Press, 1986; hereafter "O'Brian, vol. 1"), xix; Thomas Kessner, *The Golden Door* (New York: Oxford University Press, 1977).

4   "GOT ANOTHER ONE": Florence Rubenfeld, *Clement Greenberg: A Life* (New York: Scribner, 1997), 33.

4   "WOULD NOT BE TOO HARSH": Irving Howe, *A Margin of Hope: An Intellectual Autobiography* (San Diego: Harcourt Brace Jovanovich, 1982), 137–38.

5   "SAY WE WERE RICH": *Twentieth Century Authors (First Supplement)*, (New York: H. W. Wilson, 1955), reprinted in O'Brian, vol. 1, xix–xx.

5   "LAST SCRAP OF ARTWORK": Tim Hilton, "The Critic as Guardian and Inspiration," *Times Literary Supplement*, March 27, 1987, 330–31; Deborah Solomon, "Catching Up with the High Priest of Criticism," *New York Times*, June 23, 1991.

5   "BECOME AN ART CRITIC": Rubenfeld, *Clement Greenberg*, 31; Adam Gopnik, "The Power Critic," *New Yorker*, March 16, 1998, 70.

6   "IS NOT WITHOUT FRIGHT": Howe, *A Margin of Hope*, 6.

6   "IT WAS LIBERATING": Rubenfeld, *Clement Greenberg*, 36, 87.

6   "INTELLECTUAL NO-MAN'S-LAND": Thorstein Veblen, "The Intellectual Pre-eminence of Jews in Modern Europe," *Political Science Quarterly*, March 1919, 34.

7   "RESULTS WERE PLAUSIBLE": Rubenfeld, *Clement Greenberg*, 36; *Historical Statistics of the United States*, vol.1 (Washington, D.C.: Department of Commerce, 1975), 73.

7   "LET YOU GO TO ART SCHOOL": James Faure Walker, interview with

CG, 1978, published in Robert C. Morgan, *Clement Greenberg: Late Writings* (Minneapolis: University of Minnesota Press, 2003), 165.

7 IN DOWNTOWN BROOKLYN: YMCA Brooklyn-Queens, *The Marquand School for Boys*, 1916–17, 9, 11, 15, 21, 23, 28, 44–45 (copy in New York Public Library).

8 THREE YEARS OF FRENCH: Transcript Record Form, Syracuse University, Sept. 19, 1934, Clement Greenberg Papers, Special Collections, Getty Research Institute for the History of Art and Humanities, Los Angeles, California (hereafter "Getty").

9 KEPT NONE OF HAROLD'S: An abbreviated version of the letters, with many written at different times, shortened and conflated under one date, was edited and published by Greenberg's widow, Janice Van Horne, as *The Harold Letters, 1928–1943: The Making of an Intellectual* (Washington, D.C.: Counterpoint, 2000). The originals are housed in the Clement Greenberg Papers, Getty.

9 NEVER MADE IT: Rubenfeld, *Clement Greenberg*, 38–39.

9 ELEGANTLY LACONIC "A": Undergraduate papers, Box 23, folder 1, Getty.

10 "FICTION'S FUNERAL MOUND": Undated green notebook, Box 23, folder 1, Getty.

10 "I LACK DIRECTION": CG to Harold Lazarus (hereafter "HL"), Aug. 1, 1929, and Nov. 12, 1931, Getty.

11 "VERY COSMOPOLITAN": CG to HL, June 11 and 18, 1928, Getty.

11 RIVERSIDE DRIVE IN MANHATTAN: *Harold Letters*, 1.

11 WEIGHTY SEXUAL EQUIPMENT: CG to HL, June 22 and July 7, 1928, Getty.

11 "IN LOUD HORSEPLAY": CG to HL, July 18 and Aug. 1, 1928, Getty.

12 "TOO MANY JEWS IN N.Y": CG to HL, June 10, 1929, Getty.

12 "LIFE IS OK": CG to HL, June 15, 1929, Getty.

13 "THE REST OF MY LIFE": CG to HL, June 25, July 3, Aug. 1, 1929, Getty.

13 "GAUCHE, VICE VERSA, ETC.": CG to HL, Sept. 15, 1929, Getty.

13 OMITTED HIS ADDRESS: *Phi Beta Kappa Directory, 1776–1941*, New York Public Library.

13 "INDECISION AND GERMAN POETRY": CG to HL, July 7 and Aug. 12, 1930, Getty.

14 "VENT SKEPTICAL SNEERS": Poetry, 1920–1930, Box 23, folder 2, Getty.

14 HARVARD IN THE FALL: CG to HL, Aug. 2 and 18, Sept. 9, 1930, Getty.

14 "IN MY TWENTIES": CG to HL, Oct. 1, 1930; CG to John O'Brian, Oct. 18, 1984, private collection, Vancouver, B.C.

15 "PICASSO IS SIMPLY DECADENT": CG to HL, July 14, 1930, Getty.

15 "PLUCKING EVERY CHORD": CG to HL, Oct. 9 and 30, 1930, Getty.

15   COPY EDITOR APPROVED IT: CG to HL, Nov. 13, 1930, "January's middle days" and Feb. 22, 1931, Getty.

16   BOARD EXAMS: CG to HL, Oct. 1 and 30, 1930; March 13, 1931; and Nov. 25, 1933, Getty; Peter Harris, "Against Clembashing" *World Sculpture News*, http://www.sharecom.ca/Greenberg/-harris.html, July 2001.

16   "FROM THE SUBWAY STATION": CG to HL, July 8 and 24, 1931, Getty.

17   FRENCH AND LATIN: CG to HL, Sept. 23, 1931; *Twentieth Century Authors* quoted in O'Brian, vol. 1, xix.

17   NO DIRECTION OR PLAN: CG to HL, Sept. 29, Oct. 14, and Nov. 12, 1931, Getty.

17   "TILL NEXT JANUARY, EVEN": CG to HL, Dec. 17, 1931.

17   "AN EQUILATERAL TRIANGLE": CG to HL, May 13, 1931, Getty.

18   "LOUSY, BY THE WAY": CG to HL, May 13, Dec. 6 and 17, 1931 and Feb. 3, 1932, Getty.

18   "LAMB CHOPS AND MASHED CARROTS": CG to HL, Oct. 1, 1932, Getty.

19   HEARD SOPHIE TUCKER: CG to HL, Jan. 30; Feb. 9, 15, and 18, 1933, Getty.

19   "EAT THEIR OWN SNOT": CG to HL, March 23, 1933, Getty.

19   "WHAT TO THINK OF MYSELF": CG to HL, May 24 and 31; July 2 and 13; Aug. 15, Sept. 6, 1933, Getty.

20   "OF THE YEAR'S EXILE": CG to HL, Sept. 6 and 8, 1933, Getty.

20   "ALL THINGS THE SAME COLOR": CG to HL, Jan 18, 1934; untitled manuscript, Box 24, folder 2, Getty.

21   "KNOW EVERY INCH OF HER": CG to HL, Aug. 23, 1933, Getty.

21   "SHADE OF YOUR BREAST": Untitled poetry, 1920–1930, Box 23, folder 2, Getty.

21   "CLEMENT, INSTEAD OF CLEM": CG to HL, Nov. 9, 1933, Getty.

CHAPTER II: WHAT NEXT?

22   "I'M LOST": CG to HL, Jan. 26, 1934, Getty.

22   "IN THE SUN": Poetry, 1920–1930, Box 23, folder 4, Getty.

24   "REALIZING HER PAST": This account was in a folder of short stories, 1920s and 1930s, Box 24, folder 2, Getty.

24   "I HATE MYSELF": CG to HL, Feb. 22, 1934, Getty.

25   "COULDN'T HELP MYSELF": CG to HL, March 27, 1934, Getty.

25   "TRUE TO HER FOREVER": CG to HL, April 5 and 9, 1934, Getty.

25   "PISS ON THE SIDEWALK": CG to HL, April 24, May 17 and 25, 1934, Getty.

26   "TO BE MARRIED": CG to HL, July 24, 1934, Getty; Florence Rubenfeld, *Clement Greenberg: A Life* (New York: Scribner, 1997), 42.

26   "YOUNG TO BE ONE": CG to HL, Aug. 6, 1934, Getty.

27 A MEXICAN REVOLUTIONARY: CG, "Mutiny in Jalisco," *Esquire*, March 1935, 37, 167–69.

27 "THE TYPEWRITER IS OUT": CG to HL, Nov. 2, 1934, Getty.

28 REMAINED IN HIS FILES: Helene Richards, *Esquire* magazine, to R.H. Torres, Dec. 28, 1934; James Poling to Robert H. Torres, March 15, 1935; C. B. Lister to "My Dear Mr. Torres," March 25, 1935; W. H. Robertson, Syndication Department, *London Evening Standard, Daily & Sunday Express*, to Robert Herman Torres, Esq., June 3, 1935; Genevieve Pfleeger, secretary to *Esquire* editor Arnold Gingrich, to R. H. Torres, July 2, 1935; Antonio Delgado to Mr. Torres, Dec. 30, 1936, Getty.

28 PRODUCING MORE SERIOUS WORK: Trish Evans and Charles Harrison, "Conversation with Clement Greenberg," *Art Monthly*, Feb. 1984, reprinted in Robert C. Morgan, ed., *Clement Greenberg: Late Writings* (Minneapolis: University of Minnesota Press, 2003), 171.

28 "LOW AND CHEAP": CG to HL, Nov. 17 and Dec. 8, 1934, Getty.

29 AFTER ONLY SIX DAYS: CG to HL, Feb. 19 and Aug. 30, and December 14, 1935, Getty; Rubenfeld, *Clement Greenberg*, 44.

29 "OF THAT NOTHING, MUCH": Undated fragment in Poetry, 1920–1930, Box 23, folder 4, Getty.

30 "WITH THE LITTLE BASTARD": CG to HL, Dec. 14, 1935, and Jan 11, 1936, Getty.

30 "OH WEARY ROAD": Untitled poetry, 1930s, Box 23, folder 7, Getty.

31 "FOR THE LITTLE STINKER": CG to HL, Feb. 3, March 3, and March 25, 1936, Getty.

31 ON A CAREER: CG to HL, April 7 and 14, 1936; Dec. 12, 1937, Getty.

31 "EXCHANGING SOUL KISSES": CG to HL, Sept. 20, 1936, Getty.

33 "STRUGGLE OF THE WORKERS": William Phillips [under pseudonym Wallace Phelps], "Three Generations," *Partisan Review*, Sept.–Oct. 1934, 49–55; quoted in Terry A. Cooney, "Cosmopolitan Values and the Identification of Reaction, *Partisan Review* in the 1930s," *Journal of American History*, Dec. 1981, 580.

33 "AND GARBAGE COLLECTORS": CG to HL, June 22, 1928, Getty. When *New Masses* published Greenberg's poem "Sacramento 1935" in its September 24 issue, the work was immediately denounced as plagiarism of a poem by Mary deLorimer Welch (who coincidentally lived in Carmel), published two years earlier in the *New Republic*. Many years later, Greenberg denied any plagiarism, suggesting that he might have copied the poem into his notebook and then mistaken it as his own—or perhaps that it was "mystical correspondence between people." See Rubenfeld, *Clement Greenberg*, 43.

33 HAD BEEN LYNCHED: CG to HL, Oct. 27 and Dec. 10, 1933, Getty.

34 "INTELLIGENT MARXIST": CG to HL, Sept. 27, 1937, Getty.

34 "WE COULD NOT JOIN": Irving Howe, *Steady Work* (New York: Harcourt, Brace & World, 1966), 358, 360.

35 ITS FIRST ISSUE: Terry A. Cooney, *The Rise of the New York Intellectuals: Partisan Review and Its Circle* (Madison: University of Wisconsin Press, 1986), 116–17.

35 "SCIENCE AND HUMANISM": Philip Rahv, "Trials of the Mind," *Partisan Review*, April 1938, 3–4.

35 "BLACKJACKS, CLUBS, AND KNIVES": Max Shachtman, "Radicalism in the Thirties: The Trotskyist View," in Rita James Simon, ed., *As We Saw the Thirties: Essays on Social and Political Movements of a Decade* (Urbana: University Press of Illinois, 1967), 19–20.

36 DEATH IN THEIR WAKE: Max Shachtman, *Behind the Moscow Trial* (New York: Pioneer, 1936), pass.

36 "CALLING UPON DIALECTICAL MATERIALISM": Rubenfeld, *Clement Greenberg*, 44–45; Lionel Abel, "New York City: A Remembrance," *Dissent*, Summer 1961, 257.

37 POUND ON ARTHUR RIMBAUD: *New Act*, Jan. and June 1933, and April 1934, New York Public Library.

37 "A NASTY CUSTOMER": CG to HL, June 2, 1938, Getty.

37 "ANNOYED ME TO DEATH": CG to HL, Aug. 4, 23; and Oct. 7, 1938, Getty.

38 AGAINST STALIN'S SLANDERS: Ben Raeburn, "Harold Rosenberg, 1906–1978," *Art in America*, Sept.–Oct. 1978, 8–10; Abel, "New York City: A Remembrance," *Dissent*, Summer 1961, 251.

38 "DESTRUCTIVE QUARRELSOMENESS": Irving Howe, *A Margin of Hope: An Intellectual Autobiography* (San Diego: Harcourt Brace Jovanovich, 1982), 32–33.

39 ONLY AS M.M.: Harry Roskolenko, *When I Was Last on Cherry Street* (New York: Stein & Day, 1965), 157, 161; CG appointment books, Box 18, Getty.

39 "THAT INTELLECTUAL ARISTOCRACY": Irving Kristol, "Memoirs of a Trotskyist," *New York Times Sunday Magazine*, Jan. 23, 1977, 57.

40 "POLEMICAL ANNIHILATION": Daniel Bell, "First Love and Early Sorrows," *Partisan Review*, n. 4, 1981, 532, and *The End of Ideology* (Glencoe, IL: Free Press, 1960); Alfred Kazin, *Starting Out in the Thirties* (Ithaca: Cornell University Press, 1989), 86–87; Irving Howe, "Range of the New York Intellectual" in Bernard Rosenberg and Ernest Goldstein, eds., *Creators and Disturbers* (New York: Columbia University Press, 1982), 276–77.

41 SHE HAD DEMANDED: CG to HL, Jan. 19, March 16, and May 13, 1937,

Getty; CG, *The Harold Letters, 1928–1943: The Making of an Intellectual*, ed. Janice Van Horne (Washington, D.C.: Counterpoint, 2000), 174.

41 "PRODUCED NO EFFECT": CG to HL, July 13, 1937, and Feb. 8, 1938, Getty.

42 "TAKE THE LAD ANY TIME": CG to HL, June 6, 1936; Sept. 17, Nov. 1 and 9, 1938, Getty.

42 "NICE PROLETARIANS": CG to HL, Aug. 6 and Sept. 27, 1937, Getty.

43 "MIDDLEBROW CULTURE": CG to HL, Sept. 27, 1937, Getty; Robert Warshow, "The Legacy of the 30s," *Commentary*, Dec. 1947, 538–39.

44 "OF DECORATIVE DESIGN": Edward Alden Jewell, "Abstract Artists Open Show Today," *New York Times*, April 6, 1937, 21.

44 THEIR MORE INTIMATE MOMENTS: "Guggenheim Fund for Art Is Set Up," *New York Times*, Feb 11, 1937, 1, 19; "Foundation Names Board and Curator," *New York Times*, June 30, 1937, 21; Jewell, "In the Realm of Art: Challenge of the Nonobjective," *New York Times*, July 4, 1937, Sec. X, 7; Joan M. Lukach, *Hilla Rebay: In Search of the Spirit of Art* (New York: Braziller, 1983), 135.

45 "OTHER ABSTRACT ART, MUSIC": "Copper into Art," *New York Times*, July 1, 1937, 26; "Topics of the Times," *New York Times*, July 5, 1937, 16.

46 MEMBERS OF AAA: Jewell, "In the Realm of Art: Representation vs. Abstraction," *New York Times*, July 11, 1937, Sec. X, 12; Jewell, "Abstraction: A Debate Rages," *New York Times Magazine*, July 18, 1937; "Opinions Under Postage," *New York Times*, July 25, 1937, Sec. X, 7; Merle Armitage, "Opinions Under Postage," *New York Times*, Aug. 1, 1937, Sec. X, 7; Hananiah Harari, Rosalind Bengelsdorf, Byron Browne, Leo Lances, and George McNeill (all AAA members), "Opinions Under Postage," *New York Times*, Aug. 8, 1937, Sec. X, 7.

47 LACKING IN "SOCIAL VALUE": Thomas Craven, "An American Painter," *Nation*, Jan. 7, 1925, reprinted in Peter G. Meyer, ed., *Brushes with History: Writing on Art from* The Nation, *1895–2001* (New York: Thunder's Mouth, 2001), 141; Polly Burroughs, *Thomas Hart Benton: A Portrait* (Garden City: Doubleday, 1981), 22.

47 "CAN PRODUCE ART": Thomas Craven, "Politics and the Painting Business," *American Mercury*, Dec. 1932, 463, 466; Craven, "Our Art Becomes American," *Harper's*, Sept. 1935, 431.

47 "ART OF THE PEOPLE": Ruth Pickering, "Grant Wood: Painter in Overalls," *North American Review*, Sept. 1935, 271–72; Alfred Frankenstein, "Paul Sample," *Magazine of Art*, July 1938, 387.

48 NARROWNESS, AND IGNORANCE: Cooney, *Rise of the New York Intellectuals*, 133.

48 NEW YORK TRANSIT WORKERS: Howe, *Intellectual Autobiography*, 70.

49 TO NO AVAIL: Corliss Lamont to Lionel Trilling, Dec. 31, 1937; Trilling to Lamont, Feb. 1 and 2, 1938, and Lamont to Trilling, March 9, 1938; all Trilling Papers, Butler Library, Columbia University.

49 ART TO GO FORWARD: Leon Trotsky, "Art and Politics," *Partisan Review*, Aug.–Sept. 1938, 3–4.

49 "AMONG THE PARTISANSKIS": Michael Wreszin, *A Rebel in Defense of Tradition* (New York: Basic Books, 1994), 55.

50 ABOUT $2,000 A YEAR: Ibid., 52–54.

50 THE MAGAZINE'S BOOKKEEPER: Roskolenko, *When I Was Last on Cherry Street*, 158.

51 "AGAINST REACTIONARY PERSECUTION": André Breton and Diego Rivera [*sic*], "Manifesto: Towards a Free Revolutionary Art," trans. Dwight Macdonald, in *Partisan Review*, Fall 1938, 49–53.

CHAPTER III: AN OPENING ON THE LEFT

52 "LEAVING ADVERTISING ASIDE": CG, notes for "Avant-Garde and Kitsch," Box 24, folder 9, Getty.

53 "THE COMMON SEWER": CG to Dwight Macdonald, Feb. 5, 1939, Getty.

54 EUROPE THE FOLLOWING MORNING: CG to HL, March 27 and April 18, 1939, Getty.

54 "A BIT OF SWITZERLAND": CG to HL, April 18, 23, and 26, 1939; CG to "Family," April 23, 1939, Getty.

54 "THE ARCHITECTURAL VANITY": CG to "Family," April 28–30, and to "Dear Folks," May 5, 1939, Getty.

55 "MORE IMPORTANT THAN DOS PASSOS": CG to "Dear Folks," May 5, 1939, Getty; Florence Rubenfeld, *Clement Greenberg: A Life* (New York: Scribner, 1997), 52.

55 "CALLED THE SISTINE CHAPEL": CG to "Greenberg *famille*," May 15, 1939, Getty; Rubenfeld, *Clement Greenberg*, 53.

55 "NO WONDERS LEFT": CG to "*famiglia* Greenberg," May 20, 1939.

56 REWROTE THE ENTIRE ESSAY: CG to HL, June 27, 1939, Getty; Rubenfeld, *Clement Greenberg*, 53.

56 "UMBILICAL CORD OF GOLD": CG, "Avant-Garde and Kitsch," *Partisan Review*, Fall 1939, reprinted in John O'Brian, ed., *Clement Greenberg: The Collected Essays and Criticism, Volume 1: Perceptions and Judgments, 1939–1944* (Chicago: University of Chicago Press, 1986; hereafter "O'Brian, vol. 1"), 8–10.

57 "DISCARDS THE REST": Ibid., 12.

57 "WE HAVE RIGHT NOW": Ibid., 22.

58 ON HIS NEXT PIECE: CG to HL, Nov. 29 and Dec. 12, 1939; March 2 and 20, 1940, Getty.

59 "AS I SHOULD BE": CG to HL, July 11, Aug. 4 and 23, 1939, Getty.

59 "NOT TO BOTHER ME": CG to HL, Sept. 26, 1939, Getty.

59 PICKED UP ON THEM: Rubenfeld, *Clement Greenberg*, 58.

59 "MY IDEAS, OF COURSE": Transcript of an interview with Florence Rubenfeld, Feb. 16, 1990, Getty.

60 FAVORING EUROPEAN MODERNISTS: CG, "New York Painting Only Yesterday," *Art News*, Summer 1957, reprinted in John O'Brian, ed., *Clement Greenberg: The Collected Essays and Criticism, Volume 4: Modernism with a Vengeance, 1957–1969* (Chicago: University of Chicago Press, 1993), 19–20.

60 "FOR THE MASSES": Edward Alden Jewell, "Abstraction and Music," *New York Times*, Aug. 6, 1939; Stuart Davis, "Opinions under Postage," and Jewell, "The Cheshire Grin Again," *New York Times*, Aug. 20, 1939.

61 "LOOKING AT SOMETHING": Jewell, "Soundings Off a Treacherous Coast," *New York Times*, Aug. 27, 1939, and "Exploring a Dark Realm," *New York Times*, Sept. 3, 1939.

61 "A SPECIAL CIVILIZATION": Peyton Boswell, Jr., *Modern American Painting* (New York: Dodd, Mead, 1940), 15, 56; Thomas Craven, *Modern Art* (New York: Simon & Schuster, 1940), xix–xxi, 311–12.

61 "SO-CALLED EUROPEAN SCHOOLS": Boswell, "Comments: When Is Art Art?" *Art Digest*, Oct. 1939, 3; [Anon.], "Lord Duveen of Milbank," *Art in America*, Oct. 1939, 193; Christopher Lazare, "American Art on Exhibit," *North American Review*, Dec. 1939, 394–400.

62 "THOUGHT UP FOR HIMSELF": CG, "Towards a Newer Laocoon," *Partisan Review*, July–Aug, 1940, reprinted in O'Brian, vol. 1, 23–24; Jason Edward Kaufman, "Clement Greenberg as the American Art World Remembers Him," *The Art Newspaper*, June 1994, 4.

62 CUT HIS ARTICLE "OUTRAGEOUSLY": Manuscript of "Towards a Newer Laocoon," Box 25, folder 1; CG to HL, June 24, 1940; both Getty.

63 WOULD HAVE TO FOLD: CG to HL, Aug. 24, 1940, Getty.

64 "THE MORE PERNICIOUS": "Towards a Newer Laocoon," 26–28.

64 AS A CULTIVATED BEING: Ibid., 29.

65 "EXTRAORDINARILY GOOD": CG to HL, June 24, 1940, Getty.

65 "EYE IN OTHER DIRECTIONS": Steven Naifeh and Gregory White Smith, *Jackson Pollock: An American Saga* (New York: Clarkson Potter, 1989), 521.

65 "WITH THE FORM": CG to HL, Sept. 25, 1940, Getty; Karen Wilkin and Bruce Guenther, *Clement Greenberg: A Critic's Collection* (Princeton: Princeton University Press, 2001), 16.

66 "RULING THE LITERARY ROOST": Philip Rahv, "Twilight of the Thirties," *Partisan Review*, Summer 1939, 5.

66 AMERICAN LITERARY STUDIES: Charles C. Alexander, *Here the Country Lies: Nationalism and the Arts in 20th Century America* (Bloomington: Indiana University Press, 1980), 201–202.

66 ENDORSED HOFMANN'S KIND OF ABSTRACTION: Susan Noyes Platt, "Clement Greenberg in the 1930s: A New Perspective on His Criticism," *Art Criticism*, vol. 5, no. 3, 49–50; Barbara Rose, "Where Vitality Rests in Abstract Art," *Vogue*, March 1, 1971, 156.

67 AND EVELYN WAUGH: Michael Shelden, *Friends of Promise: Cyril Connolly and the World of Horizon* (London: Hamish Hamilton, 1989), 19–20.

67 A GENEROUS ALLOWANCE: Ibid., 23–25.

68 "SEX LIKE A MAN": Jeremy Lewis, *Cyril Connolly: A Life* (London: Jonathan Cape, 1997), 379–80; CG to HL, July 22, 1940, Getty.

68 "OF BEING DAZZLED": CG to HL, Aug. 13, 1940, Getty.

69 "LEAD TO DISASTER": CG, "An American View," *Horizon*, Sept. 1940, reprinted in O'Brian, vol. 1, 38–41, and "Editor's note," 41.

70 "CONSTANT AND RADICAL CRITICISM": CG and Dwight Macdonald, "10 Propositions on the War," *Partisan Review*, July–Aug. 1941, 271–78; S. A. Longstaff, "*Partisan Review* and the Second World War," *Salmagundi*, Winter 1979, 119.

70 WAR ON THE UNITED STATES: Alfred Kazin, *Starting Out in the Thirties* (Ithaca: Cornell University Press, 1989), 153; Irving Howe, *A Margin of Hope: An Intellectual Autobiography* (San Diego: Harcourt Brace Jovanovich, 1982), 87; *Partisan Review*, Nov.–Dec. 1941, 506–508.

70 "THAT HAD COUNTED": Norman Podhoretz, *Breaking Ranks* (New York: Harper & Row, 1979), 56.

71 "THE ROLE OF RADICALS": Sidney Hook, "The Radical Comedians," *American Scholar*, Winter 1984–85, 61.

71 "LITTLE MAGAZINE WORLD": S. A. Longstaff, "Ivy League Gentiles and Inner-City Jews: Class and Ethnicity around *Partisan Review* in the 30s and 40s," *American Jewish History*, Spring 1991, 329; Dwight Macdonald, "Politics Past (II)," *Encounter*, April 1957, 66.

72 SIREN-CALL OF LITERATURE: CG to HL, Sept. 16, 1940, Getty; CG, "Aesthetics as Science: Review of *The Structure of Art* by Carl Thurston," *Nation*, Feb. 22, 1941, reprinted in O'Brian, vol. 1.

72 "GOVERNMENT POLICY TOMORROW": Diana Trilling, *The Beginning of the Journey* (New York: Harcourt, Brace, 1993), 329–31.

72 "WHAT YOU LOOK FOR": CG, "The Renaissance of the Little Mag: Review of *Accent, Diogenes, Experimental Review, Vice Versa,* and

View," *Partisan Review*, Feb. 1941, reprinted in O'Brian, vol.1, 42–44, 46; Rubenfeld, *Clement Greenberg*, 62.

73 RECENT GERMAN LITERATURE: CG, "Bertolt Brecht's Poetry," *Partisan Review*, March–April 1941, reprinted in O'Brian, vol.1, 49–62.

73 "TO FEEL DEEPLY": CG to HL, Sept. 19 and 25, 1940, Getty.

73 "SO LONG TO GROW UP": CG to HL, Oct. 22 and Nov. 25, 1940, Getty.

74 "A SNOB & PRIG": CG, "Review of Exhibitions of Joan Miró, Fernand Léger, and Wassily Kandinsky," *Nation*, April 19, 1941; CG, "Art Chronicle: On Paul Klee (1870–1940), *Partisan Review*, May–June 1941, reprinted in O'Brian, vol.1., 62–73; CG to HL, Dec. 31, 1940, Getty.

74 "A LITTLE ASHAMED": CG to HL, Dec. 31, 1940, May 20 and June 10, 1941, Getty.

75 VAULTING OPINION OF HIMSELF: CG to HL, July 15, 1941, Getty; Rubenfeld, *Clement Greenberg*, 67, 81.

75 "HORRIBLE AS THE FATE": CG to HL, Sept. 19 and Nov. 25, 1940; CG to HL, March 24, 1941, Getty.

75 A NINE-PAGE ARTICLE: Dwight Macdonald to Lionel Trilling, Feb. 9, 1939, Trilling Papers, Butler Library, Columbia University.

75 "CHRONIC TRENCH MOUTH": CG to HL, Aug. 10, Oct. 13, and Dec. 16, 1942; Jan. 7 and Feb. 22, 1943, Getty.

CHAPTER IV: WAR

76 "BUT YOU DO": CG to HL, Feb. 22, 1943, Getty.

76 "SAVE YOURSELVES": CG to HL, March 10, 1943, Getty; Weldon Kees to Norris Getty, March 21, 1943, in Robert E. Knoll, *Weldon Kees and the Midcentury Generation, Letters 1935–55* (Lincoln: University of Nebraska Press, 1986), 74.

76 ROOM WITH TWO OTHERS: CG to HL, April 4, 1943, Getty.

77 "HARDLY MORE THAN THAT": CG, "Goose-step in Tishomingo," *Nation*, May 22, 1943, reprinted in John O'Brian, ed., *Clement Greenberg: The Collected Essays and Criticism, Volume 1: Perceptions and Judgments, 1939–1944* (Chicago: University of Chicago Press, 1986; hereafter "O'Brian, vol. 1"), 148–52; Rick Atkinson, *An Army at Dawn: The War in North Africa, 1942–1943* (New York: Henry Holt, 2003), 537.

77 "DID ME IN": CG to HL, June 19 and Aug. 11, 1943, Getty; editor's note to CG to Jean Connolly, July 9, 1943 (unmailed), in CG, *The Harold Letters, 1928–1943: The Making of an Intellectual*, ed. Janice Van Horne (Washington, D.C.: Counterpoint, 2000), 304–305.

78 "SAYING THEY WERE IN": *Harold Letters*, 305; Florence Rubenfeld, *Clement Greenberg: A Life* (New York: Scribner, 1997), 72–73.

78 "FELT TRAPPED": CG to HL, Aug. 11, 1943, Getty.

78   "LACK OF ANY": CG to HL, Aug. 27 and Sept. 11, 1943, Getty; CG to O'Brian, Aug. 6, 1984.

79   GREATLY GIFTED ARTIST: CG, "Review of a Joint Exhibition of Joseph Cornell and Laurence Vail," *Nation*, Dec. 26, 1942, reprinted in O'Brian, vol. 1, 131–32.

79   "THE TIME AND PLACE": CG to HL, Sept. 23 and 27, 1943, Getty.

80   "SEEM COMPLETELY SUCCESSFUL": CG "Review of Mondrian's *New York Boogie Woogie* [et al.]" *Nation*, Oct. 9, 1943, and "Reconsideration of Mondrian's *New York Boogie Woogie* [et al.]" *Nation*, Oct. 16, 1943, reprinted in O'Brian, vol.1, 153–54.

80   "THE AGE IS DOOMED": CG, "Review of Exhibitions of Alexander Calder and Giorgio de Chirico," Oct. 23, 1943; "Review of Exhibitions of Van Gogh," Nov. 6, 1943; "Review of Exhibitions of . . . Eugene Berman," Nov. 13, 1943; all in *Nation*, reprinted in O'Brian, vol.1, 159–64.

81   "RANGE OF POSSIBILITIES": Irving Howe, *A Margin of Hope: An Intellectual Autobiography* (San Diego: Harcourt Brace Jovanovich, 1982), 161.

81   PRESCRIPTIONS AND DISPUTATIONS: CG, "The Jewish Dickens," *Nation*, Oct. 16, 1943, reprinted in O'Brian, vol.1, 155–58.

81   "REMAINS UNEXPLAINED": CG to HL, Sept. 11, 1943, Getty; *Harold Letters*, 285–86.

82   FREQUENTLY DENIGRATED WOMEN: CG appointment calendar for Jan. 20, 1945, Getty.

82   "INTERVENTION OF COOLER HEADS": Rubenfeld, *Clement Greenberg*, 91–92.

83   "HIS SCRAMBLED EGGS": Carol Brightman, *Mary McCarthy and Her World* (New York: Clarkson Potter, 1992), 258–59; David Laskin, *Partisans: Marriage, Politics, and Betrayal among the New York Intellectuals* (New York: Simon & Schuster, 2000), 160; Frances Kiernan, *A Life of Mary McCarthy: Seeing Mary Plain* (New York: Norton, 2000), 215, 228.

84   "WAITING FOR HIS MOTHER": Kiernan, *A Life of Mary McCarthy*, 221.

84   "TO MARRY A JEW": Ibid., 215.

85   THROUGHOUT HIS LIFE: CG to HL, July 13, 1946, Getty.

85   "A MILE WIDE": Steven Naifeh and Gregory White Smith, *Jackson Pollock: An American Saga* (New York: Clarkson Potter, 1989), 877.

85   "OPPOSITION WAS INVINCIBLE": CG to HL, July 13, 1946, Getty.

86   "VIOLENCE BY ABUSE": Brightman, *Mary McCarthy*, 287–88; Naifeh and Smith, *Jackson Pollock*, 550; Rubenfeld, *Clement Greenberg*, 83.

87   "SOMETHING IS OFF": Elizabeth Frank, "Farewell to Athene: The Collected Greenberg," *Salmagundi*, Fall 1988, 249; Susan Noyes Platt,

"Clement Greenberg in the 1930s," *Art Criticism*, vol. 5, no. 3, 47–48; Naifeh and Smith, *Jackson Pollock*, 550.

87 "DANGEROUS TO YOUNGER PAINTERS": CG, "Obituary and Review of an Exhibition of Kandinsky," *Nation*, Jan. 13, 1945, reprinted in John O'Brian, ed., *Clement Greenberg: The Collected Essays and Criticism, Volume 2: Arrogant Purpose, 1945–1949* (Chicago: University of Chicago Press, 1987; hereafter "O'Brian, vol. 2"), 4, 6.

88 AND JAMES JOHNSON SWEENEY: "In Miniature: Art of This Century," *New York Times*, March 21, 1943, Sec. II, 7; "Local Shows," *New York Times*, May 23, 1943, Sec. II, 10.

88 "INVENTED CHIAROSCURO": CG, "Review of *The Story of Painting: From Cave Pictures to Modern Art*, by Thomas Craven," *Nation*, May 20, 1944, reprinted in O'Brian, vol. 1, 206–207.

88 "PLAYING BY GENTILE RULES": Howe, *A Margin of Hope*, 139–40.

89 "ARCHAIC" THAN DEVOTO: Philip Rahv, "The Progress of Cultural Socialism," *Partisan Review*, Summer 1944, 161, 163.

89 "OF THAT INTELLIGENCE": William Barrett: *The Truants: Adventures among the Intellectuals* (Garden City, NY: Anchor Books, 1974), 36.

89 A HALT IN 1949: Stephen J. Whitfield, "Dwight Macdonald's 'Politics' Magazine, 1944–49" *Journalism History*, Autumn 1976, 86–87; Peter Coleman, *The Liberal Conspiracy* (New York: Free Press, 1989), 75–76.

89 "WARTIME-EDUCATED PUBLIC": CG to John O'Brian, Dec. 12, 1984, O'Brian Papers; Frances Kiernan, *A Life of Mary McCarthy*, 215; Diana Trilling, "An Interview with Dwight Macdonald," *Partisan Review*, Oct. 1984, 806–807.

90 "SUBWAYS, NEWSSTANDS, THE OFFICE": Barrett, *The Truants*, 1, 36–37; Howe, *A Margin of Hope*, 130; James Atlas, *Bellow: A Biography* (New York: Random House, 2000), 111–12.

90 GREENBERG'S WAILING WALL: Barrett, *The Truants*, 41, 137.

91 "THINGS AS THEY WERE": Leslie Fiedler, *An End to Innocence: Essays on Culture & Politics* (Boston: Beacon Press, 1955), 204; Alfred Kazin, *New York Jew* (New York: Alfred A. Knopf, 1978), 44–45; Sidney Hook, "The Radical Comedians," *American Scholar*, Winter 1984–85, 45–6.

91 AND EDITED AGAIN: Rubenfeld, *Clement Greenberg*, 78–79.

92 SIX-WEEK EUROPEAN JOURNEY: Goethe essay, undated, Box 24, folder 14; On Mann's *Joseph* novels, undated, Box 24, folder 13; notes on easel painting, Box 24, folder 11; all Getty.

92 "MY EYE AGAINST WHATEVER": James Faure Walker, "Four Scottish Painters," *Art Monthly*, Dec. 1977, reprinted in Robert C. Morgan, ed., *Clement Greenberg: Late Writings* (Minneapolis: University of Minnesota Press, 2003), 165–66.

92 "NOT FOR LONG": CG, "Review of Exhibitions of Marc Chagall [et al.]," *Nation*, Nov. 13, 1943, reprinted in O'Brian, vol. 1, 164–66.

93 "DO FROM NOW ON": CG, "Review of a Group Exhibition at Art of this Century Gallery [et al.]," and "Review of Exhibitions of William Baziotes [et al.]," *Nation*, May 27 and Nov. 11, 1944, reprinted in O'Brian, vol. 1, 209–10 and 239–41.

93 WITHOUT HIS APPROVAL: Melvin Lader, "Howard Putzel: Proponent of Surrealism and Early Abstract Expressionism in America," *Arts Magazine*, March 1982, 85–88; Peggy Guggenheim, *Out of This Century* (New York: Universe, 1979), 215–16.

94 PROBABLY, JACKSON POLLOCK: Lader, "Howard Putzel," 89–90.

94 "DEALT WITH PUTZEL": Guggenheim, *Out of This Century*, 246; Lader, "Howard Putzel," 90.

95 "WOULD HAVE HAPPENED": CG, "Review of the Peggy Guggenheim Collection," *Nation*, Jan. 30, 1943, reprinted in O'Brian, vol. 1, 140–41; Lader, "Howard Putzel," 91; Naifeh and Smith, *Jackson Pollock*, 451; Jacqueline Bograd Weld, *Peggy: The Wayward Guggenheim* (New York: Dutton, 1986), 307.

95 IN FINANCIAL TROUBLE: Lader, "Howard Putzel," 92–93, 96; Edward Alden Jewell, "Toward Abstract or Away," *New York Times*, July 1, 1945; CG, "Review of the Exhibition *A Problem for Critics*," *Nation*, June 9, 1945, reprinted in O'Brian, vol. 2, 28–30.

96 "PLEASED SMILES OF DEALERS": Aline B. Louchheim, "Who Buys What in the Picture Boom," *Art News*, July 1, 1944, 12–13.

96 "FAILURE AS ARTISTS": Aline B. Louchheim, "Second Season of the Picture Boom," *Art News*, Aug. 1, 1945, 9–10; Elizabeth McCausland, "Why Can't America Afford Art?" *Magazine of Art*, Jan. 1946, 19–20.

97 WERE JEWISH: "57th Street," *Fortune*, Sept. 1946, 144–51, 197–202.

97 "EVERY WORD I WRITE": CG, "Under Forty: A Symposium on American Literature and the Younger Generation of American Jews," *Contemporary Jewish Record*, Feb. 1944, reprinted in O'Brian, vol. 1, 177.

97 OR EVEN ASSIMILATION: Oscar Handlin, "The American Jewish Committee: A Half-Century View," *Commentary*, Jan. 1957, 1–5.

98 "POWER OF THE INTELLECT": Author interview with Norman Podhoretz, New York, Oct. 28, 2002; Daniel Bell, *Winding Passage: Essays and Sociological Journeys, 1960–1980* (Cambridge: Abt Books, 1980), 132–33; Richard H. Pells, *The Liberal Mind in a Conservative Age* (New York: Harper & Row, 1985), 73.

98 "AND THEY DON'T": Pells, *The Liberal Mind*, 74; Norman Podhoretz, *Making It* (New York: Random House, 1967), 99–100.

99 "TIME IN THE OFFICE": Midge Decter, "Remembering Robert Warshow," *Commentary*, April 2002, 45–47.

99 "WITH A STRONG MIND": Howe, *A Margin of Hope*, 113.

100 "PROBABLY GOT TOO TIRED": André Breton to William Baziotes, Sept. 7, 1942, Smithsonian Institution, Archives of American Art (hereafter "AAA"); CG to Baziotes, June 17 and Aug. 23, 1944, AAA; CG, "Surrealist Painting," *Nation*, Aug. 12 and 19, 1944, reprinted in O'Brian, vol. 1, 225–26.

100 RAZOR-EDGED PROSE: CG address book for 1943–45, Getty.

101 "LOOKS UGLY AT FIRST": CG, "Review of Exhibitions of Mondrian, Kandinsky and Pollock [et al.]" *Nation*, April 7, 1945, reprinted in O'Brian, vol. 2, 14–18.

101 "EXPOSURE FOR JACKSON": CG, "Review of Exhibitions of the American Abstract Artists, Jacques Lipschitz, and Jackson Pollock," *Nation*, April 13, 1946, reprinted in O'Brian, vol. 2, 72–75; Naifeh and Smith, *Jackson Pollock*, 522.

102 "ALL HIS CONVERSATION": Naifeh and Smith, *Jackson Pollock*, 523

102 "HE'LL HELP YOU": B. H. Friedman, *Jackson Pollock: Energy Made Visible* (New York: McGraw Hill, 1974), 137; Naifeh and Smith, *Jackson Pollock*, 524.

103 CRACKING A SMILE: "The Jewish Joke: Review of *Röyte Pomerantzen*, edited by Immanuel Olsvanger," *Commentary*, Dec. 1947, reprinted in O'Brian, vol. 2, 182–87.

103 OFFER OF AN ARTICLE: Clive Fisher, *Cyril Connolly: A Nostalgic Life* (London: Macmillan, 1995), 262; Jeremy Lewis, *Cyril Connolly: A Life* (London: Jonathan Cape, 1997), 404–405; CG to Cyril Connolly, April 7, 1947, Connolly Papers, McFurling Library, University of Tulsa; Cyril Connolly to CG, July 15, 1947, Getty.

104 "MALE AND FEMALE": CG, "The Present Prospects of American Painting and Sculpture," *Horizon*, Oct. 1947, reprinted in O'Brian, vol. 2, 160–70.

105 ENTIRE YEAR TOTALED $150: David Smith to CG, Dec. 23, 1947, AAA.

106 "HUNDRED AND FORTY MILLION": CG, "The Present Prospects of American Painting and Sculpture," *Horizon*, Oct. 1947, reprinted in O'Brian, vol. 2, 160–70.

106 "CRANK'S VIEW OF AMERICAN ART": "The Best?" *Time*, Dec. 1, 1947, 55.

106 PAINTINGS WOULD BE BOUGHT: Susan Sivard, "The State Department 'Advancing American Art' Exhibition of 1946 and the Advance of American Art," *Arts Magazine*, April 1984, 92, 94–95.

107 EXHIBITIONS FOR TEN YEARS: Ibid., 96–97.

107 GUATEMALA, CUBA, AND HAITI: Ibid., 93.

108 "REMNANTS OF EARLY MODERN ART": Milton W. Brown, "After Three Years," *Magazine of Art*, April 1946, 138.

108 "BOHEMIA REALLY IS": Anton Gill, *Peggy Guggenheim: The Life of an Art Addict* (London: Harper Collins, 2001), 343, 352; CG, "A Martyr to Bohemia," *Commentary*, Sept. 1946, reprinted in O'Brian, vol. 2, 97–98.

109 EPICENTER OF CONTEMPORARY ART: CG, "Painting Only Yesterday," *Art News*, Summer 1957, reprinted in John O'Brian, ed., *Clement Greenberg: The Collected Essays and Criticism, Volume 4: Modernism with a Vengeance, 1957–1969* (Chicago: University of Chicago Press, 1993), 22–23; CG to HL, Aug. 26, 1947, Getty.

CHAPTER V: THE GURU EMERGES

110 "STACKED AGAINST THE WALL": CG, "The Situation at the Moment," *Partisan Review*, Jan. 1948, reprinted in John O'Brian, ed., *Clement Greenberg: The Collected Essays and Criticism, Volume 2: Arrogant Purpose, 1945–1949* (Chicago: University of Chicago Press, 1987; hereafter "O'Brian, vol. 2"), 192–96.

110 "TO THE NEW YORK SCHOOL": Amy Newman, *Challenging Art: Artforum 1962–1974* (New York: Soho, 2000), 22.

111 "IN PAINTING AND MUSIC": CG, "The State of American Writing, 1948: A Symposium," *Partisan Review*, Aug. 1948, reprinted in O'Brian, vol. 2, 254–58.

112 "ENJOYED BY A LARGE PUBLIC": Russell Davenport, "A *Life* Roundtable on Modern Art," *Life*, Oct. 11, 1948, 56–57.

112 "ARTIST SHOULD EXPERIMENT": Aline B. Louchheim, "ABC (or XYZ) of Abstract Art," *New York Times Magazine*, July 11, 1948, 16–17, 42–43; "Letters," *New York Times Magazine*, July 25, Aug. 1 and 15, 1948; all p. 2.

113 "IN OUR LIVES": Robert T. Elson, *The World of Time Inc.*, vol.2 (New York: Atheneum, 1973), 421; Nelson Rockefeller, "The Arts and Quality of Life," *Saturday Evening Post*, Summer 1971, 73.

113 "IT EVER DID": Elson, *The World of Time*, 422.

114 "PRODUCED IN THIS COUNTRY": Davenport, "A *Life* Roundtable," 62–63 and 79.

115 DIED TWO YEARS LATER: Francis Henry Taylor, "Modern Art and the Dignity of Man," *Atlantic Monthly*, Dec. 1948, 30–31; Howard Hibbard, *The Metropolitan Museum of Art* (New York: Harper & Row, 1980), 574.

115 "PHASE OF CUBISM": CG, "Review of Exhibitions of Worden Day, Carl Holty, and Jackson Pollock," *Nation*, Jan. 24, 1948, reprinted in O'Brian, vol. 2, 200–3.

116 "PHENOMENON OF AMERICAN ART": "Jackson Pollock: Is He the

Greatest Living Painter in the U.S.?" *Life*, Aug. 8, 1949, 42–43, 45; Elson, *The World of Time*, 422n.

116 HIS WRITING ABILITY: Ross Wetzsteon, *Republic of Dreams: The American Bohemia, 1910–1960* (New York: Simon & Schuster, 2002), 533; Steven Naifeh and Gregory White Smith, *Jackson Pollock: An American Saga* (New York: Clarkson Potter, 1989), 551.

117 "JACKSON FELT INADEQUATE": B. H. Friedman, *Jackson Pollock: Energy Made Visible* (New York: McGraw-Hill, 1972), 102–103.

117 "CLEM LIKES THAT": Naifeh and Smith, *Jackson Pollock*, 549.

118 THE CLASSLESS SOCIETY: Paul N. Siegel, ed., *Leon Trotsky on Literature and Art* (New York: Pathfinder, 1970), 59.

118 WAS NEVER PUBLISHED: Siegel, *Trotsky on Literature*, 32; John O'Brian, ed., *Clement Greenberg: The Collected Essays and Criticism, Volume 1: Perceptions and Judgments, 1939–1944* (Chicago: University of Chicago Press, 1986; hereafter "O'Brian, vol. 1"), xx.

119 "ELIGIBLE FOR THE MUSEUMS": CG, "Jean Dubuffet and 'Art Brut,'" *Partisan Review*, March 1949, reprinted in O'Brian, vol. 2, 289–91.

119 "HISTORY OF CRITICISM": Adam Gopnik, "The Power Critic," *New Yorker*, March 16, 1998, 74.

120 ASSEMBLED BY SIDNEY HOOK: Terry Teachout, "Composers for Communism," *Commentary*, May 2004, 57–60.

120 WHO HAD HIRED HIM: Florence Rubenfeld, *Clement Greenberg: A Life* (New York: Scribner, 1997), 122; Diana Trilling, *The Beginning of the Journey* (New York: Harcourt, Brace, 1993), 332.

121 REMAINED BELOW $500: CG, "The New York Market for American Art," *Nation*, June 11, 1949, reprinted in O'Brian, vol. 2, 319–22; undated accounting forms 1949–50, from Betty Parson Gallery, Jackson Pollock Papers, Smithsonian Institution, Archives of American Art (hereafter "AAA").

121 NO TRACE OF ITS DRIVER: Raphael Rubinstein, "American Criticism and How It Got That Way," *Art in America*, June 2002, 37; April Kingsley, *The Turning Point: Abstract Expressionists and the Transformation of American Art* (New York: Simon & Schuster, 1992), 93; Peter G. Meyer, ed., *Brushes with History: Writing on Art from The Nation, 1865–2001* (New York: Thunder's Mouth/Nation Books), 223; James Reidel, *Vanished Act: The Life and Art of Weldon Kees* (Lincoln: University of Nebraska Press, 2003), 3–5, 207.

122 "BOTHERED OVER NOTHING": CG and David Sylvester, "The European View of American Art," *Nation*, Nov. 25, 1950, reprinted in Meyer, *Brushes with History*, 227–32.

122 AND RALPH ELLISON: François Bondy, "Berlin Congress for Freedom:

A New Resistance in the Making," *Commentary*, Sept. 1950, 245; Description, Papers of the American Committee for Cultural Freedom, Tamiment Library, New York University; Sidney Hook, *An Unquiet Life in the 20th Century* (New York: Harper & Row, 1987), 421–22.

122 THE PREVIOUS JUNE: CG, "To the Editor of *The Nation*," Feb. 7, 1951, reprinted in John O'Brian, ed., *Clement Greenberg: The Collected Essays and Criticism, Volume 3: Affirmations and Refusals, 1950–1956* (Chicago: University of Chicago Press, 1993; hereafter "O'Brian, vol. 3"), 78–82.

123 "AN ENORMOUS MISTAKE": O'Brian, vol. 3, 79n.; Annette Cox, *Art-as-Politics The Abstract Expressionist Avant-Garde and Society* (Ann Arbor: UMI Research, 1982), 150–51; Mary Sperling McAuliffe, *Crisis on the Left: Cold War Politics and American Liberals, 1947–1954* (Amherst: University of Massachusetts Press, 1978), 113–15.

123 DENOUNCED IT AS DECADENT: "Long-range Aims of OWI Outlined," *New York Times*, Feb. 25, 1945, 39; Eva Cockroft, "Abstract Expressionism: Weapon of the Cold War," *Artforum*, June 1974, 41; Alfred H. Barr, Jr., "Is Modern Art Communistic?" *New York Times Magazine*, Dec. 14, 1952, 32–33.

123 CONVEYED THE DESIRED MESSAGE: All articles from the *New York Times*: Aline B. [Louchheim] Saarinen, "U.S.S.R. vs. Abstract," Aug. 22, 1954, Sec. II, 8; further commentary by William J. Jorden, Feb. 27, 1957, 7, and Max Frankel, Aug. 9, 1957, 2.

124 "CHRISTENED ABSTRACT EXPRESSIONISM": Robert Coates, "The Art Galleries," March 30, 1946, reprinted in Clifford Ross, ed., *Abstract Expressionism: Creators and Critics* (New York: Abrams, 1990), 230.

124 SHOW CLOSED ON DECEMBER 10: Naifeh and Smith, *Jackson Pollock*, 597–600.

124 AND LOOKING ANGRY: Ibid., 602–603; *New York Times*, May 22, 1950; *New York Herald-Tribune*, May 23, 1950; *Life*, "The Metropolitan and Art," Jan. 15, 1951, 34.

125 "YOU WERE LOUSY": Fred Camper, "In the Shadow of Giants," *Chicago Reader*, May 24, 2002, 24.

125 THIRTY-NINE-YEAR-OLD MAN: CG, desk calendar for 1948, Getty.

126 "INFLUENCE OF JACKSON POLLOCK": Weldon Kees to Norris Getty, March 22, 1949, in Robert E. Knoll, ed., *Weldon Kees and the Midcentury Generation, Letters 1935–55* (Lincoln: University of Nebraska Press, 1986), 119.

126 LOVE THAT WENT NOWHERE: Letters from Marjorie Ferguson to CG, 1949–1983, Box 1, folder 4, Getty.

127 "I FIRST LAID H.": Carter Ratcliff, *The Fate of a Gesture: Jackson*

Pollock and Postwar American Art (New York: Farrar, Straus & Giroux, 1996), 219; Rubenfeld, *Clement Greenberg*, 144–45; author interview with John O'Brian, Oct. 31, 2003, Vancouver, B.C.; CG, datebook for 1950, Getty.

127 FIRST ONE-PERSON SHOW: Ratcliff, *Fate of a Gesture*, 219–20; Rubenfeld, *Clement Greenberg*, 145; CG, datebook for 1950, Getty.

128 A LETTER FROM GREENBERG: CG, datebook for July 30, 1950, Getty; Rubenfeld, *Clement Greenberg*, 145–46.

128 "TO SEE JACKSON POLLOCK": Joseph Dorman, *Arguing the World: The New York Intellectuals in Their Own Words* (New York: Free Press, 2000), 101.

128 "ADVANTAGE OF THEM": Hilton Kramer, *The Revenge of the Philistines: Art and Culture, 1972–1984* (New York: Free Press, 1985), 198–99.

129 PUBLISHING THE VOLUME IN 1961: CG, "Chaim Soutine," *Partisan Review*, Jan.–Feb., 1951, reprinted in O'Brian, vol. 3, 72–78; "Cézanne and the Unity of Modern Art," *Partisan Review*, May–June, 1951, reprinted in O'Brian, vol. 3, 82–91.

129 "OUT OF A LOW PERIOD": CG, "Feeling Is All," *Partisan Review*, Jan.–Feb. 1952, reprinted in O'Brian, vol. 3, 105–106; CG, datebook entry for March 20, 1952, Getty.

129 "BUT WON'T BOTHER": Helen Frankenthaler, travel diary for 1952, Getty.

130 WAS SOMEHOW INEVITABLE: CG, "Cross-Breeding of Modern Sculpture," *Art News*, Summer 1952, and "Cézanne: Gateway to Contemporary Painting," *American Mercury*, June 1952; both reprinted in O'Brian, vol. 3, 107–13 and 113–18.

131 BE LIFELONG HABITS: CG papers, Box 26, folders 1, 2, 14; B. H. Blackwell, *Books New and Forthcoming*, Autumn 1952, Getty.

131 "APPREHENSIVE RIVALRY": CG, "Foreword to an Exhibition of Jackson Pollock," reprinted in O'Brian, vol. 3, 119.

132 "A COUPLE OF YEARS": Naifeh and Smith, *Jackson Pollock*, 697–98.

132 "WELL-ROUNDED HIGHBROW": Hiram Carruthers Butler, "Downtown in the Fifties," *Horizon*, June 1981, 15; Melinda A. Lorenz, *George L. K. Morris: Artists and Critic* (Ann Arbor: UMI Research, 1982), 96–97; William Barrett: *The Truants: Adventures among the Intellectuals* (Garden City, NY: Anchor Books, 1974), 132.

133 "CERTAINLY THE ENEMY": Max Kozloff, "An Interview with Friedel Dzubas," *Artforum*, Sept. 1965, 51.

133 "SEEM A STRANGER": Harold Rosenberg, "The American Action Painters," *Art News*, Dec. 1952, 22, 48.

134 "STUFF RATHER CLOSELY": O'Brian, vol. 1, xxii and 96n.

134 "MARVELOUSLY EXCORIATED": Thomas B. Hess, "Catalan Grotesque," *Art News*, Feb. 1949, 9.

134 FIFTIETH ANNIVERSARY ISSUE: "*Art News* magazine names Thomas B. Hess as Editor," *New York Times*, June 4, 1965; John Russell, "Thomas Hess, Art Expert, Dies; Writer and Met Official was 57," *New York Times*, July 14, 1978; CG, "Cross-Breeding of Modern Sculpture," *Art News*, Summer 1952, reprinted in O'Brian, vol. 3, 107–13.

135 A FEW YEARS LATER: Résumés, Harold Rosenberg Papers, Box 1, folders 1 and 2, Getty.

135 "THROUGH HIS VOICE": Irving Howe, *A Margin of Hope: An Intellectual Autobiography* (San Diego: Harcourt Brace Jovanovich, 1982), 134–35.

135 "EXHAUSTION AND EXASPERATION": Brian Winkenweder, "Art History, Sartre, and Identity in Rosenberg's America," *Art Criticism*, vol. 13, no. 2 (1998), 92; Naifeh and Smith, *Jackson Pollock*, 702–703; Simone de Beauvoir *Letters to Sartre*, ed. and trans. Quentin Hoare (London: Radius, 1991), letter dated May 8, 1947, 455–56.

136 NEAR THE POLLOCK–KRASNER HOUSE: Barrett, *The Truants*, 58; John R. Steelman, assistant to the President, to Harold Rosenberg, Feb. 24, 1950; Robert F. Delaney, archivist at U.S. Naval Intelligence School, to Rosenberg, July 28, 1950; Melvin Arnold, consulting editor at Wilfred Funk, Inc., to Rosenberg, Aug. 24, 1950; Rosenberg to Arnold, Aug. 30, 1950; Rosenberg to George Ludlam, Nov. 16, 1950; all Harold Rosenberg Papers, Getty.

136 "EXPERIMENTAL HYPOTHESES": Harold Rosenberg, *Discovering the Present: Three Decades in Art, Culture and Politics* (Chicago: University of Chicago Press, 1973), 25.

137 "YOU'RE A SMART KID": Naifeh and Smith, *Jackson Pollock*, 705.

137 IN AN ASSIMILATED WORLD: Author interview with Norman Podhoretz, New York, Oct. 28, 2002; Carol Brightman, *Mary McCarthy and Her World* (New York: Clarkson Potter, 1992), 428–29.

138 "BELLIGERENT, OR RESISTANT": Aline B. Louchheim, "Six Abstractionists Defend Their Art," *New York Times Magazine*, Jan. 21, 1951, 16–17.

138 FOR ALL OF $8,000: Naifeh and Smith, *Jackson Pollock*, 599, 600, 624, 656, 759, and 765.

138 IN THE LATE 1930S: CG, "The Plight of Our Culture," part 1, *Commentary*, June 1954, reprinted in O'Brian, vol. 3, 122–38.

139 ONLY THE YEAR BEFORE: CG Papers, Box 26, folder 7, Getty.

139 NEW ENGLAND AND QUEBEC: CG, datebook for 1953, Getty.

139 AT THE HOTEL D'INGHILTERRA: This and all other descriptions of this

trip are from Helen Frankenthaler's travel diary, Box 20, folder 2, Getty.

140 "OR PIERO DELLA FRANCESCA": CG, "Aesthetics in Art Criticism," undated lecture draft, Box 26, folder 13, Getty.

141 "OFFICE 11–2:30, HOME": CG, datebook for 1954, Getty.

141 "SEPARATION FROM H FINAL": CG, datebook for 1955, Getty.

CHAPTER VI: A VIEW FROM THE SUMMIT

142 PROMINENT ART WORLD FIGURES: Florence Rubenfeld, *Clement Greenberg: A Life* (New York: Scribner, 1997), 188–89.

143 EFFECTS OF SUCH RELATIONSHIPS: Phoebe Hoban, "Psycho-drama: The Chilling Story of How the Sullivanian Cult Turned a Utopian Dream into a Nightmare," *New York*, June 19, 1989, 45–46; Joe Conason with Ellen McGarrahan, "Escape from Utopia," *Village Voice*, April 22, 1986, 21–22.

144 "BEFORE OR SINCE": Rubenfeld, *Clement Greenberg*, 189.

144 DANNY'S INSTITUTIONALIZATION: CG, datebook, June 1955, Getty.

145 THE MONTH OF AUGUST: CG, datebook, June and July 1955, Getty.

145 "PUMPED, DRESSED UP": CG, "American-Type Painting," *Partisan Review*, Spring 1955, reprinted in John O'Brian, ed., *Clement Greenberg: The Collected Essays and Criticism, Volume 3: Affirmations and Refusals, 1950–1956* (Chicago: University of Chicago Press, 1993; hereafter "O'Brian, vol. 3"), 226; Steven Naifeh and Gregory White Smith, *Jackson Pollock: An American Saga* (New York: Clarkson Potter, 1989), 746.

146 THERAPY SESSIONS WITH KLEIN: Naifeh and Smith, *Jackson Pollock*, 747; CG, datebook, Sept. and Oct. 1955.

146 "A BLASPHEMY": David Black, "Totalitarian Therapy on the Upper West Side," *New York*, Dec. 15, 1975, 54–56; Hoban, "Psycho-drama," 53; Conason, "Escape from Utopia," 23–24, 26.

147 "HAVE STAYING POWER": CG, "American-Type Painting," 217–36.

147 "HIS OWN WAY": "A Critical Exchange with Fairfield Porter on 'American-Type' Painting,'" *Partisan Review*, Fall 1955, reprinted in O'Brian, vol. 3, 236–39.

148 "THE WORK OF ART": "How Good Is Kafka? A Critical Exchange," *Commentary*, June and Aug. 1955, reprinted in O'Brian, vol. 3, 209–16.

148 "DIFFICULT ORIGINALITY": CG, "Introduction to an Exhibition of Hans Hofmann," Bennington College, Spring 1955, reprinted in O'Brian, vol. 3, 240–41.

149 "AND IMMEDIATE EXPERIENCE": CG, "Lautrec's Art," *New York Times Book Review*, July 31, 1955, reprinted in O'Brian, vol. 3, 246–47.

150 "WERE OFF THEIR HEADS": James Laughlin, president of Intercultural

Publications, to CG, Dec. 6, 1954, and April 1, 1955, Getty.

150 "A PHILOSOPHER OF ART": CG, "Review of *Piero della Francesca* and *The Arch of Constantine*, both by Bernard Berenson," *Perspectives USA*, Nov. 1955, reprinted in O'Brian, vol. 3, 247–53.

150 ASSOCIATION WITH THE SURREALISTS: CG, "Polemic against Modern Art: Review of *The Demon of Progress in the Arts* by Wyndham Lewis," *The New Leader*, Dec. 12, 1955, reprinted in O'Brian, vol. 3, 253–55.

151 "JUST SHOWN AND SOLD": CG, "Foreword for the Tenth Anniversary Exhibition of the Betty Parsons Gallery," reprinted in O'Brian, vol. 3, 256.

151 QUADRUPLED IN VALUE: US Department of Commerce, Bureau of the Census, *Historical Statistics of the United States*, part 1, 301, 384–85, and 457.

151 "MARKET IN MODERN ART": Aline B. Louchheim, "Those Barometers of Art, Auctions," *New York Times*, March 12, 1950, Sec. II, 9.

152 OF UPHOLSTERY FABRIC: Clarence Dean, "Art Galleries Enjoy Boom Here, But Artists Are Not Prospering: Peak Demand for Pictures," *New York Times*, Feb. 25, 1957, 1, 16.

152 "DEALING IN CERTITUDES": Les Levine, "The Spring of '55: A Portrait of Sam Kootz," *Arts Magazine*, April 1974, 35.

152 "HISTORICAL IMPORTANCE": William Barrett: *The Truants: Adventures among the Intellectuals* (Garden City, NY: Anchor Books, 1974), 154.

153 SELLING IT TO THE MET: Alice Goldfarb Marquis, *Alfred H. Barr, Jr.: Missionary for the Modern* (Chicago, Contemporary Books, 1989), 117–18, 260, 297; Deirdre Robson, "The Avant-Garde and the On-Guard: Some Influences on the Potential Market for the First-Generation Abstract Expressionists in the 1940s and early 1950s," *Art Journal*, Fall 1988, 217–18.

153 "WITH MATERIAL SUCCESS": Robson, "The Avant-Garde and the On-Guard," 218; Thomas B. Hess, "Mixed Pickings from Ten Fat Years," *Art News*, Summer 1955, 36–37.

154 KNOCKED GREENBERG TO THE FLOOR: Janice Van Horne to the author, Feb. 13, 2004; Rubenfeld, *Clement Greenberg*, 198–99.

155 INTO GREENBERG'S APARTMENT: Rubenfeld, *Clement Greenberg*, 199; Van Horne to author, Feb. 13, 2004.

155 "BOX OF WHITE FLOWERS": Van Horne to author, Feb. 13, 2004; author interview with Sarah Greenberg Morse, New York, June 4, 2003.

156 "IT'S VERY COMPLICATED": CG undated recollection, dictated to Cleve Gray, Box 34, folder 1, Getty; Naifeh and Smith, *Jackson Pollock*, 785.

156 A BOTTLE OF GIN: Naifeh and Smith, *Jackson Pollock*, 789–90.

157 THE FOLLOWING MORNING: Ibid., 791–93.

157 CALLED IT ONE: Ibid., 794 and 765; Ben Heller telegram to Jackson Pollock, Feb. 17, 1956, Smithsonian Institution, Archives of American Art (hereafter "AAA").

158 POST-1950 POLLOCK OEUVRE: Loan Receipt, Dorothy H. Dudley, MoMA registrar, to Lee Krasner, Oct. 10, 1956; Sam Hunter, MoMA associate curator, to Krasner, Feb. 26, 1957; both AAA; Hilton Kramer, "The Jackson Pollock Myth," first published in *Arts Magazine*, Feb. 1957, reprinted in Kramer, *The Age of the Avant-Garde: An Art Chronicle of 1956–1972* (New York: Farrar, Straus & Giroux, 1973), 336–38.

158 "ALWAYS GOT UP TIRED": CG undated recollection, dictated to Cleve Gray, Box 34, folder 1, Getty.

158 "MADE HIM MISERABLE": Ibid.

158 "FRIGHT AND TENSION": James Reidel, *Vanished Act: The Life and Art of Weldon Kees* (Lincoln: University of Nebraska Press, 2003), 193.

159 LIKE STUART DAVIS: Deirdre Robson, "The Market for Abstract Expressionism," *Archives of American Art Journal*, vol. 25, no. 3, 1985, 21–22. At the time, a Matisse might sell for up to $75,000.

159 5 TO 7 PERCENT: "Sidelights: Of Art, Stocks, and Inflation," *New York Times*, Jan. 1, 1958.

159 IN THE SPRINGS: Dorothy Dudley, MoMA registrar, to Lee Krasner, loan receipts, June 6 and 26, 1957, and May 1959; Porter McCray, MoMA curator of international exhibitions, to Krasner, Nov. 27, 1957; all AAA; Elizabeth M. Fowler, "All that Glisters Is Not Gold: It's Old Furniture, Even Steel Sheets," *New York Times*, Jan. 1, 1960, 26–27.

160 "AS WROUGHT IRONWORK": CG, "Impress of Impressionism: Review of *Impressionism* by Jean Leymarie," *Art News*, May 1956; "Methods of the Master: Review of *Leonardo's Treatise on Painting*, annotated by A. Philip McMahon," *New York Times Book Review*, Aug. 26, 1956; "Review of *Four Steps Toward Modern Art* by Lionello Venturi," *Arts Magazine*, September 1956; and "Roundness Isn't All: Review of *The Art of Sculpture* by Herbert Read," *New York Times Book Review*, Nov. 25, 1956; all reprinted in O'Brian, vol. 3, 257–65, 270–73.

160 APPRECIATION OF SMITH: CG, "Review of Exhibitions of Hyman Bloom, David Smith, and Robert Motherwell," *Nation*, Jan. 26, 1946, and "Review of Exhibitions of David Smith, David Hare, and Mirko," *Nation*, April 19, 1947; both reprinted in John O'Brian, ed., *Clement Greenberg: The Collected Essays and Criticism, Volume 2: Arrogant Purpose, 1945–1949* (Chicago: University of Chicago Press, 1987), 51–55, 140–43.

161 "OF HIS GENERATION": CG, "David Smith," *Art in America*, Winter 1956–57, reprinted in O'Brian, vol. 3, 275–79.

161 MORE ABSTRACT FORMS: Karen Wilkin and Bruce Gunter, *Clement Greenberg: A Critic's Collection* (Princeton: Princeton University Press, 2001), 186.

162 VISIT TO DIEBENKORN'S STUDIO: Jean Dubuffet to CG, Feb. 13, 1950, Getty; News release, Betty Parsons Gallery, Nov. 28, 1950, New York Public Library (hereafter "NYPL"); Robert Motherwell postcard to CG, May 11, 1957, AAA; Richard Diebenkorn to CG, Aug. 8, 1961, AAA.

162 "THAT PAID YOU": Rubenfeld, *Clement Greenberg*, 225.

163 "A NATURAL.": Norman Podhoretz, *Making It* (New York: Random House, 1967), 101–102, 153.

163 "BRILLIANT IN THAT WAY": Neil Jumonville, *Critical Crossings: The New York Intellectuals in Postwar America* (Berkeley: University of California Press, 1991), 64; Joseph Dorman, *Arguing the World: The New York Intellectuals in Their Own Words* (New York: Free Press, 2000), 97.

164 "TILL AFTER 5:30": CG to John O'Brian, Oct. 18, 1984, O'Brian Papers.

164 EFFORTS TO SPITE COHEN: Author interview with Norman Podhoretz, New York, Oct. 28, 2002.

164 WRITE FOR *COMMENTARY* AGAIN: Ibid.; Podhoretz, *Making It*, 129–30, 147; *Commentary* for January, February, April, May, and June 1957.

165 PAWNED FOR $250: Rubenfeld, *Clement Greenberg*, 208–209; CG, datebook for 1958, Getty; author interview with Sarah Greenberg Morse, New York, May 22, 2003.

166 "AND SELF-CRITICISM": CG, datebook for 1958, Getty; Amy Newman, *Challenging Art: Artforum 1962 to 1974* (New York: Soho, 2000), 71–72, 164.

166 LATE-NIGHT PARTY: CG, "Gauss Seminars 1–3," Box 25, folder 6; datebook for 1959; both Getty.

167 AND THE CEDAR TAVERN: Rubenfeld, *Clement Greenberg*, 214.

167 BANKRUPTCY IN 1938: Undated documents on French & Co. bankruptcy, Box 1, folder 1, French & Co. Papers, Getty.

168 SPENCE-CHAPIN ADOPTION SERVICE: "French & Co. Art Will Go on Tour," *New York Times*, Feb. 11, 1958; French & Co. Inaugural Exhibition, pamphlet file, Art & Architecture Library, NYPL.

169 ONLY $5,200 EACH: Audit for second half of 1958, Box 3, folder 6, and comparative figures executive and sales salaries, March 27, 1959, Box 1, folder 1, French & Co. Papers, Getty.

169 "DILATORY TACTICS": City Investment Co. cash and advances to

French & Co. as of April 4, 1959; Spencer A. Samuels to Robert W. Dowling, president, City Investment Co., May 5, 1959, Box 2, folder 7; Brach, Grosswein, & Lane to Spencer Samuels, Feb. 23, 1959; Arthur O. Hirshberg of Brach, Grosswein, & Lane to Samuels, Jan. 24 and Feb 12, 1959, Box 3, folder 6; all French & Co. Papers, Getty.

169   LEFT HIM "EXHILARATED": Andre Emmerich, "Morris Louis: The French & Co. Show of 1960," catalog essay for exhibition at Riva Yares Gallery, Santa Fe, NM, Aug. 13–Sept. 7, and Scottsdale, AZ, Nov. 6–Dec. 27, 2004, 6; CG, catalog blurb for Barnett Newman exhibition, May 4–24, 1958, at Bennington College; all Getty.

170   "STORM OF RENOWN": Peter Schjeldahl, "Lord Barney," *New Yorker*, April 15, 2002, 82.

170   ANOTHER TWO HUNDRED WORKS: James Fitzsimmons, "A Critic Picks Some Prominent Painters," *Art Digest*, Jan. 15, 1954, 10; Biographical Outline in "Morris Louis: The French & Co. Show of 1960," 42–43.

171   OF PLATITUDINOUS ADMIRATION: CG, *Henri Matisse* (New York: Abrams, 1953), unpaged, and CG, *Joan Miró* (New York: Quadrangle, 1948). See also John Russell, *Matisse: Father and Son* (New York: Abrams, 1999), 270–71; Robert Goldwater, "The Painting of Miró," *Nation*, Feb. 26, 1949, 250–51; Weldon Kees, "Miró and Modern Art," *Partisan Review*, March 1949, 324–26; Thomas B. Hess, "Catalan Grotesque," *Art News*, Feb. 1949, 9.

171   ONLY FIVE THOUSAND VISITORS: CG to Spencer Samuels, June 25, 1959, Box 8, folder 7, and Analysis of Operations to date, June 30, 1959, Box 1, folder 6; Proforma Statement of Profit and Loss, July 15, 1959, Box 1, folder 1, and Contemporary Art Report, June 30, 1959, Box 1, folder 6; all French & Co. Papers, Getty.

172   BOTH HER AND POLLOCK'S SHOWS: Piri Halasz, *From the Mayor's Doorstep*, http://piri.home.mindspring.com/, April 15, 1998.

172   "EUPHUISTIC LYRICAL VERSE": CG, "The Case for Abstract Art," *Saturday Evening Post*, Aug. 1959, 18–19, 69–72, reprinted in John O'Brian, ed., *Clement Greenberg: The Collected Essays and Criticism, Volume 4: Modernism with a Vengeance, 1957–1969* (Chicago: University of Chicago Press, 1993), 75–84.

173   CONTEMPORARY ART STORE: Peggy Guggenheim, *Out of This Century* (New York: Universe, 1979), 363; Financial statements, Dec. 31, 1959, Box 2, folder 16; Spencer Samuels, Jr., to his father, undated, Luigi Laura to Spencer Samuels, Dec. 21, 1959, and Spencer Samuels to Madelle L. Hegeler, Sept. 21, 1959; all Box 7, folder 9, French & Co. Papers, Getty.

CHAPTER VII: THE NEXT BIG THING

174 "LOGIC, AND MEANING": Hilton Kramer, "A Critic on the Side of History," *Arts Magazine,* Oct. 1962, 60; Barbara Rose, *Autocritique: Essays on Art and Anti-Art, 1963–1987* (New York: Weidenfeld & Nicolson, 1988), 220.

174 MARTINIS IN THE AFTERNOON: CG, datebook for 1961, Getty.

175 "STEADY AND CLEAR": "Unawed by New York," *Newsweek,* May 15, 1961, 106–107.

175 "A CLASS OF THINGS": Harvey Shapiro, Sunday editor, *New York Times,* to CG, Feb. 1, 1961, Box 34, folder 1, Getty; CG, "The Jackson Pollock Market Soars," *New York Times Magazine,* April 16, 1961, and CG, letter to *New York Times Magazine,* April 30, 1961; both reprinted in John O'Brian, ed., *Clement Greenberg: The Collected Essays and Criticism, Volume 4: Modernism with a Vengeance, 1957–1969* (Chicago: University of Chicago Press, 1993; hereafter "O'Brian, vol. 4"), 107–15.

176 "MORE APPROPRIATE RANK": CG and Thomas B. Hess, letters to the editor of the *New York Times Book Review,* July 9, 1961, reprinted in O'Brian, vol. 4, 115–17.

176 "PAINTER OF HIS GENERATION": Robert Goldwater, "Art and Criticism," *Partisan Review,* May–June 1961, 688; Jack Kroll, "Some Greenberg Circles," *Art News,* March 1962, 35.

176 NOLAND LIVED THERE: James McC. Truitt, "Art Criticism's Angry Man," *Washington Post,* May 21, 1961.

177 HISTORY, AND COMMUNICATIONS: William Phillips and Philip Rahv, eds., *The Partisan Reader, 1934–1944* (New York: Dial Press, 1946); Bernard Rosenberg and David Manning White, eds., *Mass Culture: The Popular Arts in America* (abridged ed.: Glencoe, IL: Free Press, 1957); James B. Hall and Barry Ulanov, eds., *Modern Culture and the Arts* (New York: McGraw-Hill, 1967); Gillo Dorfles, ed., *Kitsch: The World of Bad Taste* (abridged ed.: New York: Universe, 1969); Francis Frascina, ed., *Pollock and After: The Critical Debate* (New York: Harper & Row, 1985).

177 "EVERYBODY'S ATTENTION": Leo Castelli speech at the La Jolla (CA) Museum of Contemporary Art, Feb. 6, 1980; Florence Rubenfeld, *Clement Greenberg: A Life* (New York: Scribner, 1997), 211–12.

178 "OF THE MODERNIST ERA": Hilton Kramer, "Does Abstract Art Have a Future," *New Criterion,* Dec. 2002, 1–2.

178 "WHAT WAS TO COME": CG, "New York Painting Only Yesterday," reprinted in O'Brian, vol. 4, 19; CG, *Art and Culture* (Boston: Beacon Press, 1961), 230–31.

179 "RUDE, UNEDUCATED BOOR": O'Brian, vol. 4, 20; Rubenfeld, *Clement*

Greenberg, 105, 228; Alfred H. Barr, Jr., to CG, Oct. 15, 1962; translation of undated review in unnamed Soviet publication, Getty.

179 "THAT ONCE CAPERED": John Canaday, "Good-by Forever," *New York Times*, May 19, 1963.

180 "ELEVATED COMMERCIAL ART": Harold Rosenberg, "Tenth Street: A Geography of Modern Art," *Art News Annual*, 1964, reprinted in Rosenberg, *Discovering the Present: Three Decades in Art, Culture, and Politics* (Chicago: University of Chicago Press, 1973), 105; "The Premises of Action Painting," *Encounter*, May 1963, 50; "After Next, What?" *Art in America*, no. 2, 1964, 72–73.

180 "HELLO SCHMUCK": Tony Scherman, "When Pop Turned the Art World Upside Down," *American Heritage*, Feb. 2001, http://web7.info-trac.galegroup.com/itw/infomark/547/180/35387953w7/purl=rc.

180 RENT-CONTROLLED AT $600: Author interview with Sarah Greenberg Morse, New York, May 27, 2003.

181 END OF HIS LIFE: CG to Robert L. Polley, executive editor, *Country Beautiful*, March 12, 1963, Getty; Edward Lucie-Smith. "An Interview with Clement Greenberg," *Studio International*, Jan. 1968, 4.

181 3:15 IN THE MORNING: CG, datebook for 1961, Getty.

182 "THE GREENBERG WAVELENGTH": Amy Newman, *Challenging Art: Artforum 1962 to 1974* (New York: Soho, 2000), 71–72, 197; Michael Fried to CG, March 24, 1963, Smithsonian Institution, Archives of American Art (hereafter "AAA").

182 "AMERICAN ART CRITICISM": CG, datebooks for 1961 and 1962, Getty; Carbon copy of Henry Geldzahler to Robert Samuels (French & Co.), April 4, 1963, Greenberg Papers, AAA; Henry Geldzahler, *American Painting in the Twentieth Century* (New York: Metropolitan Museum of Art, 1965).

183 WATCHED TELEVISION: CG, datebook for 1961, Getty.

183 ESPECIALLY SLEEPING PILLS: Ibid.

184 COMBINATIONS OF SLEEP MEDICINES: CG, datebook for 1962, Getty.

184 CLIPPINGS ABOUT POLLOCK: CG Papers, Box 34, folders 1–3, Getty.

185 WORKING AS AN EDITOR: Margaret Marshall to Harold Rosenberg, June 14, 1963, Harold Rosenberg Papers, Getty.

185 TURNED DOWN HIS BOOK PROPOSAL: CG, datebook for 1962, Getty.

186 "HAS NO STAYING POWER": CG, "After Abstract Expressionism," *Art International*, Oct. 25, 1962, reprinted in O'Brian, vol. 4, 121–34.

186 "ISOLATED ABSTRACTIONISTS": Max Kozloff, "Letter to the Editor," *Art International*, June 1963, 88.

186 GREENBERG WAS PUBLISHED: Max Kozloff to CG, Feb. 16 and 19, 1962, AAA.

187 "AMERICA'S GREATEST ARTIST": CG, "How Art Writing Earns Its Bad Name," *Encounter*, Dec. 1962, reprinted in O'Brian, vol. 4, 135–36.

187 "AMPHIGORIC": The OED lists this adjective as derived from an eighteenth-century noun of unknown origin, *amphigouri*, defined as "a burlesque writing filled with nonsense."

187 "COMEDIANS LIKE MR. ROSENBERG": CG, "How Art Writing Earns Its Bad Name," 137–38, 141–42.

187 "EVERY SINGLE DAY": Ibid., 143.

188 O'HARA ON POLLOCK: Ibid., 143–44, and editor's note, 144.

188 "MADE TO LOOK SILLY": Ibid., 144

189 MORE JABS AT ROSENBERG: "A Critical Exchange with Herbert Read on 'How Art Writing Earns Its Bad Name,'" *Encounter*, Feb. 1963, reprinted in O'Brian, vol. 4, 145–49; CG, datebook for 1962, Getty.

189 BOOK ON HERMAN MELVILLE: Charles H. Kahn to Harold Rosenberg, Nov. 8, 1962; Selma Rosen to Rosenberg, Jan. 10, 1962; Norman Podhoretz to Rosenberg, June 11 and 19, 1962; MoMA news release: "Is there a 'New' Figure Painting?" May 18, 1962; author's questionnaire, May 24, 1962; Phil Leider to Rosenberg, Sept. 10, 1962; Baxter Hathaway, chair of Festival of Contemporary Arts, Cornell, to Rosenberg, Feb. 20, 1962; Rosenberg to Hathaway, Feb. 27, 1962; all Harold Rosenberg Papers, Getty.

190 "AS FIRST CAUSE": Harold Rosenberg, "The Premises of Action Painting," *Encounter*, May 1963, 47–50.

190 "THEIR GRAVITATIONAL FIELD": Amy Newman, *Challenging Art: Artforum 1962–1964* (New York: Soho, 2000), 162.

191 HISTORICAL OR CULTURAL CONSCIOUSNESS: Max Kozloff, "The Critical Reception of Abstract Expressionism," *Arts Magazine*, Dec. 1965, 28–9, 33.

191 INTO LUCRATIVE BOOKS: Milton Greenstein (*New Yorker* vice-president) and Robert Coates to Harold Rosenberg, both Dec. 30, 1966; Allene Talmey, editor at *Vogue*, to Rosenberg, March 16, 1966; Rosenberg to Melvin Lasky, editor of *Encounter*, March 8, 1966; Rosenberg to Dan Goodall, Art Department, University of Texas, Feb. 23, 1966; all Harold Rosenberg Papers, Getty.

192 "THREAT TO ESTABLISHED TASTES": CG, "Introduction to *Three New American Painters: Louis, Noland, Olitski*," exhibition at Norman Mackenzie Art Gallery, Regina, Saskatchewan, Jan.–Feb 1963, reprinted in O'Brian, vol. 4, 149–50.

192 "IN AMERICAN PAINTING": CG, catalog for exhibition of paintings by Jules Olitski, March 12–30, 1963, artists' files, New York Public Library (hereafter "NYPL").

193 A CERTAIN PROVINCIALISM: CG, "Painting and Sculpture in Prairie Canada Today," *Canadian Art*, March–April 1963, reprinted in O'Brian., vol. 4, 153–55.

194 AMONG THE FEW VISITORS: CG, datebook for 1963, Getty; author interview with Sarah Greenberg Morse, Sept. 30, 2003, New York.

194 IN THAT PARENTAL BIBLE: CG, datebook for 1963, Getty.

195 FEELING SLIGHTLY NAUSEATED: Ibid.

195 TWO WEEKS BEFORE CHRISTMAS: CG, proposal for a grant from the Ford Foundation, Sept. 20, 1963; W. McNeill Lowry to CG, Dec. 12, 1963; both Getty.

196 DISMEMBER AT WILL: CG, "The 'Crisis' of Abstract Art," *Art Yearbook* 7, 1964, and *Preuves*, Feb. 1964; "A Famous Art Critic's Collection," *Vogue*, Jan. 1964; "Four Photographers," *New York Review of Books*, Jan. 23, 1964; all reprinted in O'Brian, vol. 4, 176–87; Allene Talmey, associate editor of *Vogue*, to CG, Dec 10, 1963, Getty.

197 "MY OWN TRAJECTORY": Annette Michelson, "Paris," *Arts Magazine*, June 1959, 18; Newman, *Challenging Art*, 60, 171.

197 "SAME AMOUNT OF TIME": "Best Known Critic Due, Art Show Flies High," *Daily Oklahoman*, July 6, 1961; "After Pop Art," draft of a lecture at the Guggenheim Museum; both Box. 30, folder 8, Getty.

198 "ILLUSION OF SPATIAL DEPTH": Kay Woods, "The Renascence of Canadian Art 1950–1960," *Artscanada*, Dec. 1979–Jan. 1980, 28; Jack Bush to CG, Nov. 5, 1961, AAA.

198 "MAKING ME SELF-CONSCIOUS": Jack Bush to CG, Feb. 27, 1965, Getty.

198 A TINY, LUKEWARM PARAGRAPH: CG, datebook for 1964, Getty; Jack Bush to CG, Feb. 24 and May 25, 1964, AAA; untitled clippings, *New York Times*, Oct. 24, 1964, artists' files, NYPL.

198 "DENY GREENBERG'S INFLUENCE": Jack Bush to CG, Feb. 27, 1965, AAA; Harry Malcolmson, "Of course Jack Bush is good, but where's all that applause?" *Toronto Telegram*, Sept. 24, 1966, Getty; untitled clipping, *New York Times*, Sept. 30, 1969, artists' files, NYPL.

198 ONLY A YEAR LATER: CG, datebooks for 1962 and 1963, Getty; Morris Louis to CG, Nov. 20, 1960, and Oct. 15, 1961, AAA; carbon of Andre Emmerich to Lawrence Rubin, Feb. 25, 1963, Box 34, folders 6 and 7, Getty; *Morris Louis: The French & Co. Show of 1960*, catalog for exhibition at Riva Yares Gallery, Santa Fe, NM, Aug. 13–Sept. 7, and Scottsdale, AZ, Nov. 6–Dec. 27, 2004.

199 PAINTINGS AS A GIFT: Gene Davis to CG, April 10, May 29, and Oct. 5, 1962, Sept. 30 and Oct. 8, 1963; all AAA.

200 "FULL OF HOLES": John Coplans, "Post-Painterly Abstraction," *Artforum*, Summer 1964, 5–8.

200 "YOUR CLASSIFICATION": James Elliott, director for Fine Arts at LACMA, to CG, Sept. 25, 1963, Getty; Robert Irwin to CG, April 2, 1964, AAA.

200 LECTURE IN PHILADELPHIA: CG, datebook for 1964, Getty; CG, "David Smith's New Sculpture," *Art International*, May 1964, reprinted in O'Brian, vol. 4, 188–92.

201 DAUGHTER WAS BORN: "Clemente Greenberg viene a Montevideo," *El Plata*, Oct. 5, 1964, Getty; CG, datebook for 1965, Getty.

202 "GET MY BEARINGS": Rubenfeld, *Clement Greenberg*, 284.

202 END OF THE YEAR: CG, "Contemporary Sculpture: Anthony Caro," *Arts Yearbook 8*, 1965, reprinted in O'Brian, vol. 4, 205–208.

202 EXHIBITION IN LIVERPOOL: Jane Harrison to CG, April 17, 1963; Jules Langsner to CG, Sept. 25, 1963; Anthony Caro to CG, May 4 and June 21, 1963; Frank Martin, sculpture department chair at St. Martin School, London, to CG, July 5, 1963; all Getty; John A. Walker, "A Vexed Trans-Atlantic Relationship: Greenberg & the British," *Art Criticism*, vol. 16, no. 1 (2001), 44–61, http://vnweb.hwwilsonweb.com1.

203 LIKE THIS SERIOUSLY: CG, "Why the Old Masters . . . ," Box 25, folder 4, Getty.

204 SEEPING SLOWLY OUT: CG, drafts for "Art Outside Metropolises" and "Painting in a One-City Culture," both Box 30, folder 2, Getty.

CHAPTER VIII: THINGS FALL APART

205 "ONE IN FIVE BUYS": Thomas B. Hess to Harold Rosenberg, March 23, 1967, Harold Rosenberg Papers, Getty; Richard F. Shepard, "Pop Arty Dealer Turns Novelist, *New York Times*, June 26, 1965, 26.

206 GAVE HIM SOME DETAILS: Author interview with Virginia Dorazio, New York, May 22, 2003.

206 DUNHILL'S IN NEW YORK: Alfred L. Green to CG, Aug. 25, 1965; Ira M. Lowe to Robert Motherwell, Feb. 23, 1966; both Getty.

207 AN ADDITIONAL $71,433: CG, "David Smith: Comments on His Latest Works," *Art in America*, Jan.–Feb. 1966, reprinted in John O'Brian, ed., *Clement Greenberg: The Collected Essays and Criticism, Volume 4: Modernism with a Vengeance, 1957–1969* (Chicago: University of Chicago Press, 1993; hereafter "O'Brian, vol. 4"), 222–28; CG, request for compensation, Probate Court of New York, undated draft [1968], and U. S. Court of Appeals for the Second Circuit, IRS vs. David Smith Executors, #74-1617; both Getty.

207 IN EXCESS OF $38,000: CG, request for compensation, Probate Court of New York, undated draft [1968], CG, "Memoranda," in datebook for 1970; both Getty.

208 "WAY BACK WHEN": Amy Newman, *Challenging Art: Artforum 1962 to 1974* (New York: Soho, 2000), 280.

209 "PUT AN ARTIST ACROSS": Harold Rosenberg, "The American Art Establishment," *Esquire*, Jan. 1965, reprinted in Rosenberg, *Discovering the Present: Three Decades in Art, Culture, and Politics* (Chicago: University of Chicago Press, 1973), 110–11; Newman, *Challenging Art*, 8.

209 "AND VICE VERSA": CG, "Avant-Garde Attitudes," John Power Lecture in Contemporary Art, University of Sidney, May 17, 1968, Getty.

210 BLACK-AND-WHITE ILLUSTRATIONS: Newman, *Challenging Art*, 9; *Artforum*, July 1963; Yves-Alain Bois, "Phil Said, They Said," *Artforum*, Oct. 2000, 21.

210 NEWSPAPER AND MAGAZINE CLAN: Newman, *Challenging Art*, 88, 209–10.

211 "CLEMENT GREENBERG'S IDEAS": CG, "Modernist Painting," *Forum Lectures* (Washington, D.C.: Voice of America, 1960), reprinted in O'Brian, vol. 4, 92; David Cohen, "Challenging art," *Art Bulletin*, vol.84, no. 3, 535–38, http://vnweb.hwwilsonweb.com/hww, 4; Florence Rubenfeld, *Clement Greenberg: A Life* (New York: Scribner, 1997), 253.

211 "A FEW STATIONS": Newman, *Challenging Art*, 293.

212 "TRUST FIRST IMPRESSIONS": Newman, *Challenging Art*, 316–17, Rubenfeld, *Clement Greenberg*, 294.

212 ON THE NEW YORK SCENE: Newman, *Challenging Art*, 173, 361, 364.

213 "WITH ITS MATTER": CG, "Complaints of an Art Critic," *Artforum*, Oct. 1967; CG, "Critical Exchange with Max Kozloff," *Artforum*, Nov. 1967; both reprinted in O'Brian, vol. 4, 265–74.

213 APRIL ISSUE WITH ADS: *Ayer Directory: Newspapers, Magazines, and Trade Publications* (Philadelphia: Ayerpress, 1930, 1940, 1950, 1960, and 1970); *Art in America*, Sept.–Oct. 1970; *Art News*, Sept. 1970.

214 HOPELESSLY CLOUDY FORMULATIONS: CG, "The Agony of Painting," Box 26, folder 2; "The Newness of Color," Box 25, folder 5; "The Decline of Art," Box 26, folder 1; "Art Criticism and American Art," Box 26, folder 3; "Outline for TV Show: Why Modernist Painting Looks the Way It Does," Box 27, folder 16; all Getty.

215 "WELCOME MR. GREENBERG": William O'Brien, program officer, Division for Americans Abroad, State Department, to CG, Sept. 1, 1966, CG to O'Brien, Sept. 2, 1966; itineraries in Japan, Box. 44, folder 1, and "Mr. Greenberg Roundtable . . . ," Oct. 20, 1966; all Getty.

215 "CLOSEST TO ART": Joseph Lelyveld, "Modern U.S. Art Stirs New Delhi," *New York Times*, April 9, 1967.

216 IN THE SOVIET EMPIRE: See Theodore Shabad, "Khrushchev Visits U. S. Embassy Fete," July 5; "Krushchev and Jazz," July 5; Theodore

Shabad, "Soviet Artists Union Is Accused of Restraining Taste and Talent," July 8; "'Thaw' for Arts Hinted in Russia," Oct. 11; Seymour Topping, "Khrushchev Scolds Abstract Painters," Dec. 2; Topping, "Soviet Orders Disciplining for Cultural Avant-Garde," Dec. 1; "Liberal Loses Soviet Art Post; Scores Foes of Abstract Trend," Dec. 6; Shabad, "Soviet Extends Campaign on Art," Dec. 8; "Cultural Stalinism, Dec. 11; all articles in *New York Times*, 1962.

218 "QUALITATIVE COMPARISONS": CG, "Avant-Garde Attitudes," *Studio International*, April 1970, reprinted in O'Brian, vol. 4, 292–303.

218 AND ALMA-TADEMA: CG, Interview conducted by Edward Lucie-Smith, *Studio International*, Jan. 1968, reprinted in O'Brian, vol. 4, 277–82.

219 "TO OVERVALUE ART": CG, Interview conducted by Lily Leino for "USIS Feature," United States Information Service, April 1969, reprinted in O'Brian, vol. 4, 303–14.

219 A PARTICULAR ARTIST'S WORK: Stephanie Noland to CG, April 11, 1965; Leslie Waddington to CG, Jan. 21, 1966; both Smithsonian Institution, Archives of American Art (hereafter "AAA").

220 EXAMPLE OF CONCEPTUAL ART: Eva Vermandel, "Generation Games," *Art Review*, May 2001, 1; John A. Walker, "A Vexed Trans-Atlantic Relationship: Greenberg and the British," *Art Criticism*, vol. 16, no. 1 (2001), 44–61, http://vnweb.hwwilsonweb.com; Tim Hilton, "Clement Greenberg," *The New Criterion*, Sept. 2000, 15.

220 "INCOMPATIBLE WITH MARXISM": Patrick Heron, "A kind of cultural imperialism?" Feb. 1968, 63; Donald Judd, "Complaints, Part I," April 1969, 183–84; Andrew Higgens, "Clement Greenberg and the Idea of the Avant-Garde," Oct. 1971, 145; all articles in *Studio International*.

220 "KINDNESS, OR DISMISSIVENESS": Tim Hilton, "Clement Greenberg," *New Criterion*, Sept. 2000, 14–15.

221 HE WAS UNFORGETTABLE: Ibid., 20.

221 SPENT CHRISTMAS DAY ALONE: CG, datebook for 1968, Getty.

221 "NEVER AN ISSUE": Author interview with Sarah Greenberg Morse, New York, May 27, 2003.

222 "SHOW OF SMOKING THEM": Author interviews with Sarah Greenberg Morse, New York, June 4 and Sept. 30, 2003; CG, datebook for 1975, Getty.

223 DID NOT LAST LONG: Author interview with Sarah Greenberg Morse, New York, Sept. 30, 2003.

223 IN HER HOME: Esme Berman, Art Institute of South Africa, to CG, Sept. 30, Nov. 12, and Dec. 17, 1974; Jan. 29 and June 17, 1975; CG to Berman, Nov. 25, 1974, and June 17, 1975, Box 44, folders 3 and 4, Getty;

author interview with Sarah Greenberg Morse, New York, May 27 and Sept. 30, 2003.

223 PIPES IN THE FLOOR: Frank Lloyd Wright, *The Natural House* (New York: Bramhall House, 1954), unpaged.

224 TOWARD THE HORIZON: Author interviews with Sarah Greenberg Morse, New York, Sept. 30, 2003, and Bonnie Gale, Norwich, New York, Sept. 27, 2003.

225 EVEN HEARD OF HIM: Author interview with Sarah Greenberg Morse, New York, June 4, 2003.

226 "THOUGHT IN THE WORLD": See CG, datebooks for 1972–74, Getty.

226 PREPARED BY THE MOMA: Bernard Karpel, MoMA librarian, to CG, July 1, 1966; CG to Karpel, July 16, 1966; Gray Williams, MoMA director of publications, to CG, Aug. 3, 1967; all AAA.

226 "WAS RARELY CIRCUMSPECT": Author interview with Rosalind Krauss, New York, Oct. 21, 2002; Newman, *Challenging Art*, 165; Rubenfeld, *Clement Greenberg*, 260–61.

227 "TO AUTHORITY FIGURES": Newman, *Challenging Art*, 292–93 and 347; author interview with Rosalind Krauss, New York, Oct. 21, 2002.

227 "STILL A SMITH": Rosalind Krauss, "Issues and Commentary," *Art in America*, Sept.–Oct. 1974, 30.

228 WERE FREQUENTLY CITED: Rosalind Krauss, "Changing the Work of David Smith," *Art in America*, Sept.–Oct. 1974, 32; Carl R. Baldwin, "Art and the Law: 'Property Right' vs. 'Moral Right,'" ibid., 34.

228 "IF ONLY PRIVATELY": David Smith to CG, undated [post-1956] and March 31, 1964, AAA; George Schloss to the editor, *Newsweek*, Oct. 21, 1974, 21; Hilton Kramer, "Altering of Smith Work Stirs Dispute," and "Questions Raised by Art Alterations," Sept. 13 and 14, 1974; undated carbon of Kenneth Noland to Hilton Kramer and Stanley E. Marcus to Kramer, Sept. 25, 1974; draft of CG letter to *Christian Science Monitor*, Oct. 9, 1974; all Getty.

229 "THE NAKED METAL": Amei Wallach, "Discussing the demerits of posthumous changes," *Newsday*, Dec. 11, 1974; Newman, *Challenging Art*, 413; Deborah Solomon, "Catching Up with the High Priest of Criticism," *New York Times*, June 23, 1991.

229 COLOR JUST RIGHT: Robert Hughes, *American Visions: The Epic History of Art in America* (New York: Alfred A. Knopf, 1997), 504; author interview with Irving Sandler, New York, May 23, 2003.

230 "AFFAIRS WITH OTHERS": Rubenfeld, *Clement Greenberg*, 284, 294; author interview with Sarah Greenberg Morse, New York, June 4, 2003.

230 "HEAD OF A PIN": Tom Wolfe, "The Painted Word," *Harper's*, April 1975, 72, 77, reprinted New York: Farrar, Straus & Giroux, 1975.

231 "BOUND TO FIND UNINTELLIGIBLE": William Phillips to CG, April 3, 1975, and CG to Phillips, April 14, 1975, Getty; Barbara Rose, "Wolfeburg," *New York Review of Books*, June 26, 1975, 28.

231 "HE REALLY RELISHED": CG, "Matisse and the Fauves," Box 30, folder 21, Getty; author interview with Sarah Greenberg Morse, New York, May 27, 2003.

232 WHAT HER COUSINS RECEIVED: Estate of Joseph Greenberg, New York Surrogate's Court, #4527-1977, photo #3226.

233 "A MUCH-MELLOWED MAN": Sandra McGrath, "Greenberg on His Own," *Weekend Australia Magazine*, Oct. 27–28, 1979, Getty.

CHAPTER IX: IN THE POSTMODERN WILDERNESS

234 SUCCEEDING HENRY GELDZAHLER: Harry Roskolenko, "Harold Rosenberg: 1906–1978," *Art International*, Sept. 1979, 62–63 (reprinted from *Quadrant*, April 1979); John Russell, "Harold Rosenberg Is Dead at 72, Art Critic for the New Yorker," *New York Times*, July 13, 1978; Robert Storr, "Book Review," *Art Journal*, Winter 1987, 325; John Russell, "Thomas Hess, Art Expert, Dies; Writer and Met Official Was 57," *New York Times*, July 14, 1978; "A Hess Update," *Soho Weekly News*, Nov. 16, 1978, Artists' files, Art and Architecture Library, New York Public Library.

235 "FEATURE IN HIS FACE": "Hess May Get Met Job," *New York Times*, Jan. 13, 1978; articles by Donald Barthelme (pp. 8–9), Elizabeth C. Baker (p. 8), John Russell (p. 12), John Jacobus (p. 9), and Milton Gendel (p. 9) in "Thomas B. Hess, 1920–1978," *Art in America*, Nov.–Dec. 1978.

236 "FANTASIES ABOUT ART": Barbara Rose, "Thomas B. Hess: 1920–1978," 11–12; Dan Seidell, "Two Views of de Kooning, *Art Criticism*, vol. 10 (1994), 29.

236 TO THE SOVIET UNION: 1978 Salzburg Seminar Pamphlet; John Tuthill, president, Salzburg Seminar in American Studies, to CG, July 16 and Aug. 15, 1977; Salzburg Seminar report for 1978, 14–15; both Getty.

236 "LESS SIGNIFICANT HIS ART": CG, Hans Platschek, and Christian Gneus, "Wohin geht die Avantgarde?" radio interview reprinted in *Das Kunstwerk*, Dec. 1978, 43.

237 CONDEMNED AS "DAMNABLE": Irving Howe, *The Decline of the New* (New York: Harcourt, Brace & World, 1970), 259; "New York and the National Culture," *Partisan Review*, no. 2, 1977, 178–79; William Barrett, *The Truants: Adventures Among the Intellectuals* (Garden City, NY: Anchor Books, 1974), 155–56.

238 "WILL BE UNMENTIONED": CG, "The State of Criticism," *Partisan Review*, vol. XLVII, no. 1 (1981), 36–37.

238 PROPOSED BY DUCHAMP'S FOLLOWERS: John Jacobus, "Picasso: A Symposium," *Art in America*, Dec. 1980, 9; see also: Alice Goldfarb Marquis, *Marcel Duchamp: The Bachelor Stripped Bare* (Boston: MFA Publications, 2002).

238 WHATEVER SUBJECT HE WISHED: CG, datebook for 1979, Getty.

239 "REACTIONARY OR RETARDED": CG, *Fourth Sir William Dobell Memorial Lecture: Modern & Postmodern* (Sydney: University of Sydney, 1980), reprinted as "Modern and Postmodern," *Arts Magazine*, Feb. 1980, 66.

239 CONFIRMED IN NEW YORK: CG, "Decline of Taste," Box 31, folder 1; Carolyn R. Henning, Kalamazoo Art League, to CG, Feb. 26, March 6, and Sept. 5, 1980; all Getty.

239 "RESIST DECLINE": CG, "To Cope with Decadence," and Serge Guilbaut, "The Relevance of Modernism," in Benjamin H. D. Buchloh, Serge Guilbaut, and David Solkin, eds., *Modernism & Modernity* (Halifax: Nova Scotia College of Arts and Design, 1983), 161–64, xii–xiii; see also: Serge Guilbaut, *How New York Stole the Idea of Modern Art* (Chicago: University of Chicago Press, 1983).

240 "AMERICA AND EUROPE": Diane Waldman to CG, April 14, 1980; Henry A. Million, dean, and Rosalind Krauss, senior fellow, National Gallery of Art, Center for Advanced Study in the Visual Arts, to CG, Dec. 16, 1980; Constance Schwartz, curator of exhibitions at Nassau County Museum of Art, to CG, May 1 and 15, 1980, and Jan. 7, 1981; Jorge Glusberg, vice president, International Assn. of Art Critics, to CG, Nov. 28, 1980; all Getty.

241 "MEANS TO SUBLIMATE": Donald B. Kuspit, *Clement Greenberg: Art Critic* (Madison: University of Wisconsin Press, 1979), 4–5, 87, 126.

241 "IDEOLOGY OF THE MARKETPLACE": Franz Schulze, "Books: Designer and Manipulator," *Art News*, Nov. 1980, 35; Joyce Brodsky, "Review of Kuspit's *Greenberg*," *Journal of Aesthetics and Art Criticism*, Fall 1980, 107; John Adkins Richardson, "Review of Kuspit's *Greenberg*," *Leonardo*, Autumn 1982, 326.

242 "PATERNALISTIC WOMAN BAITER": Kay Larson and Carry Rickey, "In Critical Condition: A Double Take on Clement Greenberg," *Village Voice*, April 21, 1980, 79–80; CG, "Art of the State," and Carry Rickey, "Art: Taste Test," *Village Voice*, May 5, 1980, 23–24, 83; CG, "Arts and Letters," *Village Voice*, May 19, 1980, 34.

243 HE CONTACTED GREENBERG: John O'Brian, undated curriculum vitae and letter to CG, May 9, 1983, Getty; T. J. Clark, "Clement

Greenberg's Theory of Art," *Critical Inquiry*, Sept. 1982, 139–56; author interview with John O'Brian, Oct. 31, 2003, Vancouver, B.C.

243 "ALWAYS SMOKED CAMELS": Author interview with O'Brian, Oct. 31, 2003; O'Brian, notes on a phone conversation with CG, July 24, 1982, O'Brian Papers.

244 "BOW TO EXPERIENCE": O'Brian, copy of draft of proposal for CG collected writings for Beacon Press, Nov. 1, 1982; CG to O'Brian, Dec. 3, 1982; Marie Cantlon, senior editor, Beacon Press, to O'Brian, April 13, 1983; all Getty; CG to O'Brian, Oct. 1, 1983, O'Brian Papers.

245 "THE TRUE MESSIAH": O'Brian to CG, April 29, 1983; Wendy Strothman, director, Beacon Press, to CG, Feb. 10, 1984; both Getty; author interview with John O'Brian, Oct. 31, 2003; O'Brian to CG, March 14, April 6 and 13, 1984, and CG to O'Brian, March 25 and Dec. 12, 1983, O'Brian Papers.

245 "MORE THAN THE FORMER": CG to O'Brian, April 9, 1984, O'Brian Papers.

245 BLAMED ON "LAZINESS": CG to O'Brian, Nov. 13, 1983; CG to O'Brian, April 9, Oct. 18, and Nov. 19, 1984; O'Brian to CG, Jan. 17, 1985; all O'Brian Papers. Orthodontia was an exceedingly rare procedure during the 1920s. As late as 1929, the annual per capita outlay for dental services was $3.90: see *Historical Statistics of the United States* (Washington, D.C.: Department of Commerce, 1975), vol.1, 73.

246 APPENDED TO EACH VOLUME: CG to O'Brian, Nov. 16, 1986, O'Brian Papers; author interview with John O'Brian, Oct. 31, 2003.

246 "THAT OF PHILISTINES": CG, "Contemporary Taste," Box 31, folder 1, Getty; "Beginnings of Modernism," *Arts Magazine*, April 1986, 78–79.

246 "FROM NATURE, TOO": Author interview with Sarah Greenberg Morse, June 4, 2003, New York; CG, untitled talk at Butler Institute of American Art, Youngstown, Ohio, Box 31, folder 20, Getty.

247 A LUNCHEON AFTERWARD: Robert G. Boyers, dean of Skidmore College, to CG, Aug 23 and Oct. 17, 1984; James Cuno, dean of Vassar College, to CG, Sept. 7, 1984; John T. Bernhard, president of Western Michigan University, to CG, Dec. 2, 1983; John Link, WMU art department chair, to CG, Jan. 27 and Feb. 22, 1984; Sheila K. Smith, asst. to Rhode Island School of Design president Tom Schutte, to CG, May 16, 1984; all Getty.

247 PREVIOUSLY PURSUED ELSEWHERE: Elaine King, asst. professor of art, Carnegie-Mellon University, to CG, Nov. 9, 1983, and Jan. 18 and March 27, 1984, Getty.

248 "BUT AN IMPORTANT ONE": Author interview with Elaine King, April 19, 2004; Jonathan D. Glater, "Raw Eggs? Hair of the Dog? New

Options for the Besotted," *New York Times*, Dec. 7, 2004.

248   AT A SYMPOSIUM: CG, "Abstract Painting and Sculpture," Box 31, folder 19; David Mickenberg to CG, Nov. 23, 1983, and July 5, 9, 24, and Aug. 21, 1984; all Getty.

249   "A POLITICAL AGNOSTIC": CG, "Art and Culture," *Partisan Review*, Oct. 1984, 854–55.

249   "THEY GET CERTIFIED": CG, "Response to New York in the Eighties," *New Criterion*, Summer 1986, 18.

250   PROFILED JACKSON POLLOCK: CG, "The New York Market for American Art," *Nation*, June 11, 1949, reprinted in John O'Brian, ed., *Clement Greenberg: The Collected Essays and Criticism, Volume 2: Arrogant Purpose, 1945–1949* (Chicago: University of Chicago Press, 1987), 319–22.

251   CURRIER & IVES PRINTS: John O'Brian, ed., *Clement Greenberg: The Collected Essays and Criticism, Volume 1: Perceptions and Judgments, 1939–1944* (Chicago: University of Chicago Press, 1986; hereafter "O'Brian, vol. 1"), xvii–xxv.

251   SUPERIOR TO ROBERT RAUSCHENBERG'S: Robert Storr, review in *Art Journal*, Winter 1987, 323, 325.

252   "A MORAL IMPERATIVE": Sidney Tillim, "Criticism and Culture, or Greenberg's Doubt," *Art in America*, May 1987, 122, 201.

252   "AROUND MUCH ANY MORE": Elizabeth Frank, "Farewell to Athene: The Collected Greenberg," *Salmagundi*, Fall 1988, 246, 249, 263.

252   "CHANCE AND HISTORY": Sanford Schwartz, "Clement Greenberg— The Critic and His Artists," *American Scholar*, Fall 1987, 536, 545.

252   BENEFITED THE ART WORLD: Ken Januski, "The Collected Essays and Criticism, v. 1 and 2," *Jewish Exponent*, Nov. 6, 1987, Getty; CG, "Under Forty: A Symposium on American Literature and the Younger Generation of American Jews," *Contemporary Jewish Record*, reprinted in O'Brian, vol. 1, 177.

253   "ARGUING WITH HIM": Michael Auping, ed., *Abstract Expressionism: The Critical Developments* (New York, Abrams, 1987), 84.

253   "COME MORE READILY": Roberta Smith, "Famous Eye Speaks in a House of Memory," *New York Times*, Oct. 3, 1991.

254   "I LOVED TO DANCE": Saul Ostrow, "'Avant-Garde and Kitsch' Fifty Years Later," *Arts Magazine*, Dec. 1989, 57.

255   "ABILITY TO PAINT": Author interview with Jacquie Littlejohn, Oct. 3, 2003, New York; Dodie Kazanjian, "On Target," *Vogue*, Feb. 1990, 326.

256   "TO THE DEATH": Donald Kuspit, "Arms Against a Sea of Kitsch," *New York Times Book Review*, May 16, 1993, 14–15.

256   PUBLISHED IN 1997: Robert Hughes, "The Medium Inquisitor," *New*

York Review of Books, Oct. 21, 1993, 43, 44, 46; see also: Robert Hughes, *American Visions: The Epic History of Art in America* (New York: Alfred A. Knopf, 1997).

257 FOR A NIGHTCAP: http://www.sharecom.ca/Greenberg/anecdotes.html.

257 "I DON'T MEAN TO": Peter Plagens, "Thoroughly Modern, Really," *Newsweek*, April 19, 1993, 66; John O'Brian, ed., *Clement Greenberg: The Collected Essays and Criticism, Volume 3: Affirmations and Refusals, 1950–1956* (Chicago: University of Chicago Press, 1993; hereafter "O'Brian, vol. 3"), xxix–xxxi; author interview with O'Brian, Oct. 31, 2003; O'Brian to CG, June 7, 1993, private collection, Vancouver, B.C.

257 "DIDN'T LIKE HIS NEARNESS": CG, *The Harold Letters, 1928–1943: The Making of an Intellectual*, ed. Janice Van Horne (Washington, D.C.: Counterpoint, 2000), 307–308.

258 "HOLD IN HIGH REGARD": CG, datebook for 1993, Getty; Frank DiGiacomo, "The Transom: Greenberg Mending," *New York Observer*, Aug. 30, 1993; Karlheiz Lûdeking, "Clement Greenberg: Modernism or Barbarism," *Kunstforum* (Berlin), 1994, reprinted in Robert C. Morgan, ed., *Clement Greenberg: Late Writings* (Minneapolis: University of Minnesota Press, 2003), 217.

259 "FROM THE GRAVE": Author interview with John O'Brian, Oct. 31, 2003; Andrew Hudson to O'Brian, Feb. 12, 1994, private collection, Vancouver, B.C.; death certificate in File 3321/1994, Surrogate's Court of the State of New York.

CHAPTER X: THE LEGACY

261 "MORE READILY": Raymond Hernandez, "Clement Greenberg Dies at 85; Art Critic Championed Pollock," *New York Times*, May 8, 1994.

262 "ANALYZING ITS MECHANISM": ~~Michael Kimmelman~~, "The Art Critic Whose Viewpoint Remains Central," *New York Times*, May 10, 1994.

262 "NOT JUST AN ART CRITIC": Jason Edward Kaufman, "Clement Greenberg as the American Art World Remembers Him," *Art Newspaper*, June 1994, 4.

263 ALWAYS INSPIRED PEOPLE: William Feaver, "Clement Greenberg: An Unerring Demolisher of Pretension," *Art News*, Sept. 1994, part 4; Nick Zangwill, *The Metaphysics of Beauty* (Ithaca: Cornell University Press, 2001), reviewed in *Leonardo*, vol. 36, no. 2, 164–65.

263 "SHROUD OF THE MARKET": Robert C. Morgan, *The End of the Art World* (New York: Allworth, 1998), xix–xxi.

263 "PERENNIAL GADFLY": Hilton Kramer, "Clement Greenberg, 1909–1994," *New Criterion*, June 1994, 1–2; Karen Wilkin, "Greenberg's Eye," *Partisan Review*, Fall 1994, 561.

264   MOVEMENTS WERE SLIGHTED: Robert Hughes, *American Visions: The Epic History of Art in America* (New York: Alfred A. Knopf, 1997), 545, 548–49.

264   "STILL DOES NOW": David Anfam, review of O'Brian, vols. 1–4, *Archives of American Art Journal*, no. 2, 1996, 19, 22; Robert Hughes, "The Medium Inquisitor," *New York Review of Books*, Oct. 21, 1993, 49.

265   EARLIER, IN 1980: Report of Gail Blumenthal, guardian *ad litem* for Daniel Ewing Greenberg, Sept. 16, 1994, Surrogate's Court of the State of New York, File 3321/1994.

265   FEDERAL ESTATE TAX: CG will and related papers and list of assets dated Jan. 27, 1995, Surrogate's Court of the State of New York, File 3321/1994.

265   NEST EGG FOR THE WIDOW: Florence Rubenfeld, *Clement Greenberg: A Life* (New York: Scribner, 1997), 273–76.

266   "I DUSTED IT": Janice Van Horne, in Karen Wilkin and Bruce Guenther, *Clement Greenberg: A Critic's Collection* (Princeton: Princeton University Press, 2001), 11; author interview with John O'Brian, Oct. 31, 2003, Vancouver, B.C.

266   BY NO MEANS COMPREHENSIVE: John E. Buchanan, Jr., in Wilkin and Guenther, *Clement Greenberg: A Critic's Collection*, 7; Guenther, *Portland Art Museum*, Summer 2001, 7.

267   OTHER COLOR FIELD PAINTERS: Askart database, Art and Architecture Library, New York Public Library.

267   LIVING ROOM IN 1964: Sue Taylor, "Clem's Cache," *Art in America*, Nov. 2001, 104–106; Marina Vidas, research assistant at MoMA, to CG, July 20, 1984, Getty; Howard Mehring to CG, undated [1965?], Getty; Dodie Kazanjian, "On Target," *Vogue*, Feb. 1990, 324–25, 327.

267   "TO DETERMINE SUCCESS": Susan Platt, "Portland," *Art Papers*, no. 6, 2001, 83–84, http://vnweb.hwwilsonweb.com/hww.

268   "MISS THE POINT": Hilton Kramer, "Critics, Style-setters," *Art and Antiques*, Feb. 2003, 86–87; CG, "Review of an Exhibition of Arnold Friedman," *Nation*, April 14, 1944, reprinted in John O'Brian, ed., *Clement Greenberg: The Collected Essays and Criticism, Volume 1: Perceptions and Judgments, 1939–1944* (Chicago: University of Chicago Press, 1986), 205; CG, essay in "Arnold Friedman Memorial Exhibition," Feb. 15–March 13, 1950, Jewish Museum, New York, and George Walter Vincent Smith Museum, Springfield, MA, Getty.

INDEX

Index

Index

Index

PHOTOGRAPH CREDITS

page i:

Greenberg yearbook and fraternity photos: Courtesy of Syracuse University Archives

page ii:

"The Irascibles": Photo by Nina Leen / Time & Life Pictures / Getty Images

The Rosenbergs in Washington Square: Photo by Ibram Lassaw

page iii:

Pollock in 1953: Photo by Tony Vaccaro / Hulton Archive / Getty Images

Jackson Pollock (American, 1912–1956), *Troubled Queen*, 1945. Oil and enamel on canvas, 188.28 x 110.49 cm (74.13 x 43.5 in.). Charles H. Bayley Picture and Painting Fund and Gift of Mrs. Albert J. Beveridge and Juliana Cheney Edwards Collection, by exchange. Museum of Fine Arts, Boston 1984.749. © 2006 Pollock-Krasner Foundation / Artists Rights Society (ARS), New York

page iv:

Greenberg, Pollock, and others on the beach: Courtesy of the Jackson Pollock papers, 1912–1975, in the Archives of American Art, Smithsonian Institution

page v:

Helen Frankenthaler (American, born 1928), *Dawn After the Storm*, 1957. Oil and alkyd on canvas, 167 x 177.8 cm (65.75 x 70 in.). Sophie M. Friedman Fund. Museum of Fine Arts, Boston 1976.141. Copyright © 2006 Helen Frankenthaler

Greenberg by Halsman: Photo by Philippe Halsman, © Halsman Estate *page vi:*

Greenberg at window: Photo by Hans Namuth. © 1991 Hans Namuth Estate. Courtesy Center for Creative Photography, University of Arizona

Morris Louis (American, 1912–1962), *Theta*, 1961. Acrylic resin (Magna) on canvas, 259.1 x 426.7 cm (102 x 168 in.). Anonymous gift. Museum of Fine Arts, Boston 67.623. Copyright © 1961 Morris Louis. Reproduced by arrangement with Whiteford, Taylor & Preston L.L.P.

page vii:

David Smith (American, 1906–1965), *Cubi XVIII*, 1964. Polished stainless steel, 294 x 152.4 x 55.2 cm (115 3/4 x 60 x 21 3/4 in.). Gift of Susan W. and Stephen D. Paine. Museum of Fine Arts, Boston 68.280. Art © Estate of David Smith / Licensed by VAGA, New York, NY

John O'Brian: Courtesy of John O'Brian

page viii:

Greenberg studio critique: Photo by Toni Onley, courtesy of John O'Brian

Greenberg looking at Noland's *Target*: Photo © Estate of Cora Kelly Ward/ Licensed by VAGA, New York, NY. Art © Kenneth Noland / Licensed by VAGA, New York, NY

ABOUT THE AUTHOR

Alice Goldfarb Marquis was born in Munich, Germany, and immigrated to New York in 1938. She attended Hunter College and earned a Master's degree in art history from San Diego State University and a Ph.D. in modern European history from the University of California at San Diego. For the past twenty-two years, she has been a Visiting Scholar in the Department of History at UCSD, and has lectured at numerous other institutions. For much of her life, she has also worked as a journalist and in 1972 was named Suburban Journalist of the Year by the Suburban Newspapers of America. In 2002, she published *Marcel Duchamp: The Bachelor Stripped Bare* (MFA Publications), which the *Washington Times* called "the most sober appraisal yet of this artist." Ms. Marquis's other published works include *Art Lessons: Learning from the Rise and Fall of Public Arts Funding*, which was chosen as the best nonfiction book of the year by the San Diego Book Awards (1995); *The Art Biz: The Covert World of Collectors, Dealers, Auction Houses, Museums, and Critics*; *Alfred H. Barr, Jr.: Missionary for the Modern*; *Hopes and Ashes: The Birth of Modern Times 1929-1939*, which was made an Alternate Selection of the History Book Club; and numerous articles and reviews for *The Nation, The Journal of American History, American Historical Review, Biography, Chronicle of Higher Education, American Heritage,* and others. She makes her home in La Jolla, California.

contact Washington Arts Assoc
Wash DC

denise@arubastreet.com

"Bidding for Class"

telephone cell ? change contract.

M